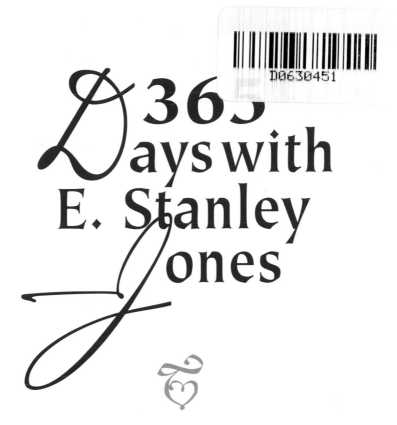

365 Days with E. Stanley Jones

edited by
Mary Ruth Howes

DIMENSIONS
FOR LIVING
NASHVILLE

365 Days with E. Stanley Jones

Copyright © 2000 by Dimensions for Living

This book is printed on recycled, acid-free paper.

Library of Congress Cataloging-in-Publication Data

Jones, E. Stanley (Eli Stanley), 1884-1973.
365 days with E. Stanley Jones / edited by Mary Ruth Howes.
    p. cm.
Includes bibliographical references.
ISBN 0-687-07309-X
1. Devotional calendars.   I. Howes. M. R. (Mary Ruth)   II. Title.

BV4811 .J5994 2000
242'.2—dc21

00-029472

00 01 02 03 04 05 06 07 08 09 — 10 9 8 7 6 5 4 3 2 1

ontents

Preface . . . 5

Editor's Note . . . 7

List of Abbreviations . . . 9

How to Change Your Life . . . 11

The Kingdom of God: Homeland of the Soul . . . 46

Finding God Through Jesus Christ . . . 74

Learning to Pray . . . 109

Discovering the Power of the Holy Spirit . . . 137

Living Under God's Guidance . . . 172

Living with Health . . . 200

Conquering Anger and Anxiety . . . 228

Learning to Live Positively . . . 256

Living with Maturity . . . 284

The Way of Grace and Discipline . . . 319

Growing in the Fruits of the Spirit . . . 347

A Daily Exercise . . . 375

reface

E. STANLEY JONES, A MISSIONARY TO INDIA AND THEN TO THE WORLD since 1907, wrote twenty-nine books in his lifetime, finishing the last book just before he died in 1973 at age eighty-nine. His son-in-law James K. Mathews estimated that he preached more than sixty thousand sermons in his lifetime, including fifty in his last year after a stroke, when doctors told him he would never be able to preach again.

"For thirty-five years I knew him intimately," Mathews writes, "and had occasion to observe him closely for prolonged periods. He rang true! Of course, he had weaknesses. These were before the Lord, for he was completely surrendered to Jesus Christ. Once, when I asked a Hindu how he was, he replied, 'As you see me.' So it was with Brother Stanley, as he was called. He was as you saw him."[1]

What strikes me as I have read and worked on these devotionals is how convinced—and convincing—Jones was about the truth and the power of the gospel. He himself lived and worked in the power of the Holy Spirit, demonstrating the reality of what he preached. His highest joy was to share what he had learned and experienced and to challenge others to experience abundant living, mastery, power and poise, Christian maturity and transformation by surrendering themselves to Jesus Christ.

—Mary Ruth Howes, editor

[1]James K. Mathews, "Postscript," in E. Stanley Jones, *The Divine Yes* (Nashville: Abingdon Press, 1975; Abingdon Classics edition, 1992), pp. 151-60.

Editor's Note

THE 365 DAILY DEVOTIONALS IN THIS BOOK ARE GARNERED FROM many of the books that E. Stanley Jones published in his lifetime. Although every book has a different focus and slant, Dr. Jones touched on many of the same topics in each one, always emphasizing his basic themes—the centrality of Jesus Christ, the need for self-surrender to Christ, and the power of the Holy Spirit for daily living.

These devotionals are selections. Often they are shortened versions of the originals. They have been edited to eliminate repetitions, as well as to take out references to generic "man" with the accompanying pronouns "he," "his," and "him." Occasionally punctuation has been changed and updated. Unless otherwise noted, the Scripture quotations have been changed to the wording of the New Revised Standard Version of the Bible, which has carefully avoided most sexist language. In addition, Scripture references have been added to biblical quotations and references.

The comments or questions that follow each devotional are often the editor's reaction to the material, though sometimes Jones himself provides such a reaction. The prayers belong to Jones in thought, if not in direct language. They have been edited in order to address God as "you" rather than "thee" or "thou," to update the language, and often to shorten them. And where one original devotional has provided material for two or more new devotionals, or the material was taken from books other than devotional books, new prayers have had to be created.

In some of his books Jones provided an affirmation for the day, but in a number of them he did not. Where possible I have reproduced Jones's affirmations or taken an idea, if not the wording, from the text. The suggestions for further reading or study are sometimes Jones's suggestions and sometimes the editor's. They provide further illumination on the devotional, and allow Scripture to comment on Scripture.

List of Abbreviations

THE SOURCE OF EACH DEVOTIONAL IS INDICATED BY AN ABBREVIATION and a page number or numbers. These are the abbreviations and the works they stand for:

AL	*Abundant Living*
CM	*Christian Maturity*
COTM	*The Christ of the Mount*
GS	*Growing Spiritually*
HBTP	*How to Be a Transformed Person*
MAS	*Mastery*
TW	*The Way*
WBF	*The Word Became Flesh*
WPP	*The Way to Power and Poise*

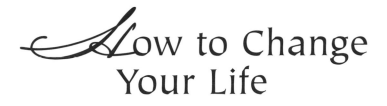

How to Change Your Life

A Craving for Right Direction

Who are they that fear the Lord?
He will teach them the way that they should choose.
—Psalm 25:12

There is an inherent urge to go beyond ourselves, to be a different and better person.... [But] we not only want to go beyond ourselves, we want to go ... in the right direction. We want to be oriented. But oriented to what? Here the psychologist puts up a vast question mark. But religion steps into that vacuum and says ... : You must be oriented to God. If there is a God, that's important. You cannot be at cross-purposes with Reality and not get hurt.

There is also a third basic urge ... the longing for unity. ... You desire basically a reunion with God—with God your Father. You are homesick.... Not basically related to God, you are like lungs without air, a heart without love, an aesthetic nature without beauty. You are centrally starved.

What are you longing for?
Could it be God?

O God, I'm starved—starved for you. Nothing this side of you can satisfy me. So I'm on a search for nothing less than You.

Affirmation: My homesickness for my heavenly Father is going to lead me to him.

For further reading: Psalms 25:4-12; 23; 63

HBTP 2

11

2 — Finding Scapegoats

Teach me your way, O Lord,
and lead me on a level path
because of my enemies.
—Psalm 27:11

"When the Greeks made the gods responsible for man's situation, the point they reached was spelled out in one word: *Nonsense,* to the Greeks more dreadful than tragedy."[1]

When we go wrong, our first impulse is to look around to find some way of evading responsibility, some scapegoat upon which we can lay our sins. But deep down we know that this won't do. Our moral nature revolts and says with the Greeks one word, "Nonsense." Something within us sides with the moral universe against ourselves. We have the feeling that in any struggle with the moral universe we will come out badly.

Do you try to avoid responsibility for your actions?

O God, maybe I'll have to side with you against myself if I'm to get out of what I am. Help me to do it.

Affirmation: If I try to find scapegoats, in the end I know I shall become the goat!

For further reading: Ephesians 2:1-6

AL 3

---

[1]Lewis J. Sherrill, *Guilt and Redemption* (Philadelphia: John Knox Press).

Taking Responsibility

" 'Father, I have sinned against heaven and before you.' "
—Luke 15:21a

Transformation will begin in any life—in yours—when you stand up and say: "I'm responsible for the kind of person I am. I am what I've wanted to be. Now I've changed my mind. I'm sorry for what I am and have done. I'm going to be different. God help me." Immediately the healing, transforming forces of the universe set in—the work begins. The grace of God begins to operate. In that moment you cease to be a whining evader, laying blame here and laying it there, and you become a person. There the birth of a soul begins. You're taking no longer the role of a puppet, but of a person.

Are you looking for change?

O God, I'm through with being a supposed victim of this and that. I'm now going to be a person—your person. Make me over again.

Affirmation: I have been and am what I have decided to be; today I decide to be another person.

For further reading: Luke 15:11-24; Acts 2:22-24, 38

HBTP 7

13

The Divided Self

Now discipline always seems painful rather than pleasant at the time, but later it yields the peaceful fruit of righteousness.
—*Hebrews 12:11*

The struggling person sees that there is a division [in the self] and hates it.... That fact that you are struggling... shows that there is not only hope, but the very great possibility of your becoming a transformed person.

God is disturbing you, like friends walk a man who has taken an overdose of sleeping powders, lest if he lies down, he will never awaken again. So the everlasting Mercy pursues us, sets us at war with our lower selves, disturbs us until we beg to be let alone—to die. Love will not let us die. Our very pangs are his prods—prodding us to be a transformed person. As long as the prod is there—the Person is there.

Where might God be disturbing you?

Gracious Father, you are the Love that will not let me go. I am grateful at least that I feel your prods, prodding me to you.

Affirmation: I shall accept my pangs as God's prods.

For further reading: Hebrews 12:15-17; Acts 26:12-15

HBTP 10

14

5

God Personalized

In these last days [God] has spoken to us by a Son.
—Hebrews 1:2

A little boy, child of missionaries, was in school in the United States at Christmas time. The principal said to him, "Son, what would you rather have most of all for Christmas?" The boy looked at the picture of his father framed on his desk and remembered acutely the absence of the father in a far-off land, and then quietly said, "I want my father to step out of that frame." The little boy voiced the cry of humanity: We want God our Father to step out of the frame of the universe, out of his impersonal relationship, and meet us personally. Jesus is God stepping out of the frame of the universe—God simplified and God personalized, God become intimate and tender and redemptive.

What does Jesus tell you about God?

How amazing, O God, that you are willing to come to meet me.

Affirmation: Jesus is God made personal to me.

For further reading: Romans 1:1-7

HBTP 14

15

6 Jesus, the Inescapable

Jesus said . . . , "I am the way, and the truth, and the life."
—*John 14:6*

Jesus is the personal approach from the unseen God coming so near that he becomes inescapable. . . . You don't have to find him—you simply have to consent to be found. No one is farther than one step from God. And that one step is a short step; turn around and say "Yes" and you are at once in the arms of redemptive Love. But that yes must carry with it *you*—you must be behind the yes, not a lip-yes, but a life-yes. God's yes has been said; the Incarnation is God saying "Yes." When your yes of response meets his yes of invitation, you are simply there—at the place of transformation. . . . You don't have to ascend to heaven to bring God down by your efforts— he's down by his love. All you have to do is to "let go and let God"—let go of yourself and take his self.

What or whom are you saying "Yes" to?

Gracious God, I begin to see that I may be at the door even before I begin.

Affirmation: I accept the gift and gladly belong forever to the Giver.

For further reading: Romans 3:23-26; 5:6-11

HBTP 15

16

Life Is Not What It Ought to Be

All have sinned and fall short of the glory of God.
—Romans 3:23b

We are led in our quest to the very center: *It is the conviction that life is not what it ought to be.*

God apparently is convinced of that, hence the extraordinary step of becoming human that humans may become like God. Are we convinced?...We know that there is a cleft in our natures, a cleft we cannot heal. James Smetham wrote the confession for each of us: "One of the most formidable enemies was a vivid and ill-trained imagination. Against outward and inward evils of this kind there existed a very powerful love of truth and purity.... The antagonism of these two forces...went nigh to threaten my reason."

...We know that we haven't within ourselves the resources to heal ourselves. We may run to cults of self-realization, of self-healing, of self-cultivation, but in our heart of hearts we know that what we need is not self-realization...but self-release. We know we need conversion—fundamental and radical.

Is your life what it ought to be?

O God, I see that I need your help to become not the person I am but the person I am meant to be.

Affirmation: I will accept God's help to be different.

For further reading: Romans 3:19-25; 5:1-5

HBTP 15

17

8 ~ Freedom and Release

*All this is from God, who reconciled us
to himself through Christ . . . in Christ God
was reconciling the world to himself.*
—2 *Corinthians 5:18-19*

We come to the very central thing the divine invasion offers—a freedom and release from what we are and what we have done. . . .

"Thou shalt call his name Jesus, for he shall save his people from their sins" (Matthew 1:21 KJV). The first mention of sin in the New Testament is not a fierce invective against it, but a promise of its removal as the central thing the Incarnation would mean. It meant a double saving: *from* their sins, *to* himself, the Savior. "To himself" meant the opening of amazing possibilities in being made over again into a new pattern—after his image.

This fundamental change here sounded as the keynote of the gospel is variously described in the New Testament: conversion, a new birth, a new creation, partakers of the divine nature, alive to God, being transformed. All language has been laid hold on to describe this most important thing that can happen in human living.

Are you looking for freedom?

O God, I want to accept the possibilities you offer me in your salvation.

Affirmation: Becoming a changed person is the most important thing that can happen to me.

For further reading: 2 Corinthians 5:16-19; Ephesians 2:1-10

HBTP 16

Stunted Souls

All of us once lived ... in the passions of our flesh,
following the desires of flesh and sense,
and we were by nature children of wrath.
—Ephesians 2:3

Stanley Hall, the psychologist, says, "Every life is stunted unless it receives the metamorphosis, called conversion, in some form or other. . . . " "Every life is stunted"—is that true? Yes, there is a fundamentally tied-up condition within until this central release takes place. The Japanese very cleverly stunt great forest trees and make them into potted plants by a simple expedient of tying up the taproot. The tree then lives off its surface roots only, with no taproot going down into the soil and drawing sustenance from the depths. Every person, religious, irreligious, or nonreligious, is an inwardly tied-up person until conversion in some form releases him. And there are no exceptions. Many are tied up with fears, guilts, resentments, inferiorities, and self-preoccupations. They are stunted and runted.

Where is your spiritual nourishment coming from?

O God, my Father, I know I'm a 25 percent person until you touch me and change me into 100 percent and beyond. I need that touch.

Affirmation: A full-sized person in a full-sized job with a full-sized goal—that's the me I want to be.

For further reading: Romans 6; Ephesians 2:1-10

HBTP 16

19

Born from Below or from Above?

*"What is born of the flesh is flesh,
and what is born of the Spirit is spirit."*
—John 3:6

Human beings stand between the animal kingdom and the kingdom of God. We are pulled between the two, for we have a foot in each. We are akin to the animal with our physical desires, and we are akin to God in that we are made "a little lower than divine" (Psalm 8:5). We can "be born from above," or born from below; we can be controlled from above or controlled from below.

The animal kingdom stands for self against the rest; the kingdom of God stands for the divine Self for the sake of the rest. The animal kingdom is "red in tooth and claw" (Tennyson); the kingdom of God is red with the blood of the Son of God in self-sacrifice. The animal kingdom is the survival of the fittest in terms of the sharpest tooth and claw; the kingdom of God is the revival of the unfit in terms of redemption. The animal kingdom is life organized around the hunger motive; the kingdom of God is life organized around the love motive. The animal kingdom is a feud; the kingdom of God is a family. We can be born from below, or we can be born from above—life can be dominated by animal instincts or life can be dominated by God.

"The choice is always ours." We decide to be transformed from above or from below.

Would you rather be in a feud or in a family?

O God, I need transformation. I want to be born from above and become part of your family.

Affirmation: My life will be organized around the love motive with God's help.

For further reading: 1 John 5:1-3; Colossians 1:21-22; 3:1-3

HBTP 19

The Way Up
Is the Way Down

Do not be conformed to this world, but be transformed by the renewing of your minds.
—Romans 12:2a

How can we get from the kingdom of man to the kingdom of God?...Here is foul, polluted mud in a swamp, and above it is a lotus flower. How can the slime be transformed into a lotus flower? It cannot lift itself; there is only one possible way...the higher kingdom comes down into the lower, and the lower kingdom surrenders itself to the roots of the plant and is lifted up and transformed and transfigured and blooms in the beauty of the flower. It is born from above....

There is only one way up and that is the way down—the kingdom of God, personalized in Jesus, comes down into our polluted world and says, "Let go your old life, be willing to surrender to my life, and I'll transform you into my image." We do "let go and let God," and we are transformed into a new image, infused with a new life. We are born from above.

Where have you seen transforming power at work?

O God, I'm like that mud—I'm polluted, but I cannot purify myself. But I can consent. I do.

Affirmation: I'm consenting to God's redemptive power.

For further reading: 1 Corinthians 1:23-31; 2 Corinthians 5:20-21

HBTP 19, 20

Born of Water
and of the Spirit

*To all who received him, who believed in his
name, he gave power to become children of God,
who were born, not of blood or of the will of the
flesh or of the will of man, but of God.*
—John 1:12-13

The new birth John says (1:13) is "not of blood"—it cannot be inherited from the bloodstream of our parents. It is not "of the will of the flesh"—you cannot get it by the efforts of the will, lifting yourself by the bootstraps. It is not "of the will of man"—no man can give it to you, neither pastor nor priest nor pope. It is "of God." It is directly from God or not at all.

To Nicodemus Jesus said, "No one can enter the kingdom of God without being born of water and Spirit" (John 3:5). The being "born of water" is the coming by baptism into an outer fellowship—the Christian fellowship; the being born of the Spirit is the inner birth. It is possible to be born of water and not be born of the Spirit—to be outwardly in and not inwardly in. . . . A lot of people are horizontally converted, but not vertically converted; their labels changed but not their lives. The new birth means life and label changed.

Lifting oneself up by the bootstraps is impossibly hard work.

O God, I cannot tolerate this birth into a physical universe unless it is supplemented by a spiritual birth. I cannot stand being half born.

Affirmation: God wills total conversion, inward and outward—so do I.

For further reading: 1 John 5:18-19; Colossians 3:5-11

HBTP 20

The Old Becomes New

So if anyone is in Christ, there is a new creation: everything old has passed away; see, everything has become new!
—2 Corinthians 5:17

Paul tells us that the basic drives—self, sex, and the herd—have been cleansed and united and directed toward new ends. Note that they have not been eliminated. By no known process can these instinctive urges be eliminated. Put them out by the door, and they will come back by the window. If they cannot be eliminated, neither can they be repressed without setting up complexes and conflicts. There is one thing, and one thing only, that can be done— they can be cleansed, redirected, and united under a single controlling purpose by the Spirit of God.

Note this passage says, "everything old has passed away; everything [old] has become new." Self has passed away as the center of one's life and the center of festering interests, and yet, behold, it has become new—it is back again, an old thing and yet forever a new thing. The self now cleansed from its conflicts and its guilts is a self you can live with, and live with it with joy. You can love yourself now for you love something beyond yourself.

Have you been afraid to give yourself to God for fear you'd have nothing left?

Father, you are taking away with your left hand to give back with your right hand. Take all I have and give it back cleansed.

Affirmation: All my old things are new things because they are directed to new ends.

For further reading: 2 Corinthians 5:11-21; Colossians 3:12-17

HBTP 21

25

Three Steps
to Transformation

*"Assuredly, I say to you, unless you are converted
and become as little children, you will by no
means enter the kingdom of heaven."*
—Matthew 18:3 NKJV

In this transformation called conversion there are three steps.

1. *A new direction*—"unless you are converted." The word *converted* is *con*, "with," and *vertare*, "to turn"—a new direction. Conversion is first of all a new direction, a reversal. But it is a turning *with*, it is not turning around in general. It is a turning around specifically—with Christ. He joins you the moment you turn.

2. *A new spirit*—"and become as little children." A fresh beginning, the spirit of a child possesses you, you are reduced to simplicity from the complexities and complications of evil. "I feel like a newborn babe," said a very sophisticated and able, but now radically changed person.

3. *A new sphere of living*—"enter the kingdom of heaven." You pass out of the sphere of the kingdom of self and enter the sphere of the kingdom of God. You change worlds.

How wonderful that we do not have to change by ourselves!

O God, I am ready to begin this new life with you.

Affirmation: Christ is with me.

For further reading: Acts 3:19-20; 1 Corinthians 6:9-11; 1 Thessalonians 1:9

HBTP 22

26

Working Life Together

*[God] is the source of your life in Christ Jesus,
who became for us wisdom from God, and
righteousness and sanctification and redemption.*
—1 Corinthians 1:30

There is a difference of heaven and hell between the two worlds [of the kingdom of self and the kingdom of God]. Here in the new sphere of living you and God work out life *together.* You supply willingness and he supplies power. . . . The lonely, orphaned striving is gone, and now a sense of being together with One who has all the answers and all the resources for carrying out those answers takes possession of you. You feel you *belong* and belong to Adequacy.

In the first step [to transformation] you are responsible. No one, not even God, can turn around for you. You are endowed with free will and you decide. In the second step God is responsible. You cannot give yourself a new spirit—only God can do that. But you can consent, and that consent looses the power of God upon your inner life. In the third step it is the part of both God and you—you offer willingness and the surrendered you, and he offers power and his presence. Life now takes on power, direction, adequacy. You are a transformed person.

How wonderful to have Someone who has the answers!

O God, thank you that I am no longer adrift at sea. I know my goal, I know my resources, and I know whose hand is on the helm.

Affirmation: "In him who strengthens me, I am able for anything" (Philippians 4:13 Moffatt).

For further reading: Acts 3:19-21; 1 Corinthians 1:27-31

HBTP 22

18 — "Immediate Luminousness"

It is the God who said, "Let light shine out of darkness,"
who has shone in our hearts to give the light of the
knowledge of the glory of God in the face of Jesus Christ.
—2 Corinthians 4:6

William James says in *Varieties of Religious Experience*, "The best fruits of religious experience are the best things that history has to show," and he gives three signs as the tests of the validity of this experience: "Immediate luminousness, philosophical reasonableness and moral helpfulness are the only available criteria."

Pascal describes this change thus: "The year of grace 1654. Monday, 23 November.... From about half past ten in the evening until half past midnight. FIRE. 'God of Abraham, God of Isaac, God of Jacob,' not of philosophers and scholars. Certainty, certainty, heartfelt, joy, peace. God of Jesus Christ...."[3]

To put it in the words of a converted Lancashire drunkard: "Religion has changed my home, my heart, and you can all see that it has changed my face. I hear some of these London men call themselves Positivists. Bless God, I'm a Positivist. I'm positive God for Christ's sake has pardoned my sins, changed my heart, and made me a new creation."

The experience of God brings glorious light.

O God, my Father, thank you that I am not left to grope in darkness; you come bringing an invincible certainty with you.

Affirmation: Illuminated, I become luminous and illuminating—today I shall be all three.

For further reading: Romans 8:14-17; 2 Corinthians 3:17-18; 4:3-6

HBTP 26

---

[3]Blaise Pascal, *Pensées*, translated by A. J. Krailsheimer (New York: Penguin Books, 1966), p. 309.

"Philosophical Reasonableness"

Be careful then how you live,
not as unwise people but as wise.
—Ephesians 5:15a

The philosophical reasonableness of the conversion experience comes not merely from the sense of verbal consistency of argument, but from a vital consistency of life meaning. . . . There is a sense of being drawn together from a scatterbrained, scatter-affectioned, and scatter-souled condition.

A missionary writes after undergoing a spiritual change: "Since I returned I have worked harder than ever—on that which was my greatest problem. It was impossible for me to sit down and stick to the Santali language. I preferred to do other things, with the result that I felt the Santali in my tummy! But now I like sitting with difficult books. I enjoy the studies. And feel well!"

A coherent soul made a coherent mind and set him to work to make a coherent world.

What change are you looking for in your life?

O God, I'm grateful that life is no longer at loose ends—it's been gathered into a pattern. It means something now. Thank you.

Affirmation: The rest of my life is going to be coherent, to make sense, the sense of God.

For further reading: Ephesians 4:25–5:20

HBTP 27

20 — Total Renovation

Do you not know that wrongdoers will not inherit the kingdom of God?... And this is what some of you used to be. But you were washed....
—1 Corinthians 6:9, 11

The third test of the worth of an experience is moral helpfulness. Said Mark Rutherford in *Catherine Furze:* "I can assure my incredulous literary friends that years ago it was not uncommon for men and women suddenly to awaken to the fact that they had been sinners and to determine that from henceforth they would keep God's commandments by the help of Jesus Christ and the Holy Spirit. What is more extraordinary is that they did keep God's commandments for the rest of their lives."

It was said of Thomas Chalmers that in his early days he preached morals alone and with no moral result. Then he became filled with the love of Christ, and with that power behind him, he engraved the ethical precepts upon the heart of Scotland....

This is illuminating—preach morality, and the moral life is largely unchanged; preach the atoning love of God in Christ, and conversion and a total renovation of the total life results, especially by a moral renovation.

Total renovation is no impossible dream.

O Christ, you are a redeemer, for you redeem us. Redeem me, now, from what I have been and am.

Affirmation: I am no longer a part of the disease—I am part of the cure.

For further reading: 1 Corinthians 6:9-11; 2 Corinthians 3:2-3

HBTP 28

21 — The Gift of Grace

*For by grace you have been saved through faith,
and this is not your own doing; it is the gift of God
—not the result of works, so that no one may boast.*
—Ephesians 2:8-9

Richard W. Church, in *The Gifts of Civilization*, describes the redemptive impact of conversion in these words:

> It seems to me that the exultation apparent in early Christian literature...at the prospect...of a great moral revolution in human history...that at last the routine of vice and sin had met its match, that a new and astonishing possibility had come into view, that men, not here and there, but on a large scale, might attain to that hitherto hopeless thing to the multitudes, goodness—is one of the most singular and solemn things in history.
>
> But it was not really an attainment—it was an obtainment, a gift of grace. Had it been an attainment, it would have shut out the multitudes, but because it was an obtainment, a gift of grace, it opened the door to the multitudes. And this miracle still takes place today.

God offers grace and salvation to all.

O God, you provide grace for all my needs. I accept your grace and your goodness for my life.

Affirmation: I am saved by God's grace.

For further reading: Ephesians 2:1-10; Romans 8:1-2

HBTP 29

22

True Freedom

The law of the Spirit of life in Christ Jesus has set you free from the law of sin and of death.
—Romans 8:2

This miracle [of conversion] still takes place today. A few weeks ago this letter came from an Indian teacher: "When I came out of the sitting room after talking and praying with you, I felt that a heavy load was taken from my heart and body. I became so light that the whole night I dreamed, semiconsciously, of flying about in the air. Five years' bondage was broken in five seconds. It is really so amazing." It is. But it is a fact and a recurring fact to the degree it is tried.

Just two days ago a student said to me: "Why, I am so free from condemnation that I am afraid. I expected to be depressed and it is the opposite. I'm surprised at the freedom from guilt and condemnation—I'm free and released." And he looked like it, for his face glowed!

Are you heavy laden?

O God, my Father, this is breath-taking. I need be under the tyranny of nothing. I can be free and free now. Thank you.

Affirmation: I am being redeemed. Today I shall look redeemed, think redeemed, act redeemed, and be redeemed.

For further reading: Romans 6:5-14; 7:21–8:4

HBTP 29

Saved and Sobered

*To set the mind on the flesh is death, but
to set the mind on the Spirit is life and peace.*
—Romans 8:6

A leading editor recently said to me: "I was an alcoholic. It
had me. I was beaten and I knew it. I went to a sanitarium
to get scientific help. One day a case was brought in and I
said to the doctor, 'That man is in a terrible condition.' And
the doctor replied: 'Yes he is. But within a year he'll be well,
but in a year you won't be.' It struck me like a blow. That
night I went out under the stars, lonely and defeated, and
raised my hands toward heaven and repeated what the
leper said to Jesus, 'If thou wilt, thou canst make me clean.'
Immediately the answer came back, 'I will, be thou clean.'
From that moment the power of alcohol was broken in my
life. I have never touched a drop since. Have never even
wanted it."

Christ is more powerful than anything binding us.

O God, my Father, this miracle of inner change is taking
place in me. My old life is dropping away. I'm becoming a
new creature.

*Affirmation: "Be not afraid;...here am I alive for evermore, holding
the keys that unlock death and Hades"* (Revelation 1:17-8 Moffatt).

For further reading: Romans 6:1-6; 8:3-6

HBTP 30

24

"My Heart
Strangely Warmed"

*You are not in the flesh; you are in the Spirit,
since the Spirit of God dwells in you.*
—Romans 8:9a

John Wesley, whose conversion produced an epoch in the life of Britain, according to Lecky, the historian, tells of his change:

"In the evening I went very unwillingly to a society in Aldersgate Street, where one was reading Luther's preface to the Epistle to the Romans. About a quarter before nine, while he was describing the change which God works in the heart through faith in Christ I felt my heart strangely warmed. I felt I did trust in Christ, Christ alone for salvation; and an assurance was given me that He had taken away *my* sins, even *mine,* and saved *me* from the law of sin and death." This strange warming of the heart sent a moral cleansing through the soul of Britain and the world.

"You seem to be a very temperate people here," Augustine Birrell once observed to a Cornish miner. "How did it happen?" The miner replied, solemnly raising his cap, "There came a man among us once and his name was John Wesley."

**"The world has yet to see what God will do
with a man fully consecrated to him."[4]**

O God, my Father, I open the depths of my being to the moral cleansing of your Spirit. Make me clean within.

Affirmation: Whether or not I can be another John Wesley, I can at least be fully consecrated to God.

For further reading: Romans 8:6-11; 12:1-2

HBTP 31

---

[4]"This remark was made by an ex-butcher, Henry Varley, in the hearing of Dwight L. Moody on his 1872 visit to Britain. Quoted in John D. Woodbridge, editor, *Great Leaders of the Christian Church* (Chicago: Moody Press, 1988), p. 340.

25 — "The Only Jet of Light"

If Christ is in you, though the body is dead because of sin, the Spirit is life because of righteousness.
—Romans 8:10

I once asked leaders of the Khasi Hills people of Assam: "Can you give me cases of transformed lives through Christianity among your people?" They looked bewildered and said, "Why, everybody and everything has been transformed by our becoming Christians." They had been head-hunters! The Hindu governor of Assam said to me: "The only jet of light in the hills is the work of Christian missions. Take that out and all will be darkness. The houses of hill people are notoriously filthy, but the homes of these people are neat and clean.". . .

I asked a Japanese aviator to tell the story of his conversion before a large audience. He had hated Americans, and through undernourishment and resentments he developed tuberculosis. In the hospital he found he was eating food supplied by Americans. "What makes Americans give food to their former enemies?" he asked himself. "It must be because they are Christians." He got hold of a Bible, made a surrender to Christ, and his resentments dropped away. His tuberculosis healed at once.

Our spirits and bodies are inextricably entwined.

O God, thank you that your power is available for the best of human living, to be lived anywhere—with you.

Affirmation: I will live in God's light so that I may be God's light in my world.

For further reading: Romans 8:9-14; 2 Corinthians 4:5-7

HBTP 32

26 — A Daybreak

Scripture

Where sin increased, grace abounded all the more.
—Romans 5:20

Some lives are transformed with less spectacular change.
. . .

"Oh, Father Latimer," cried one, "I prithee hear me, when I read in the New Testament, Christ Jesus came into the world to save sinners, it is as if the day suddenly broke." It is a daybreak.

Hugh Fawcett describes his change thus: "I became conscious of a subtle change stealing over me. I was invaded by some will in which was infinite love, peace, wisdom, and power. I felt a never-before-known humility and gladness, an inexpressible certainty that within all the discords of life there was divine intention and a final harmony, that the darkness in me was in this timeless moment resolved in light and the error redeemed in the ultimate comprehension."

Comment

Conversion may be sudden or a gradual, subtle change.

Prayer

O God, I am ready for your invasion, ready to experience humility and gladness.

Affirmation: I will live today in the daylight of Christ's salvation.

For further reading: Romans 5:20-21; Colossians 3:5-10

HBTP 33, 34

Guilt, a Divine Gift

" 'God, be merciful to me, a sinner!' "
—Luke 18:13

Conversion is the penitent, receptive response to the saving divine initiative in Christ, resulting in a change, gradual or sudden, by which one passes from the kingdom of self to the kingdom of God and becomes a part of a living fellowship, the church. . . .

First, it has to be a *penitent* response, no bluffing it through and acting as though nothing had happened.

A trusted man had taken $200,000 but had covered it up with clever bookkeeping. He thought himself safe. But he developed stomach ulcers and migraine headaches, the result of the strain of living a double life. The increasing incidence of nervous disease is the direct result of passing by repentance and forgiveness and trying to take the way of denial of anything about which to feel guilty.

I believe guilt is one of the divinest gifts of God. Guilt can be pushed into the subconscious and there fester, or guilt can take you by the hand and lead you to God. . . . The attempt to get rid of our guilts by removing moral standards is like the two children of a friend of mine who moved the position of a sundial and then said, "Look, it's such-and-such an hour, the sundial says so." But the sun said otherwise.

What do you do with your guilt?

O Christ, you are the Way, the Way that stretches clear to the mouth of hell. It begins where I begin—in penitence. Thank you.

Affirmation: Today I will make a penitent, receptive response to God's highest for me.

For further reading: Luke 18:9-14

HBTP 44, 45

28 Active Faith

Scripture

> She said to herself, "If I only touch his cloak,
> I will be made well."
> —Matthew 9:21

Conversion is the penitent, *receptive* response to God's initiative. . . . Faith is receptivity—receptivity to God's invading grace. It is passive activity. Jesus says, "Whatever you pray for and ask, believe you have got it, and you shall have it" (Mark 11:24 Moffatt). Note, "have got it." The word of Jesus is accomplishment, and when I take his word as accomplishment, then it is accomplishment. For behind that word is the character of Jesus, and behind the character of Jesus is the character of the universe—the nature of Reality backs it.

. . . Here is a case of active faith: a woman had a neurotic mother, a father who was killed in a drunken brawl, a brother who was an alcoholic and in an institution, and she was on the point of suicide. A pastor gave her a prescription just as a doctor would: "Go home and read a page of *Abundant Living*[5] every day and do what it tells you." She did. Today she is transformed, radiant, and in charge of a young people's society. She had nothing to act on save the pastor's word: she acted on it and it worked. Jesus says, " 'Your faith has made you well; go in peace' " (Luke 8:48). He would never say, "Go," except to mean, "Go into release."

Question

Where do you need to exercise active faith?

Prayer

Dear Lord and Savior, I'm grateful that you will my release. I will it too. Our wills meet. Mine is released by that meeting.

Affirmation: Jesus' word is his prescription for me today.

For further reading: Matthew 9:20-22; Luke 8:42-48

HBTP 46

---

[5]E. Stanley Jones, *Abundant Living* (Nashville, Abingdon Press, 1951; Festival edition 1978).

Gradual or Sudden Conversions

*"Let the little children come to me,
and do not stop them; for it is to such as
these that the kingdom of heaven belongs."*
—Matthew 19:14

Conversion results "in a *change, gradual or sudden.*" Some conversions are gradual and some are sudden. Some unfold like a flower to the sun—the gradual type. Others take a sudden leap to the breast of God. Some children who were brought up in a Christian home can "testify that 'from childhood' they knew, not the Scriptures, but God himself. . . . "

. . . Jesus said of little children, "To such belongs the kingdom of heaven" (RSV). They are in the kingdom of God and get out only by sinning out. If therefore we can keep them in from the beginning, then so much the better. Many wanderings and wounds would be saved. . . . But most of us need a definite and decisive round-about-face resulting in an unfolding or sudden conversion. . . . Both types are valid if they are vital.

The important thing is to come to Christ.

O God, if I have any lingering doubts left, I lay them at your feet in a self-surrender.

Affirmation: I rest on the promise of Christ's word.

For further reading: Luke 18:1-4; 19:13-15

HBTP 47

30

"I'm In"

Therefore, since we are justified by faith, we have peace with God through our Lord Jesus Christ.
—Romans 5:1

At the close of one of a series of luncheon addresses for the bankers and businessmen of Wall Street, one of these men said: "Where do you go next? I'd like to take you in my car."...We had scarcely started when he said..., "How do you get hold of the thing you are talking about?" ...As we went through the roaring traffic I told him the steps: self-surrender, acceptance, obedience. I felt he was inwardly taking them. Then we came to the moment when I felt we should talk with God. "Do you think we could pray going through the traffic of this city?" I asked. "Well, I'd like you to pray, but I'll have to keep my eyes on the traffic," he replied. "All right," I said, "you watch and I'll pray." I'm not sure but what I kept my own eyes open!

But we were borne up into God's help, for God was looking for this hour of self-surrender and acceptance. As I jumped out of the car to go to my appointment he grabbed my hand in both of his and said very simply, "Thank you. I'm in." And he was!

Nobody is ever farther than three steps from the kingdom of God.

We can find God at any time and in any place.

My Father, I want "in" to your kingdom.

Affirmation: God is looking for me.

For further reading: Acts 15:8-11; 16:23-34

HBTP 49

Found by God

31 ~

"Believe on the Lord Jesus, and you will be saved."
—Acts 16:31

Nobody is ever farther than three steps from the kingdom of God.

(1) Self-surrender, which includes sin-surrender.

(2) Acceptance of the gift of God—the gift of salvation.

(3) Obedience—obedience to the unfolding will of God.

Anybody, anywhere, any time, can take these three steps and will be "in." It works with an almost mathematical precision. The infallibility of the Bible is in this. If anyone will take the way of Jesus, he will infallibly find God. This is an infallibility not to be argued about but to be experienced here and now. But really we don't find God; we let God find us. These three steps put us in the way of being found by God. In reality no one is ever more than one step from God—just turn and you are in the arms of redeeming love. If this sounds too good to be true, remember it is too good not to be true.

We do not need to be afraid of being found by God.

My Father, I am so close to being found that I am found in the very fact of grasping this truth—that your love is just waiting for me to turn.

Affirmation: I do not hold God—he holds me.

For further study: Acts 9:1-19; 2 Corinthians 5:14-15

HBTP 49

41

32   Coiled the Wrong Way

"You are a stumbling block to me; for you are setting your mind not on divine things but on human things."
—Matthew 16:23

We come now to another step in our definition of conversion: "By which we pass from the kingdom of self to the kingdom of God."

The center of sin is self-centeredness—all else is marginal. Halford Luccock has defined sin as "disharmony with the moral nature and purpose of God as revealed in Christ.".... To be centered in self is the center of the disharmony.... That is an attempt to arrange the universe around the wrong center.

An animal importer was looking for an expert snake winder who could unwind a fifteen-foot python. It was so bad tempered that no one could approach the box in which it was coiled. "It's because the snake was coiled into the box the wrong way. I am trying to find someone who can rewind it the right way." When we are coiled around self as the center, then we are coiled the wrong way. We are ill-tempered, out of sorts with ourselves and people and situations. When the inner life is coiled around God as the center, then we are good-tempered, in harmony with ourselves and people and situations. Conversion is changing us from an unnatural coil around the wrong center to a natural coil around God as the center.

What is the center of your life?

O Christ, you have come to make me well at the center. Make me new there and I am new everywhere.

Affirmation: With God at my center I will live in harmony with myself and others.

For further reading: Matthew 16:21-26

HBTP 50

42

Self-Punishment to Self-Surrender

*Did you receive the Spirit by doing the works
of the law or by believing what you heard?*
—Galatians 3:2b

The crux of the transformation [of conversion] is that we pass from the kingdom of self to the kingdom of God. [But] there is no use trying to repress the self; that only makes it fester.

A prominent man in a personal conference told me how he tried to master his ego by penances. As a penance for his sins he would tie his arm to the bedpost, so that he would be so uncomfortable in that position with his arm up that he couldn't sleep. It ended in frustration, for penance is not repentance. Penance is a religious masochism where you inflict punishment on the self. But in repentance and self-surrender the self ceases its own rule and takes God's rule, abdicates the throne and kneels before the throne of God. This man saw this, ceased his self-punishment and passed to self-surrender.

God waits to receive us, not to punish us.

God, my Father, I know you have your finger on the center of my problem, myself. Help me not to dodge or evade or excuse, but to surrender.

Affirmation: Today, no criticism; only love, sympathy, compassion.

For further reading: Galatians 2:15–3:7

HBTP 52

43

In Alignment

" 'If then your whole body is full of light, with
no part of it in darkness, it will be as full of light
as when a lamp gives you light with its rays.' "
—Luke 11:36

"With no part . . . in darkness"—that is total conversion.
But until the self is surrendered to God, then the center and
the margin are both dark. Centered in yourself, you are
like an electric lightbulb out of its socket trying by its own
efforts to be light. But centered in God, then you are that
bulb fastened in the socket, glowing with light and warmth.

When steel is magnetized, the electrons are aligned with
each other. Before being magnetized, the electrons are helter-
skelter, at cross-purposes, but being magnetized, they are
together, working together, hence magnetism has drawing
power. Until we surrender our self to God we are inwardly
at cross-purposes, life is helter-skelter, canceling itself
out; it is ineffective and repels people rather than draws
people. But when the self is surrendered to God, then it is
aligned to God, which puts us into alignment with ourselves, which in turn makes us inwardly a cooperative
order, which makes us magnetic persons.

To what are you aligned?

O God, I do not want to be at cross-purposes with you or
with myself. Take me and make me your magnetic person.

Affirmation: Today I shall live by the first law of life—the law of self-
surrender.

For further reading: Luke 11:33-36; Galatians 5:22-25

HBTP 54, 53

A Living Fellowship

35

We are members of one another.
—*Ephesians 4:25*

The last portion of the definition of conversion is that one "becomes a part of a living fellowship, the church."

Suppose one tries to take the conversion without the fellowship of the church. Will it work? Across the years I have found that where the fellowship of the church fades out, conversion and its fruits fade out.

In one day two people came to see me, both in spiritual trouble. One was a youth who told me he was staying away from church because he and his girl friend had broken up some months before. He became very unhappy, for he was deteriorating. He came to church that night, surrendered to Christ and became radiantly happy. Another was a pastor's wife who had given up resentments against her husband, but pulled out of the church when she felt he had let her down. She simply stayed away. She deteriorated. . . .

A. J. Muste, after leaving the church for Marxian communism, came back to it. "I return to the church," he said, "because these years have taught me that the church of the redeemed is the only redeeming agency."

**You cannot break fellowship
any more than you can break a bone
and not get hurt.**

O Christ, thank you that your church is the mother of my spirit. Here I find fellowship, and most of all, here I find you.

Affirmation: I belong to the body of Christ and will live connected to it.

For further reading: Ephesians 5:25-30; 1 Corinthians 12:14-27

HBTP 55

The Kingdom of God: Homeland of the Soul

36

The Kingdom of God Is Within You

Behold, the kingdom of God is within you.
—Luke 17:21 KJV

When Jesus said, "The kingdom of God is within you," he voiced one of the most important things ever uttered. The seeds of a new humanity are in that statement....

If the kingdom of God is within us, written into the constitution of our beings, the way we are made to live, then sin is not less tragic, but more so. For then we sin not only against a God afar off, but also against a God who is that kingdom within us—it is intimate rejection, intimate slaying. Moreover, we sin not only against God; we sin also against ourselves. Sin, therefore, is not the nature of our being; it is against nature—our nature—and against the God who made it.

Can it be that God's kingdom is within me?

O God, I see that when I sin, it is against the kingdom within. I disrupt myself, my possibilities, my future, my all. And I sin against you.

Affirmation: The kingdom of God is within me.

For further reading: Romans 8:9-13; Micah 6:8

AL 191

Within You—
At Your Doors!

Scripture

"Whenever you enter a town and its people welcome you
. . . say to them, 'The kingdom of God has come
near to you.' "
—Luke 10:9

There are two great streams of religious thought in the world today. One maintains, "Everything is within you; all you need to do is to awaken your latent powers; you have the spark of the Divine within you—kindle it.". . .

The other stream maintains, "You are a sinful creature; there is nothing good within you; you need the invading grace of God from without to awaken you, to redeem you.". . .

Each has a truth, but it is only a half-truth. The truth is beyond each; the truth is in the kingdom of God. . . . "The kingdom of God is within you.". . . "The kingdom of God is upon you" (Mark 1:15 REB) . . . at your doors.

Humans are sinful, sinning not only against the God who made us but also against the kingdom written into the texture of our being. We are sinning against ourselves. If sin is not only sinful but also unnatural, then sin is doubly bad—it is revolt against God and myself. Sin is anti-life.

How might you be sinning against yourself?

O God, you have not created me and then abandoned me, turning me over to forces too strong for me. You are protesting every step of my self-ruin.

Affirmation: I will not consent to my own ruin.

For further reading: Romans 7:24-25; 8:1-4

AL 192

Moral Tension

Do not let sin exercise dominion in your mortal bodies, to make you obey their passions.
—Romans 6:12

This kingdom-within-you emphasis heightens...tensions and leads more definitely to crisis, for now we see that we are in revolt against God and ourselves....

When people do right, do they feel less than human? They feel their personalities heightened; they are at home in the universe;...they walk the earth conquerors. Therefore goodness is native to us, and sin is unnatural, an aberration,...a defeat, a degradation. It is the accustomed but not the natural.

Where do you feel tension and stress?

O God, I do set up a tension between myself and my sin. In your name I revolt against it, repudiate it, break with it forever. I accept my native land—you, your kingdom.

Affirmation: I am at home in the kingdom of God, free and at my best.

For further reading: Romans 6:1-2, 11-23; 1 John 4:4

AL 193

Original Sin

The way of peace they do not know,
and there is no justice in their paths.
—Isaiah 59:8

There is a truth in original sin, which we should call racially acquired sin. The [human] race has sinned generation after generation and has passed on to posterity unnatural bents to evil. The natural urges—self, sex, and the herd—have been twisted by unnatural use to unnatural bents. . . .

If we are made in the image of God, then sin is not natural; it is the acquired—it is an attempt to live against nature, to live against life and escape the consequences. We pay tribute to this fact when we say of a bad man, "He is crooked," implying that he is departing from goodness, from the straight. . . . When we say of a person, "He is impure," we thereby suggest he has departed from the pure, the original intention. Impurity is therefore unnatural; purity is natural. . . . The sum total of reality is behind the pure person.

How might you be living against your God-given nature?

O God, you are teaching me your ways, written in your word and also written in me. Help me surrender to your purposes that I may live abundantly.

Affirmation: I will surrender my whole being to God's purposes and his vibrant life.

For further reading: Isaiah 59:1-8, 19-20; Deuteronomy 32:3-7

AL 194

49

The Kingdom of God
Is the Norm

[The Father] has rescued us from the power of darkness and transferred us into the kingdom of his beloved Son.
—Colossians 1:13

"The kingdom of God is within you." . . . There is a norm written within us, and . . . to depart from that norm is to end in disruption and self-frustration. . . . We who believe that our origin is in God would spell it with a capital N—Norm. To depart from it is to lose ourselves, to frustrate ourselves. . . .

Trying to live against the Norm [is] an impossible attempt. . . . It is bound to end in only one way—in self-defeat and self-frustration . . . for the nature of things works that way. Sin and its punishment are one and the same thing, for sin is "missing the mark"—the meaning of the Greek word *hamartia*, a departure from the Norm.

One does not have to impose punishment on a cancer for being a cancer, because being a cancer is its own punishment—it is bound to destroy itself and the other tissue in the body by its very nature. The end is death. "The wages of sin is death" (Romans 6:23)—"the wages," the natural outcome, the pay-off, is bound to be death, for the sin itself is death, a departure from Normal.

Are you missing the mark anywhere?

Father God, I stand in awe of your goodness. I see your footprints everywhere. They are within me. When I turn within, I am on holy ground.

Affirmation: I am God's temple. May everything within God's temple say, "Glory."

For further reading: Colossians 1:12-19; 1 Corinthians 2:15-16

AL 195

50

The Natural Man

The spiritual person is controlled by the kingdom of God and hence is a truly natural person. The unspiritual person is living against that kingdom within and hence is the unnatural person. . . .

When you discover the Christian way, you discover your own way as a person. To adopt the Christian way is to have your personality heightened. For it is unified, adjusted to the nature of Reality, and is therefore no longer under the law of self-frustration but of self-fulfillment. "The Spirit enabled them to express themselves" (Acts 2:4 Moffatt). True self-expression began when they were filled with the Spirit.

How are you looking for self-fulfillment?

O God, I have been afraid to surrender myself to your will lest my own will be lost. I now see that your will is my own deepest will and that to find your purposes is to find my person.

Affirmation: I will open myself to God's Spirit within me.

For further reading: 1 Corinthians 2:6-16; Ephesians 5:8-18

AL 196

51

42 The Kingdom of God Is the Cause

*"The kingdom of heaven is like treasure hidden in a
field, which someone found and hid; then in his joy he
goes and sells all that he has and buys that field."*
—Matthew 13:44-45

Education . . . has come to the conclusion that if a person
centers on self, the self will go to pieces. Only as we lose
our self in some great Cause beyond ourselves do we find
our self coming back to us integrated and heightened.
That is a law of human living as deeply imbedded in our
moral and spiritual universe as the force of gravity is
embedded in our material universe. . . . The laws of the
moral and spiritual world written into the constitution of
things . . . are self-authenticating—one doesn't have to
argue them. . . . They argue themselves. . . .
  The people who heard Jesus wondered at his authority—
it was the authority of the facts.

Have you submitted to the authority of the facts?

O God, we have been feverishly trying to support your universe with our puny arguments. Forgive us and help us to
trust implicitly in your self-authenticating truth.

Affirmation: I give myself to God's kingdom.

For further reading: Matthew 25:31-44; 16:24-28

AL 197

The Kingdom of God and Business

Scripture

" 'You shall love your neighbor as yourself.' "
—Matthew 22:39

When someone asked Daniel Willard, the head of the Baltimore and Ohio Railway, what was the outstanding qualification for a successful executive, he replied: "The ability and the willingness to put yourself in the other man's place." That is distinctly Christian—it is loving your neighbor as you love yourself,... projecting yourself in understanding sympathy and making the other person's difficulties and troubles your own. [Willard] came to that conviction not through dogmatic assertion from a pulpit, but through the method of trial and error—nothing else would work....

Goodwill is written into the constitution of things; ill will is sand in the machinery. Life will work with goodwill but not with ill will. You may try with infinite cleverness to make your universe hold together by ill will, but sooner or later it will topple and fall to pieces. Ill will is against the nature of reality.

**How might you be putting sand
in the machinery of your life?**

O God, how can I thank you enough for constituting me within so I can take you as naturally as the lungs take air? You and my soul have been separated but are not separate. You are my life.

Affirmation: God is my life, my breath, my being, my all.

For further reading: Luke 10:25-37

AL 198

44 — The Kingdom of God Is Among You

"The kingdom of God is not coming with things that can be observed; nor will they say, 'Look, here it is!' or 'There it is!' For, in fact, the kingdom of God is among you."
—Luke 17:20-21

If there is a way to get along with yourself, there is a way to get along with other people. In both cases it is God's way. If the kingdom of God is stamped into the constitution of your personal beings, it is also stamped into your social relationships with one another. Unless your relationships with one another proceed along the lines of certain inherent laws, they break down. You do not make or pass those laws—you only discover them; and if you break them you break yourself and the relationship.

For instance, you needn't love your neighbor as you love yourself; but if you don't you cannot get along with your neighbor. You do not get rid of your neighbors by not loving them; you transform them into a problem or a pain—but they are still on your hands. You broke the law of human relationships and so those relationships broke down.

Do your relationships with your neighbors need to be changed?

Gracious Father, you have written the family spirit into our relationships with the rest of the Family. Help me to catch your mind in my relationships with others.

Affirmation: My neighbor is part of God's Family—and part of mine.

For further reading: Luke 10:29-37; Proverbs 3:29

AL 199

54

45 — Trying to Dominate

Scripture

Do not be deceived; God is not mocked,
for you reap whatever you sow.
—Galatians 6:7

There are five ways in which we try to get along with one another. (1) Some try to dominate others. . . . What happens? The relationships break down and get snarled up. One man summed this up rather sadly when he said: "In the home I tried to be *it*, and I found my wife oppos*ite*." The type of action determined the reaction. . . .

"Do not be deceived" over initial success in domination, for "God is not mocked"—the nature of reality is against you and in the end will break you. "If you sow to your own flesh," the flesh of domination, "you will reap corruption from the flesh" (Galatians 6:8)—the situation and you will be corrupted, will deteriorate, will go to pieces and will collapse. The nature of reality foredooms the collapse.

"But if you sow to the Spirit"—if you align yourself with the eternal realities, "you will reap eternal life from the Spirit"—the sum total of reality will back you; you will have the power of survival, for you are living with and not against the grain of the universe. You reap an everlasting way to live—eternal life.

Are any of your relationships snarled? Why?

O Designer of eternal realities, I want to be fully surrendered to your purposes and your reality and thus live abundantly.

Affirmation: I set my heart on living by eternal realities.

For further reading: 1 John 4:7-12; Colossians 3:12-14

AL 200

46

Mutual Aid

The commandment we have from him is this: those who love God must love their brothers and sisters also.
—*1 John 4:21*

You cannot violate the law of love any more than you can violate the law of gravity and not get hurt. Suppose the law of mutual aid, which is the law of life among the organs and members of our bodies, should be violated by the members—the stomach falling out with the heart and refusing to give it nourishment; the heart retaliating and refusing to cooperate, . . . the arteries withholding pure blood and the veins holding up the elimination of impurities. . . . If the organs of the body became selfish and competitive instead of unselfish and cooperative, the whole system would collapse, and with it the parts. If the parts should save their life in self-centeredness, they would lose it. Only as they lose themselves in the interest of the whole do they find themselves again.

The law of mutual aid is not something imposed on the body from without as a decree; it is written into the very constitution of its being.

Where might you be violating the law of love by withholding aid to others?

Father, we come to you as foolish children, children who try to live against your ways and end only in hurting ourselves. Forgive us and give us the sense to live in your ways.

Affirmation: God's laws are God's love, and God's laws are my life.

For further reading: 1 John 4:12-21; 5:1-4; 2 John 5-6

AL 201

56

The Retreat
Away from People

*I appeal to you ... by the name of our Lord
Jesus Christ, that all of you be in agreement ...
united in the same mind and the same purpose.*
—1 Corinthians 1:10

(2) [The second way we try to get along with others is to]
try to live aloof from others. This is the opposite [of trying
to dominate them.] ...

Can we cut all human relationships, retreat into a shell,
and not be affected in our own being? Not at all. We will
deteriorate. If we cannot have a world of real human relationships, we build up a world of false relationships. We fill
our minds with fantasies and daydreams of superior personal
grandeur ... and so we remain aloof from the common herd.
Or we look at ourselves as inferior and ... not worthy to get
into relationships with others. In either case we are recessive
and we hurt our own mental and moral nature. Humans are
made inherently for relationships with others, and any
attempt to live apart brings inherent penalties.

To try to recede from people in order to protect oneself
morally and spiritually from temptation is also false strategy. I find more temptations when I am alone than when
I am with people. People can help us to be at our best by
their expectancy.

Have you taken your place in God's kingdom?

Gracious Father, you have set us within your Family. Teach
us not to run away from others but to enter into loving
relationships with one another.

Affirmation: God meets me in others. I will see God in them.

For further reading: Galatians 2:11-13; 1 Corinthians 1:10-13

AL 202

48 — Aloofness and Reserve

We have spoken frankly to you Corinthians;
our heart is wide open to you. There is no
restriction in our affections, but only in yours.
—2 Corinthians 6:11-12

(3) If receding from people will not work, neither will the third attitude of being indifferent to them produce any other result. It too will end in self-frustration and a breakdown of relationships.

(4) The fourth attitude we can take toward others is to work with others. This sounds like a great advance over the other positions, and yet, so imperious and so demanding is the kingdom of God that even this turns out to be inadequate. For we may work with others and yet reserve our inner life from others. So sensitive are these laws of the kingdom that an outer conformity to them will not do. If the inner self is withheld the relationships break down.

How might you be withholding yourself from other people?

O God, give me grace not only to trust your power but to trust my brothers and sisters in Christ. For we are together part of your kingdom.

Affirmation: I will open my heart to God and to others.

For further reading: 2 Corinthians 1:8-11

AL 202, 203, HBTP 256

Working with and for Others

For we are God's servants, working together.
—1 Corinthians 3:9

(5) There is only one attitude toward others that will work—the fifth one. Work with and for others. You must not only work with people; you must work for them as well. There must be positive outgoing good will, a desire to help the other person as you would be helped.

Labor and capital can work together, but in a suspicious, semihostile mood, fulfilling the letter of contracts, the relationship is only suppressed war. It will break out into overt hostility at the first provocation. Only minimum production results—each does as little as possible for the other. Only when the relationship is built on a generous and just basis—say a half-and-half division of profits between capital and labor—will there be relaxed attitudes of good will, a new spirit in the relationships, and a new increase in total output and hence in profits. Just generosity is literally the best policy. It obeys the law of the kingdom, "You shall love your neighbor as yourself" (Mark 12:31). This law is written into the constitution of our relationships, and hence it has the backing of the universe.

How might working for and with others be good for you?

God our Father, we have tried to live together on anti-kingdom principles, and we see the results in messed-up relationships and wars and poverty and general ruin. Forgive us.

Affirmation: I will live by the law of the kingdom: I will love my neighbor as myself.

For further reading: Philippians 1:27; 2 Corinthians 9:6-15

AL 203

50

The Kingdom of God Is at Your Doors!

Scripture

The time has arrived; the kingdom of God is upon you.
—Mark 1:14 REB

The kingdom of God is at your doors!...The kingdom is within us, among us; but it is also above us, beyond us, and is prepared to invade us from without.

This kingdom is within history and beyond history. It is within time and beyond time—eternal. It is within us and yet stands at our doors awaiting our consent for an invasion in fullness from without....If you insist only on a kingdom-within emphasis, you end in a vague mysticism which often flattens out into humanistic techniques for awakening your latent powers. But if you insist only on the kingdom-from-without, then you end in making sin natural, in rendering human beings helpless, in becoming pessimistic about human nature. God becomes more or less absentee and wholly Other....

How do we see the nature of this kingdom...? Only as we look at the historical Christ do we really see the full meaning of the kingdom.

"You are the new order," was said to a certain Christian. But only in Christ do we really see the new Order.

What is your relationship to Christ?

O Christ, we turn to you to see the meaning of God's kingdom, so that we do not get it wrong or go astray.

Affirmation: I will look steadily at Christ for the pattern of God's kingdom.

For further reading: Mark 1:16-20; 2:13-14; Matthew 12:28

AL 204

God Rules in Terms of Christ

Scripture

*"If I do [the works of my Father]...believe the
works, so that you may know and understand
that the Father is in me and I am in the Father."*
—John 10:38

The kingdom of God is at your doors! The divine invasion
is near! The nature of that divine invasion is seen in
Christ. He is the personal approach from the unseen. In
Christ...we see into the nature of God and also into the
nature of God's reign....

In Christ the kingdom is...given a personal content....
When I give myself to the kingdom I give myself to the
Person who embodies that kingdom. That makes my relationship with the kingdom warm and tender and personal.
...In Christ it is possible both to be loyal to and to love the
kingdom. For in him the kingdom looks out at me with
tender eyes, loves me with warm love, and touches me
with strong, redemptive hands—it is personal.

Is God's kingdom personal for you?

O Christ, in you I see into the heart and meaning of God's
kingdom, and I surrender to that kingdom with complete
abandon.

Affirmation: I belong to Christ who shows me the nature of God's
kingdom.

For further reading: John 1:1-5; 14:7-11

AL 205

The Kingdom
and Repentance

"Very truly, I tell you, no one can see the kingdom
of God without being born from above."
—John 3:3

Two awakenings [to the kingdom of God] are necessary.
(1) We are to be awakened to the kingdom within us—to
discover the latent powers hidden away in the recesses of
our beings, to become alive to our possibilities, to become
aware of our divine origin and our divine destiny.

(2) We are to be awakened to the kingdom outside us—
the invading kingdom that precipitates crisis. We sense a
tension between this kingdom and what we are. . . .

The crisis demands that we repent, that we submit, that
we be changed, that we be converted, that we let this kingdom outside us invade us with its healing, its reconciliation, its life. When we fling open the doors of our being and
let this kingdom invasion possess us, we are not letting in
something strange, something alien. We are letting in the
very Fact for which we are made. The kingdom within us
rises up to meet the kingdom without us, and together they
cast out the unnatural kingdom of sin and evil.

Perhaps the tension you are feeling is a call to repentance.

O Christ, you are the Love of my love, the Joy of my joy,
the Peace of my peace, the Being of my being. When I welcome you, I welcome my long-estranged self.

Affirmation: In Christ's kingdom I am at rest, at peace, at home.

For further reading: John 3:1-5; Luke 18:17; Romans 5:1; 8:6-11

AL 206

The Kingdom as Invasion

"The one who sows the good seed is the Son of Man."
—Matthew 13:37

When we welcome this invading kingdom, we welcome the heavenly Natural—the homeland of our soul. Jesus said, "The earth beareth fruit of herself" (Mark 4:28 KJV). The soil and the seed are made for each other. The soil of your being and the seed of the kingdom are affinities. You have tried to grow the poisonous weeds of sin in the soil of your being, but the whole process brought not comfort but conflict, not rest but rebellion. . . .

But the nature of the kingdom cannot be truly seen by looking within. . . . Only in the face of Christ do we see the nature of the kingdom. . . . We see in him what it costs God to get to us in spite of our sin. The kingdom at our doors came down to us through an Incarnation, down to us through a Cross, down to us through a Resurrection, down to the very threshold of our being, there to await our consent for entrance. . . .

The barriers have been broken down from God's side by his offensive of suffering, redemptive love.

Have you considered the cost of God's love?

Gracious Christ, you have come to me at supreme cost. Your kingdom knocks with nail-pierced hands at my doors. Help me to open with hands that are willing to be pierced.

Affirmation: I will respond to Christ with all the cost I can pay.

For further reading: Matthew 13:37-43; John 3:16; 15:1-6

AL 207

54

Choosing Life

*For the wages of sin is death, but the free gift
of God is eternal life in Christ Jesus our Lord.*
—Romans 6:23

The coming of the kingdom to our doors was costly.... It cost God and it will cost us.... "For God so loved the world that he gave his only Son, so that everyone who believes in him may not perish but may have eternal life" (John 3:16). Those who do not receive this kingdom do "perish" literally, for their life forces break down through contradiction and strife. When you let in his kingdom you have ever-lasting life—you align yourself with the eternal realities of Being; hence you live, now and everlastingly.

The coming in of that kingdom means crisis, choice, conversion.... "Wretched man that I am! Who will rescue me from this body of death?" or, literally, "this dead body" (Romans 7:24). The figure is that of a live person chained to a dead body, carrying around a decaying corpse as punishment.... Sin is anti-kingdom, therefore anti-life; therefore it is doomed to decay and the one who harbors it "perishes." But that dead body of sin is not the real person—it is a false importation into life, a useless, infecting incumbrance. The real person is the person with the kingdom of God written within.

What do you need to be loosed from?

O Christ, you have come to loose the chains of this dead body. I come to you to free me from decaying death.

Affirmation: I gladly consent to let go this sin whose embrace is death.

For further reading: Romans 7:14-25

AL 208

55 Resisting Conversion

"What does it profit them if they gain the whole world, but lose or forfeit themselves?"
—Luke 9:25

A brilliant doctor, whose inner life was a mass of conflicts, returned to me an inscribed New Testament with this written on the wrapper: "I hate Him, and I hate you." I had scarcely received this outburst when another letter came, saying: "Where is God, and where are you?"

Here is the stark first stage of kingdom invasion—a soul resisting God, and yet reaching out for him; telling him to go, and yet entreating him to stay!

Rebelling, repelling—relenting, repenting: these are the alternate heartbeats of the heart that feels the pressure of the divine invasion.

Consent—conversion: these are the alternate beats in the first stage of acceptance.

What is the heartbeat of your life?

O Christ, forgive me if I hesitate, resisting you, but I have lived with death so long that I think it is life. I want real life—your life.

Affirmation: I will open my life to Christ.

For further reading: Luke 18:18-25

AL 209, 208

56 — The Crises of Conversion and Cleansing

Scripture

"You will receive power when the Holy Spirit has come upon you."
—Acts 1:8

When we consent [to God's kingdom], the divine invasion usually takes place in two great crises: (1) the crisis of conversion; (2) the crisis of a deeper cleansing. . . . The crisis of conversion brings release from festering sins, and marks the introduction of a new life. Conversion is a glorious release, but not a full release. Festering sins are gone, but the roots of the disease are still there. . . .

While I was in an acute stage of appendicitis, I was operated on. When I came to consciousness the doctor told me, "I have drained the inflamed appendix, but I couldn't take it out, for there were too many adhesions. This will relieve you, but you'll have to have the appendix and the adhesions taken out later." After that I was better but I wasn't well. Six months later I had the appendix and the adhesions taken out. Then I was not only better; I was well.

Sin throws its adhesions around the organs of life, but neither the sin nor the adhesions are natural. Salvation, in these two great crises, drains the poison, unlooses the adhesions, and restores to the truly natural—gives health!

Question

Are there poisons in your life?

Prayer

Tender and skillful Invader of my soul, I yield my stricken life to your healing. Drain every drop of poison from my being, and then root out the adhering results of that poison.

Affirmation: I want not only to be better; I want also to be well.

For further reading: Luke 9:23-26, 24:49; Acts 1:8

AL 209

The Kingdom of God and Freedom

*"You will know the truth,
and the truth will make you free."*
—John 8:32

When we harbor sin within us... we have to live out our life under a double protest: the protest of what we really are, in contrast to the false world we have built up, and the protest of what we might be. One protest is from the kingdom within, and the other from the kingdom without. Sin is therefore caught within a pincer movement.... Evil must surrender and succumb if we are to live. When it truly surrenders, then the kingdom within and the kingdom without coalesce, and we are possessed by an inner unity; we are possessed by Life! We are now truly natural, hence rhythmical and harmonious and adequate.

The paradox is this: When we find this invading kingdom, we find ourselves.... When I belong most to the kingdom, I belong most to myself. When I try to live in un-kingdom ways, I lose both the kingdom and myself. Here then in the kingdom I find my perfect freedom.

Are you looking for a harmonious life?

My God, I take the yoke of the kingdom and I find it easy, for your yoke is my yearning. I take your burden and I find it light, for your burden is my bounty; your burden is light.

Affirmation: When I take God I find myself.

For further reading: John 8:31-32; Matthew 11:28-30; Romans 6:16-23

AL 210

67

Naturalized in the Unnatural!

"He would gladly have filled himself with the pods that the pigs were eating."
—Luke 15:16

We have been so accustomed to false ways of life that we think them our true nature. We hold to our unnaturalness and suspect God's true nature. A woman who had lived all her life in the foul, heavy air of the slums of New York said that she got physically sick when she went into the country and breathed the pure fresh air. Her lungs had become so accustomed to unnatural foulness that natural freshness was unnatural! . . .

That is the tragedy of our humanity. We see that our ways won't work, and yet we hesitate to take God's way. . . . Christ . . . sees us with our unworkable ways of life, running into roads with dead ends, ending in frustration and futility, losing our means of living, and our lives themselves, and he says again: "Seek ye first the kingdom of God . . . and all these things shall be added unto you" (Matthew 6:33 KJV). But we are seeking other things first, and all these things are being subtracted from us.

Are you living with subtraction rather than addition?

Gracious Father, we have our life strategy wrong and things won't come out right. We become all tangled up because we will not take your way. Help us to have sense—to abandon our ways of futility for your way of fruitfulness.

Affirmation: I will seek first God's kingdom.

For further reading: Luke 15:11-24; Romans 1:19-25

AL 211

Seek First the Kingdom of God

*"Strive first for the kingdom of God
and his righteousness,
and all these things
will be given to you as well."*
—Matthew 6:33

What did [Jesus] mean by "all these things"? He mentioned the simple things: food, drink, and clothing (Matthew 6:31). In other words, the kingdom of God is concerned not merely with supplying us a heavenly world after this life, but with supplying our need for bodily sustenance in this life. Get the central spiritual facts straight, says Jesus, and your material facts will be straight, too....

In seeking first the kingdom of God...the material basis of human life will be guaranteed to you. You will have what you need. "Your heavenly Father knows that you need all these things" (v. 32). Note that you will get according to your *need*, not according to your *greed*. You have a right to as much of the material as will make you mentally, spiritually, and physically fit for the purposes of the kingdom of God.

Are your central spiritual facts straight?

God, my Father, you have written your laws into matter as well as into mind and spirit. Help me to live by your laws.

Affirmation: Thank you, Father, for supplying my needs.

For further reading: Matthew 6:25-33

AL 215

60 — The Results of Too Little and Too Much

As many as owned lands or houses sold them and brought the proceeds of what was sold. They laid it at the apostles' feet, and it was distributed to each as any had need.
—Acts 4:34-35

In order to have a proper physical basis for abundant living we must surrender the will to be rich, and determine to keep only enough wealth to supply our need—and no more. We must likewise surrender the will that reconciles itself to poverty, and determine to make enough to supply our needs—and no less. . . . Need should be supplied—no less, no more. . . .

There is one, and only one, basis for the material life in the New Testament. . . . "[Money] was distributed to each as any had need." The word *need* is used in the New Testament seven times in relationship to the material. . . .

The frustrations in modern society . . . are in large measure due to the breaking of this law of the kingdom. Some have too little; some have too much. Result: war, instability, frustration. God's way is our way. And we take our way against God's way at our peril and to our frustration.

What place do possessions have in your life?

Gracious God, help me to be so related to the material that it may be my minister and not my master.

Affirmation: God will supply all that I need as I seek his kingdom.

For further reading: Acts 4:32-35; Matthew 6:8-13

AL 217, 216

Getting and Giving

You sent me help for my needs more than once....
And my God will fully satisfy every need of yours
according to his riches in glory in Christ Jesus.
—Philippians 4:16, 19

All God's promises are conditional, for God must not merely give—he must give in such a way that the person receiving is stimulated, not smothered. God must not merely make a gift; he must make a person.

Abundant living will not come through eternally receiving. One can dry up while eternally receiving. Abundant living depends upon abundant giving. If therefore we should stop at the thought "to each according to his need," we would create a parasitic society—everyone with a stretched out hand.... The other side... is "from each according to his ability." If you do not give to the good of society according to your ability, then you will not get according to your need.

The two principles imbedded in the New Testament are: "They would...distribute the proceeds to all, as any had need" (Acts 2:45), and "Anyone unwilling to work should not eat" (2 Thessalonians 3:10)....This way of life is neither socialism nor democracy but Christianity, for that is where these twin principles originally came from....If you do not give, you cannot get.

How is your life balanced between giving and getting?

Father, you have made your children for creative activity. Help me to be a channel of your creative energy—to pass on what you have so richly given me.

Affirmation: Today I will be a giver.

For further reading: Acts 2:43-47; 4:32-35; 2 Thessalonians 3:6-13

AL 218

Seeking First
the Kingdom Means Action

*"Give, and it will be given to you. A good
measure, pressed down, shaken together,
running over, will be put into your lap."*
—Luke 6:38

Abundant living means abundant giving. . . . If you are not
giving out to others, you . . . will go dry in spirit.

God will see to it that "all these things" will not "be
added unto you" if you do not "seek first the kingdom"
(Matthew 6:33 KJV). If you do not give back to society
according to ability, you will not get according to need. . . .

Seeking first the kingdom means committing the whole
of life to the proposition that the kingdom is first, last, and
always—and acting upon the committal. . . . Just as people
"seek" food, clothing, you are to "seek" the kingdom—it
must master your thinking, your emotions, your will, you.
That means that you discipline life to a one-pointedness.
In every situation you ask, "In this situation what does the
kingdom demand I should do?"—and you *do* it.

. . . "Thy kingdom come. Thy will be done in earth"
(Matthew 6:10 KJV). . . . The kingdom and the carrying out
of the will of God are one and inseparable.

How abundant is your living—and your giving?

O God, you have made me for strenuous endeavor; and
unless I work, I wither. Put your zeal within me.

Affirmation: I commit my will to God's will, to do what the kingdom
demands.

For further reading: Matthew 7:21; John 5:30; Hebrews 11:6

AL 219

The Kingdom and the Church

We must grow up in every way into him who is the head, into Christ.
—Ephesians 4:15

The kingdom of the Church must bend the knee to the kingdom of God. Just as we want our state, our race, our class to be dominant, so we want our church to be dominant....

God sometimes works through the denomination, sometimes in spite of it, but never exclusively or particularly in any of them. If that hurts your denominational pride, it may help your Christian humility! The saints are about equally distributed among all denominations....

No one denomination has the truth. The truth is in Christ, who is "the Truth." What we hold are truths about the Truth.... He is beyond us all, and more than us all....

The church is not an end in itself; it is a means to the end of the kingdom of God.

Hold your denomination up to the light of Christ.

O God, forgive us that we have made of your glorious Church an idol. We offer it to you to be the instrument of your redemption.

Affirmation: Jesus Christ is the Way, the Truth, and the Life.

For further reading: Ephesians 4:1-7; 1 Corinthians 3:1-9

AL 223

Finding God
Through Jesus Christ

64

The Hidden God

> Truly, you are a God who hides himself,
> O God of Israel, the Savior.
> —Isaiah 45:15

Here is the hidden God. Like the hidden thought...we cannot know what he is like unless he communicates himself through a word.

If you say, "I can know God in my heart intuitively and immediately, without the mediation of a word," then the answer is: "But your 'heart' then becomes the medium of communication and knowing the heart as you do with its sin and crosscurrents and cross-conceptions you know it is a very unsafe medium for the revelation of God."

God must reveal himself.

**Only as the hidden thought is put into a word
is the thought communicated.**

O God, my Father, you are the hidden God. How can I, bounded by my senses, know you unless you show yourself to me? I cannot read you unless I get a word from you.

Affirmation: If the word is the expression of the hidden thought, I shall be, in some real way, the expression of the hidden God.

For further reading: John 1:1-3, 14; Job 23:1-10

WBF 19

The Word

Scripture

*In the beginning was the Word, and the
Word was with God, and the Word was God.*
—John 1:1

Here is the hidden God, and he expresses himself through
the Word. . . .

Jesus is called the Word because the word is the expression of the hidden thought. Unless I put my thought into
words you cannot understand it. Here is God; we sense his
presence, but he is Spirit, hence hidden. We want to know
what he is like—not in omnipotence, nor in omniscience,
nor in omnipresence; a revelation of these would do little
or no good, but we would know his character, for what he
is like in character, we, his children, must be. So the
Hidden Thought—God—becomes the Revealed Word—
Christ.

Do you hear God speaking through Jesus?

O God, continue to reveal yourself to me through your
Son, Jesus Christ, my Lord.

Affirmation: I believe in God, Father of our Lord Jesus Christ.

For further reading: John 1:4-5; Hebrews 1:1-3

COTM 28, WBF 20

66

Did God Have to Become Human?

*Long ago God spoke to our ancestors
in many and various ways....
—Hebrews 1:1*

Did God have to become human to show himself?...

Well,...he can reveal himself through nature. But not perfectly.... The song we sing, "How great Thou art," tells of looking at the stars and hearing the rolling thunder and concluding that God is "great," but great in what? The stars look down on us indifferent as to our moral character, and the rolling thunder and the flashing lightning may hit a brothel or a baby with no moral discrimination. So nature's revelation of God is equivocal.

Then God reveals himself through prophet and teacher and sage, but not perfectly, for the medium of revelation is imperfect and the message...partakes of that imperfection.

Then there is...revelation through a book. We must be grateful for every inspired word which has come down to us through a book...but not satisfied....First, a book is impersonal and God is the infinitely Personal; second, a book is the Word become word, not the Word become flesh.

God *has* provided a perfect, personal revelation.

O Father, we search through various ways and media to find you. We are homesick for you—you are our Home. Apart from you we wander from thing to thing and from place to place, seeking rest.

Affirmation: My restless heart will rest in God today.

For further reading: John 1:1-3, 14-15; Hebrews 1

WBF 21

The Lived-Out Word

64

The Word became flesh and lived among us,
and we have seen his glory, the glory as of a
father's only son, full of grace and truth.
—John 1:14

Jesus [the Word] is not a Third Person standing between me and God. Rather he is God projected to me, God become available. . . .

   This Word is not a spelled-out Word, it is a lived-out Word. He is indeed the speech of eternity translated into the language of time, but the language is a Life. God's method is a Man. Jesus is . . . God meeting me in my environment, a human environment. He is God showing his character in the place where our characters are formed. He is the human life of God.

How wonderful! God speaks my language!

O Father, when I talk with you, I know I am not listening to the echo of my own voice, but hearing your Word, spelled out in Jesus.

Affirmation: I trust you, God, because you are like Jesus Christ.

For further reading: Matthew 6:43-48; John 10:25-30

COTM 30, WBF 32

68 — Jesus Puts a Face on God

No one has ever seen God. It is God the only Son, who is close to the Father's heart, who has made him known.
—John 1:18

Christianity "puts a face on God." Jesus is God's face.... The Psalmist asks: "He who planted the ear, does he not hear? \ He who formed the eye, does he not see?" (Psalm 94:9). And we may add, "He who made the human personality, shall he not be personal?" He can't be less than personal, for personality is the highest category of being we know....I don't mean he is corporeal—an enlarged Man seated in the heavens. In personality there are at least four things: intelligence, feeling, will, self-consciousness. So when we say that God is personal, we believe he thinks, he feels, he wills, he has self-consciousness....

Prayer and worship are response on the part of the person to the response of the Person.

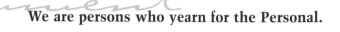

We are persons who yearn for the Personal.

O Father God, thank you for showing us your face in the face of Jesus, and for letting us hear your voice in his. I am listening.

Affirmation: I will listen for God's voice today and respond.

For further reading: John 10:11-18; 27-30

WBF 32, 33

69 — Jesus Is the Last Word About God

*Long ago God spoke to our ancestors
in many and various ways by the prophets, but in these
last days he has spoken to us by a Son,
whom he appointed heir of all things.*
—*Hebrews 1:1-2*

A great many people think Jesus was a moralist imposing a moral code upon humanity—a code for which humanity is badly made.... But Jesus was not a moralist in that sense at all. He was a revealer of the nature of reality. First of God. He said, if you want to know what God is like look at me. "Whoever has seen me has seen the Father" (John 14:9). We see the Father in the face of his Son. God is like Jesus in character. Transfer every characteristic of character from Jesus to God, and you do not lower your estimate of God—you heighten it. For there is nothing higher for God or humans than to be Christlike. Jesus is God simplified, God approachable, God understandable, God lovable. When I say "God" I think Jesus. And nothing higher can be thought or said! Jesus is the last word that can be said about God.

**To follow Jesus is to accept Truth
embodied in a Person.**

O Jesus, I accept you in every portion of my life and with the consent of all my being.

Affirmation: I will follow Jesus, today and always.

For further reading: John 14:8-13; Hebrews 12:1-2; 13:8

WBF 37

79

What Do I Want to Know About God?

No one has ever seen God; the only Son, who is in the bosom of the Father, he has made him known.
—*John 1:18 RSV*

You cannot describe God; you can only show him, make him known. Jesus has made God known in the only way he can be made known—by life.

What do I want to know about God?...I want to know what God is like in character. For what he is like in character, I must be like. I cannot be at cross purposes with Reality and not get hurt. So Jesus makes known the character of God, makes it known in the only possible way his character can be made known, namely through another character—his own.

And he reveals the central thing in God's character—Love! "The only Son, who is in the bosom of the Father"—"the bosom" represents the heart of God. Jesus is not in the arm of the Father—his omnipotence; nor in the mind of the Father—his omniscience. He is in the bosom of the Father, the revelation of his love. So Jesus came, stripping himself of everything as he came—omnipotence, omniscience, omnipresence—everything except love. "He emptied himself" (Philippians 2:7), emptied himself of everything except love. Love—his only protection, his only weapon, his only method.

Love is the only omniscience, the only omnipotence.

O Jesus, you used love and only love, and you won with love and only love. Now we see into the heart of God.

Affirmation: In some faint way I shall make my Father known in everything I do today.

For further reading: Philippians 2:1-11; 1 John 4:7-12

WBF 37

Why Did God Create Us Free?

So God created humankind in his image;
in the image of God he created them.
—Genesis 1:27

I have often wondered why God dared to create humans and to create them free. It was a risky business.... God would have to limit himself. He would have to step back and allow that free will to operate. He could not coerce it, for if he did, the will would not be free. And the will would have to be free in both directions... to choose evil as well as good or it would not be free.... But suppose that will should go wrong—it would break its own heart and the heart of God too. For God would have to live alongside that straying, rebellious will as love. And it is the nature of love to insinuate itself into the sins and sorrows of the loved one and make them its own. If love stays out of the sins and sorrows of the loved one, it is no longer love. But if it gets in it bleeds. All love has the doom of bleeding upon it as long as there is sin in the loved one....

God saw the risk and took it on one condition, that anything that falls on humans would fall on God himself. He would bear our sin and sorrow in his own body.

God is not an absentee father.

O God, my Father, I wonder at such love that would take such risks and carry through, though it meant the cross. My heart is bowed in deepest gratitude and profoundest awe.

Affirmation: God's love has me forever and forever.

For further reading: Isaiah 53:4-6; 1 Peter 2:21-24

WBF 112

81

The Unseen Cross on the Heart of God

You were ransomed...not with perishable things...but with the precious blood of Christ, like that of a lamb without defect or blemish. He was destined before the foundation of the world.
—1 Peter 1:18-20

We ended yesterday on the thought that God being love would create objects of love upon whom he could lavish his love and be loved in return. But God would be responsible for humans' sin by making humans free! Yes, and God accepted that responsibility and discharged it upon a cross.

That is what the passage means in the book of Revelation where it speaks of "the Lamb slain from the foundation of the world" (13:8 KJV). But the Gospel accounts say that he was slain two thousand years ago! No, the cross began the moment humans sinned. There was an unseen cross upon the heart of God the moment human beings began to sin. The Lamb was slain from the foundation of the world.

But how would we know that there is an unseen cross upon the heart of God? He is Spirit....We could not know unless he showed this inner cross through an outer cross. The outer cross lifted up in history shows the inner cross upon the heart of God.

In the cross we see what our sins cost God.

Father God, I know my sins hurt you, but I never saw it before I saw it in the cross. Now I know what my sins cost you. In response, I give you myself. Thank you for the cross.

Affirmation: I am a child of God's love, and in response, I will follow him.

For further reading: 1 Peter 1:18-21; Ephesians 1:3-10

WBF 113

God Was in Christ

God was in Christ, reconciling the world unto himself, not imputing their trespasses unto them.
—2 Corinthians 5:19 KJV

An Italian painter has painted the nails going through the hands of Jesus, through the wood into the hands of God back in the shadows. "God was in Christ"—in his suffering, in his bearing "our sins in his own body on the tree" (1 Peter 2:24 KJV). He isn't laying our sins on Jesus to appease his own anger—he took it on himself.

If there isn't a God like that in the universe, there ought to be one. Would the highest in humans rise higher than the highest in God? . . . He who made love, will he not love? He who put the impulse to sacrifice themselves into the souls of the highest human beings, will he not sacrifice? Will human beings rise higher than their Maker?

**The cross lights up the nature of God
as redemptive love.**

O God, our Heavenly Father, we are now at the heart of things. Take us by the hand and take us into this Divine mystery—this open secret of the universe. Open our minds, hearts, wills to it.

Affirmation: God has shown me The Way—that Way a cross. I will follow.

For further reading: 2 Corinthians 5:16-21; 1 Peter 2:21-25; Romans 5:1-11

WBF 114

What About Law?

*Do not be deceived; God is not mocked,
for you reap whatever you sow.*
—Galatians 6:7

If love is in God, if God is love, then what about the law side of things?...Do love and law meet in Jesus?...

The Hindus stress the law of sowing and reaping—the law of karma. They believe there can be no forgiveness. Whatever suffering you are undergoing is just. You are reaping what you have sown....Christianity also has this law of sowing and reaping....This is a universe where you get results or you get consequences. If you work with the moral universe, you get results—you will have cosmic backing for your way of life. But if you go against the moral universe, you will be up against it—you will get consequences. You will reap what you sow.

This is a halftruth, however. You alone do not reap what you sow—other people reap what you sow, for good or evil...family...friends...community, and, faintly, the world. This vicarious passing on to others...has far-reaching consequences—very far.

**There are results of our actions—
but there is also forgiveness.**

O God our Father, you are bound up with our sin and our sorrow—but not alone. We are bound up with one another for good or ill. Help me to come to terms with this moral universe, and to accept your redemption.

Affirmation: I reap what I sow.

For further reading: 2 Corinthians 5:21; 1 Corinthians 1:30; Romans 5:12-17

WBF 115

We Reap What He Sowed

*God made you alive together with [Christ],
...erasing the record that stood against us
..., nailing it to the cross
—Colossians 2:13-14*

We can pass on to others the fruit of our [deeds]. The greater the person the more far-reaching the effects of that passing on.... Suppose there were one who stood at the center of life as the Son of Man and the Son of God, a part of God and a part of every human being, could he not pass on to every child of the race the effects of his life and acts?... And could we reap, not what we sow, but what he sowed? That is, if we identify ourselves with him by surrender and obedience? If we are "in him," do we not reap what he sowed—his victory our victory, his love our love, his purity our purity?

At the cross we find God Incarnate sowing himself in sacrifice for his creatures.... Now we need not reap what we sowed. We all reap what Jesus Christ sowed—redemption! That is not a philosophy—the Word became word; it is a fact—the Word became flesh.

This is not good views—it is Good News!

O Jesus, Lord and Savior, when we look at you upon the cross, all our half-truths become flickering candles. You bore the consequences of my acts, my sin, so that I might reap what you sowed—redemption and life. Thank you.

Affirmation: "The free gift of God is eternal life in Christ Jesus our Lord" (Romans 6:23).

For further reading: Romans 5:15-21; 8:1-4

WBF 116

76 The Cross Cancels Our Karma

The law of the Spirit of life in Christ Jesus has set you free from the law of sin and of death.
—Romans 8:2

God does not leave us to the inexorable consequences of our sins and weaknesses. He provides in his own self-giving at the cross redemption from our sins and strength for our weaknesses. This is not only a way out of our dilemma— it is a way up!

I have lived among a people—the Indian people—who are burdened with fatalism. The Hindu gets into trouble and blames it on his karma—deeds—of a previous birth. The Muslim when he gets into trouble taps his forehead and says, "My kismet [fate] is bad." So they both turn over their hands and say. . . "What can I do?"

On the other hand the real Christian gets into trouble and says, "In Him who strengthens me, I am able for anything" (Philippians 4:13 Moffatt). . . . "It follows, my friends, that our lower nature has no claim upon us; we are not obliged to live on that level" (Romans 8:12 NEB). The tyranny of sin and fate is broken. So Jesus cancels your karma by his, cancels it by forgiveness and regeneration—from above.

The cross is the way of freedom.

O Father, you have lifted me out of the inexorable consequences of my sins. You bore them yourself in your own body on the cross. I accept your grace, your offer.

Affirmation: I am free—free in God—free to live, free to develop, free to be what God wants me to be.

For further reading: 1 Peter 2:6, 24-25; Romans 5:15-17; 6:17-19

WBF 118

A Portrait of Jesus

"You are the salt of the earth. . . . You are the light of the world. . . . Be perfect, therefore, as your heavenly Father is perfect."
—Matthew 5:13, 14, 48

The Sermon on the Mount (Matthew 4, 5, 6) is realism. First of all, it is a portrait of Jesus himself. . . . This Sermon is not preaching but revelation—a revelation of the inner life and character of Jesus. It is the Word become flesh in relationships.

Jesus is here not imposing an impossible code on human nature, a code for which humanity is badly made. He is lifting up principles underlying the universe. When he finished speaking, the people "were astounded at his teaching, for he taught them as one having authority, and not as the scribes" (Matthew 7:28-29). The phrase "as one having authority" could be translated "according to the nature of things." He lifted up out of reality the principles that were according to the nature of things. The people who heard him felt the authority of what he was saying. It hit them with an inner thud. Impossible idealism doesn't do that. It arouses you emotionally, but it doesn't come with authority.

To live some way other than the Sermon on the Mount turns out badly.

O Jesus, Lord and Master, when we take this portrait of you —these principles that produced you—and say it is unrealistic, this becomes your new crucifixion.

Affirmation: I accept the authority of Jesus. With his help I will be salt and light to the world.

For further reading: John 7:14-17; Matthew 5:1-10

WBF 159

Livable Words

*"Everyone then who hears these words of mine
and puts them into practice is like a sensible
man who builds his house on the rock."*
—Matthew 7:24 Phillips

[Jesus] met life as a man. He called on no power for his own moral battle that is not at your disposal and mine. . . . His character was an achievement. Everything he laid before us in the words spoken on the Mount had gone through his own soul. They were livable, for he was living them. . . .

The Sermon on the Mount is practicable, for the Man who first spoke these words practiced them, and the practicing of them produced a character so beautiful, so symmetrical, so compelling, so just what life ought to be, that he is as inescapable in the moral realm as the force of gravity is in the physical.

**We have in the Sermon on the Mount
not the lines of a code
but the lineaments of a Character.**

O Divine Son of God, I thank you that you lived this life. I am in awe at the wonder of it and I am drawn to emulate you by putting your words into practice. Help me to be the wise and sensible person who builds on rock.

Affirmation: "Blessed are the poor in spirit, for theirs is the kingdom of heaven" (Matthew 5:3).

For further study: Matthew 5; 7:21-28

COTM 31, 27, WBF 160

Idealism or Realism?

"Be perfect, therefore, as your heavenly Father is perfect."
—Matthew 5:48

[Jesus' call to be perfect] seems the ultimate in idealism. In fact it is the most matter-of-fact realism. For we are made in the inner structure of our being for just this—perfection and for this kind of perfection.... The perfect God made us for perfection. And this striving after perfection is written into the whole process of fuller, more abundant life. If [Jesus] says "Be perfect," then everything within me says the same: "Be perfect."

Our striving after perfection is simply the culmination of a process we see in all nature. In everything there is a cry for life, more abundant life. In the Christian this cry for life has turned qualitative—it is the cry for a particular type of life—the life we have seen in Jesus. We can be satisfied with no other type of life. He has spoiled us for any other type—it is this or nothing. In him we have seen the ultimate.

**The perfection of the heavenly Father
is interpreted by the life and character of Jesus.**

O Jesus, because we have seen you, we cannot stop this side of being made into your likeness. Stir up this divine urge so we may not sink back into the fatalities of lower nature.

Affirmation: The Divine Urge to be like Christ is upon me—I will follow it, not bury it.

For further reading: Philippians 3:7-11

WBF 163, 164

Jesus Is
"The Concrete Christ"

80

They were astounded at his teaching, for he taught them as one having authority, and not as the scribes.
—Mark 1:22

Jesus, the mystic, was amazingly concrete and practical. Into an atmosphere filled with speculation and wordy disputation, where men were "drunk with the wine of their own wordiness," he brought the refreshing sense of practical reality. He taught, but he did not speculate. He never used such words as *perhaps, maybe, I think so.* Even his words have a concrete feeling about them. They fell upon the soul with the authority of certainty—self-verifying.

**Jesus never taught theology—
he showed us who God is by his life.**

O Jesus, you do not merely tell us of the Way—you are the Way, not by claim alone but by demonstration.

Affirmation: I will live my theology today, not talk about it.

For further reading: Mark 1:21-32; John 7:45-46; Luke 12:22-34

WBF 369

Jesus Demonstrated the Way

A woman in the crowd raised her voice and said to him, "Blessed is the womb that bore you and the breasts that nursed you!" But he said, "Blessed rather are those who hear the word of God and obey it!"
—Luke 11:27-28

Jesus is "the Concrete Christ."...

He did not discourse on the sacredness of motherhood—he suckled as a babe at his mother's breast, and that scene has forever consecrated motherhood.

He did not argue that life was a growth and character an attainment. He "increased in wisdom and in stature, and in favor with God and man" (Luke 2:52 RSV).

He did not speculate on why temptation should be in the world—he met it, and after forty days' struggle in the wilderness he conquered and, "filled with the power of the Spirit, returned to Galilee" (Luke 4:14).

He did not discourse on the dignity of labor—he worked at a carpenter's bench and this made the toil of the hands honorable.

Jesus lived a fully human life.

Jesus, you demonstrated that you are the Way by the way you acted. In you I see the Way at work.

Affirmation: I will walk in the Way of Jesus Christ, hearing and doing the will of God.

For *further reading:* Luke 2:41-50; 4:1-14; John 4:1-7, 31-34

WBF 369

82 — He Raised the Dead

"My Father is still working, and I also am working."
—John 5:17

Jesus did not try to prove the existence of God—he brought him [to us]. He lived in God, and people looking upon his face could not find it within themselves to doubt God.

He did not argue...the immortality of the soul—he raised the dead.

He did not speculate on how God was a Trinity. He said, "If it is by the Spirit of God that I cast out demons, then the kingdom of God has come to you" (Matthew 12:28). Here the Trinity—"I," "Spirit of God," "God"—was not something to be speculated about, but was a working force for redemption—the casting out of devils and the bringing in of the kingdom.

He did not teach in a didactic way about the worth of children. He took them in his arms and blessed them and said, "Of such is the kingdom of God" (Mark 10:14 KJV). And he raised them from the dead.

The character of Christ can unlock the door to God.

O Jesus, Lord and Friend, I watch you in action and I see how to live—in the power and love of the Father.

Affirmation: I will be a working force for love and redemption.

For further reading: John 5:17-24; Mark 10:13-16; Luke 8:40-56; 7:11-16; John 14:16-18

WBF 370, COTM 324

88 — The Divine Illustration

*"If I, your Lord and Teacher, have washed
your feet, you also ought to wash one another's
feet. For I have set you an example."*
—John 13:14-15

Jesus did not discourse on the equal worth of personality—he went to the poor and outcast and ate with them.

He did not argue the worth of womanhood and the necessity of giving them equal rights—he treated them with infinite respect, gave them his most sublime teaching, as to the woman at the well, and when he rose from the dead he appeared first to a woman.

He did not teach in the schoolroom manner the necessity of humility—he girded himself with a towel and washed his disciples' feet. . . .

He wrote no books—only once are we told that he wrote and that was in the sand—but he wrote upon the hearts and consciences of people about him and it has become the world's most precious writing. . . .

We do not find him arguing that the spiritual life should conquer matter—he walked on the water.

**The Christian life is for living,
not for arguing.**

O Blessed Conqueror, you have conquered matter and you have conquered me—both of them miracles. Make me a miracle of your grace today, conquering where I cannot conquer, loving where I cannot love.

Affirmation: I will serve others in love today, following my Savior's example.

For further reading: John 4; 8:6-8; 11:1-6, 17-27; 13:3-5, 12-17; Luke 15:1-2; 18:18-25; 22:31-34, 54-62; Mark 6:45-52

WBF 371

93

He Loved

[Jesus] answered [the disciples of John the Baptist], "Go and tell John what you have seen and heard: the blind receive their sight, the lame walk, the lepers are cleansed, the deaf hear, the dead are raised...."
—Luke 7:22

[When] John sent to him from the prison and asked, "Are you the one who is to come, or are we to wait for another?" Jesus did not argue the question.... He simply and quietly said, "Go and tell John what you have seen and heard..." (Luke 7:18-23). His arguments were the facts produced.

He did not discourse on the beauty of love—he loved.

He greatly felt the pressing necessity of the physical needs of the people around him, but he did not merely speak on their behalf, he fed [more than] five thousand people with five loaves and two fishes.

He did not speak only in behalf of the Gentiles—he went across the lake and fed the four thousand, made up largely of Gentiles, and ate with them as a kind of corporate communion.

Actions speak louder than words.

O Jesus, Lord of all, thank you that your method was different—you did not declare so much as demonstrate. You did not merely speak, you acted.

Affirmation: I will deliberately perform loving acts today.

For further reading: Matthew 14:13-21; 15:32-39; 1 John 3:16-18

WBF 372

85

He Healed

"So that you may know that the Son of man has authority on earth to forgive sins"—he said to the paralytic—"I say to you, stand up, take up your mat and go to your home." And he stood up.
—Mark 2:10-12

Friends brought to Jesus a man with a double malady—sick in body and stricken more deeply in his conscience because of sin. Jesus attended first of all to the deeper malady and said, "Son, your sins are forgiven." In answer to the objections of the religious leaders, he asked, "Which is easier, to say to the paralytic, 'Your sins are forgiven,' or to say 'Stand up and . . . walk'?" (Mark 2:9). Then he told the paralytic "Stand up, take up your mat and go to your home." The man did. "He stood up, and immediately took the mat and went out before all of them, so that they were all amazed and glorified God, saying 'We have never seen anything like this!' " (v. 12).

The outward concrete miracle was the pledge of the inward.

Jesus did not argue the possibility of sinlessness—he presented himself and said, "Which of you convicts me of sin?" (John 8:46).

Jesus goes right to the heart of our need.

O Jesus Christ, Lord of all, your demonstration of power is more convincing than any declaration could ever be. Thank you.

Affirmation: I shall have no maladies rooted in wrong attitudes of mind or emotions.

For further reading: Mark 2:1-12; John 8:31-47

WBF 372

95

True Followers

*" 'Truly I tell you, just as you did it
to one of the least of these who are members
of my family, you did it to me.' "*
—*Matthew 25:40*

Jesus has been called the Son of Fact. We find striking illustration of his concreteness [in his parable of the final judgment]. To those on the right he does not say, "You believed in me and my doctrines, therefore come, be welcome in my kingdom." Instead he says, "I was hungry and you gave me food, I was thirsty and you gave me something to drink, I was a stranger and you welcomed me, I was naked and you gave me clothing, I was sick and you took care of me, I was in prison and you visited me." These [on the right] were true followers of his, unwilling to obtain heaven through a possible mistake and so they objected: " 'Lord, when was it that we saw you hungry and gave you food . . . ?' And the Master answered, 'Just as you did it to one of the least of these who are members of my family, you did it to me.' "

Jesus was not only concrete himself, he demanded a concrete life from these who were his followers.

Who are the least of Jesus' family?

Jesus Christ, teach me your secret of how to live; more, give me yourself to live in me so that I can do what you have done.

Affirmation: One deed is worth a hundred words.

For further reading: Matthew 25:31-46

WBF 373

True Values

"What does it profit them if they gain the whole world, but lose or forfeit themselves?"
—Luke 9:25

Jesus told us that a human soul was worth more than the whole material universe, and when he had crossed a storm-tossed lake to find a storm-tossed soul, ridden with devils, he did not hesitate to sacrifice the two thousand swine to save this one lost man.

Jesus did not merely ask us to turn the other cheek when hit on the one, to go the second mile when compelled to go the one, to give the cloak also when sued at law and the coat was taken away, to love our enemies and to bless them—he himself did that very thing. The servants struck him on one cheek, he turned the other cheek, and the soldiers struck him on that. They compelled him to go one mile from Gethsemane to the judgment hall—he went two, even to Calvary. They took away his coat at the judgment hall and he gave his seamless robe at the cross, and in the agony on the cross he prayed, "Father, forgive them."

Jesus [is] the pioneer and perfecter of our faith.
(Hebrews 12:2)

O Blessed Illustration of all your teaching, going even beyond everything you have said to give your self, I would be your true follower and give myself, by your grace.

Affirmation: By Christ's grace, I will respond in love to everything that comes my way today.

For further reading: Mark 4:35-41; 5:1-20; 14:32, 43, 53, 63-65; 15:16-20; John 19:17-25; Luke 23:32-36

WBF 373

88 — Jesus the Concrete Word

"Believe the works, so that you may know and understand that the Father is in me and I am in the Father."
—John 10:38

Jesus did not try to prove heaven to his disciples—he went up into heaven before their very eyes. . . .

He said to his disciples that in the New Order revenge should be abolished. The Old Testament limited revenge—one eye for one eye. He abolished it. When the Samaritans would not receive him because his face was set to go to Jerusalem and the disciples wanted to call down fire upon them, He rebuked them and "they went on to another village" (Luke 9:56).

When his disciples asked whether a man born blind or his parents had sinned, Jesus dismissed both hypotheses. He showed them how "God's works might be revealed in him" (John 9:3), even through suffering and disability. Then he proceeded to illustrate in his own life the principle of using suffering, turning the worst into the best. He took the worst thing that could happen to him, namely his death, and turned it into the best thing that could happen to the world, namely its redemption.

Jesus was the Concrete, for he was the Word become flesh. Had he been the Word become word, He would have spun theories about life, but since he was the Word become flesh, he put shoes on all his theories and made them walk.

God walking in my shoes—amazing!

O Lord and Savior, I hear you speak—and I see the meaning of your words in what you are. Theory and practice were one in you, and your practice makes luminous your theory.

Affirmation: Jesus did it, and so can I, by his grace—make my beliefs and my actions one.

For further reading: Luke 9:51-56; 24:50-53; Acts 1:6-11; Matthew 5:38-48; John 9:3, 14-16

WBF 375

What Jesus Christ Means to Me

*But now in Christ Jesus you who
once were far off have been brought near
by the blood of Christ. For he is our peace.
—Ephesians 2:13-14*

When the attack upon Pearl Harbor took place I was in Urbana, Illinois . . . to speak in a university convocation on "Peace." I had just come from weeks and months of efforts at Washington to head off the war. . . . On my way to the convocation I heard the voice of a radio announcer telling of the attack upon Pearl Harbor. . . .

I told that shocked audience that obviously I could not speak on peace, for peace was gone, but I would speak on "What Christ Means to Me." When that world of peace which we had tried to build up crashed, did anything remain? Yes, all the values, the real values, of my life were intact, for "Jesus Christ is the same yesterday and today and forever" (Hebrews 13:8). When things crash he remains. . . .

The war was won, but the peace has not been. We are still in a very shaken world. So I give my witness again . . . as to what Christ means to me.

Jesus Christ is our hope for peace.

O Lord and Savior, may the message I bring be not merely a message, but a message embodied in the messenger.

Affirmation: I am grateful that I, a very imperfect follower of a very perfect Lord, have Someone to talk about, for he is my message.

For further reading: Ephesians 2:11-21; 2 Thessalonians 3:16

WBF 376

90 — Jesus Christ Means to Me Redemption

[God] is the source of your life in Christ Jesus,
who became for us...redemption.
—1 Corinthians 1:30

The first thing Christ means to me is redemption. I met him first at an altar of prayer. I came there with nothing to offer except my moral and spiritual bankruptcy. To my astonishment he took me, forgave me, reconciled me to God, to myself, to my brother man, to nature, to life, and sent my happy soul singing its way down the years.

A Hindu said to a friend of mine, "I believe in prayer, but it is a very deep belief on the part of us Hindus that prayer cannot do anything about the past—the past must be paid for now or in a coming reincarnation." But the prayer of repentance and surrender to Jesus Christ did something about the past—it was gone, wiped out as though it belonged to another person, now dead, a new one alive in his place.

... After sixty years I've never gotten over the wonder of [being a ransomed sinner]. "By the grace of God I am what I am."

Forgiveness is the glory of the Christian faith!

Dear Savior, I do not want to get over the wonder of being a ransomed sinner. It sends me to my knees and to the highest heaven. It fills me with humility and hallelujahs. Thank you.

Affirmation: Grace is written across all I have and all I am—grace and gratitude.

For further reading: Psalm 103:1-14

WBF 377

Jesus Christ Means to Me
Resources

For in [Christ] every one of God's promises is a "Yes." For this reason it is through him that we say the "Amen," to the glory of God.
—2 Corinthians 1:20

The second thing Jesus Christ means to me is resources.

For about a year after my conversion I ran under cloudless skies, and then I ran into stormy weather. But the storms were within—deep within, from the fact of an unredeemed subconscious. My conscious mind was converted in conversion, but apparently my subconscious was not. So a crisis ensued. In that crisis I surrendered all I knew—the conscious, and all I didn't know—the subconscious. And then something happened. When I arose from my knees, a quiet but profound joy possessed me. I knew the Holy Spirit had moved into the subconscious and had cleansed it, coordinated it with the conscious. [They] . . . were under one control—the control of the Holy Spirit. The Holy Spirit was redemption extended to the subconscious, . . . to the deepest urges—to self, sex, the herd. Don't misunderstand me—these urges are still there, and can be and are the source of temptation. But they were under a new control, and if I cooperated by surrender and obedience, the resources were adequate for life.

Is your subconscious giving you problems?

O Son of God, I am grateful that I do not need to fumble and stumble through life. Your superior wisdom is at my disposal, your resources are never failing, and your trustable love will never let me go.

Affirmation: I have everything I need in Jesus Christ, who is God's Yes.

For further reading: Mark 7:14-23; Luke 11:37-42; Galatians 5:16-25

WBF 378

Jesus Christ Means
to Me Guidance

*When I came to Troas to proclaim the good news of
Christ, a door was opened for me in the Lord.*
—2 Corinthians 2:12

The third thing Jesus Christ means to me is guidance. My
life has become not a self- or circumstance-guided life,
but a God-guided life. In all the great crises, and in the
smaller crises—and more, in the daily round—I have felt a
Hand not my own on the helm. Not automatically. I can
still insist on my way, can take the helm myself—and pay
the penalty. But he never leaves me, and takes over again,
with my penitent consent, when I'm about to go on the
rocks. I've found it profoundly true [that] . . . "where God
guides, God provides."

Are you trusting God to guide you?

O Jesus, pioneer of our faith, thank you that none of us are
at loose ends, but that a pattern is being woven as we follow you. I would be one of your followers.

Affirmation: He who redeemed my life will guide my life—I shall not
falter nor fail.

For further reading: Hebrews 12:1-2; Romans 12:1-2; Acts 8:26-27;
13:1-3

WBF 378

Jesus Christ Means to Me Adequacy

I want you to know, beloved, that what has happened to me has actually helped to spread the gospel, so that it has become known throughout the whole imperial guard and to everyone else that my imprisonment is for Christ.
—Philippians 1:12-13

The fourth thing that Jesus Christ means to me is adequacy, the power to use everything that comes. I do not ask for special treatment, to be God's spoiled child (though sometimes I wonder if I'm not) but to be able to take what comes, good, bad, and indifferent, and make something out of it.

A blind man in our Ashram in India said, "The quintessence of Stanley Jones is his belief that you can not merely bear everything that happens, but use it, to rescue out of everything some good." But I was a long time learning that secret. After a period of fumbling it came as a revelation through the Scriptures: when you are delivered up before courts and magistrates, "it shall turn to you for a testimony" (Luke 21:13 KJV). The injustice that brought you before courts can be used for a testimony. The injustice becomes opportunity. In Jesus everything is opportunity. . . . Everything, literally everything, furthers those who follow Christ.

Do you ask for special treatment?

O Lord and Master, thank you for your mastery of me and for the power you give me to master everything that happens. Mastered, I master. It is so simple and yet so effective. Thank you.

Affirmation: I can bear everything for I can use everything.

For further reading: Philippians 1:12-18; Ephesians 6:18-20

WBF 379

94
Jesus Christ Means Education

*Jesus said to him, "I am the way,
and the truth, and the life."*
—John 14:6

The fifth thing Jesus means to me is education. . . . I have nothing but a college degree, and from a small college at that. I have some honorary degrees but I've felt uneducated when in company with the really educated. When M.A.s and Ph.Ds get their degrees by dissertations on "The Theology of E. Stanley Jones," my reaction is, "Have I a theology?" What theology I have is a by-product of evangelism among the intellectuals of India and other parts of the world. An author of twenty-three books? It all seems a mistake, for I never intended to be an author. I simply write when I see a need and the urge is upon me. Then somehow I must be educated.

The secret is in Jesus. He is the Awakener—Awakener of the total person, including the mind. . . . I've made life and people educate me—a lifelong process. My mind has become a magnet, so I pull from every person, every situation, some information, some truth to further me. . . . So Jesus Christ being the Truth awakens me to search for truths which invariably lead me to the Truth.

Have you let your lacks hinder you or impel you forward?

Jesus, the Truth, thank you that you are keeping me on the stretch to know more of truth. Convert my mind every day from error to truth, from lower truths to higher truths, from truths to the Truth.

Affirmation: Truth will take me by the hand today and will lead me to Christ.

For further reading: John 6:33-37; 7:16-17; 8:31-32

WBF 380

Jesus Christ
Means Health

Jesus . . . cried out, "Let anyone who is thirsty come to me, and let the one who believes in me drink. As the scripture has said, 'Out of the believer's heart shall flow rivers of living water.'"
—John 7:37-38

The sixth thing Jesus Christ means to me is health. . . . As a by-product of all I've said before, health emerges. In a health crisis a few years ago he said to me: "In me you are well and whole." It was important for it meant that if I stepped out of him into resentments, fear, self-preoccupation, and guilt I was not well, and I was not whole. I can only be "well" as long as I am "whole," and I am "whole" only as long as I remain in him. . . .

[I thank God] for that continuous healing which grace gives day by day, year in and year out. This continuous healing is what Paul means when he says: "He who raised Christ from the dead will give life to your mortal bodies also through his Spirit that dwells in you" (Romans 8:11). The indwelling Spirit giving life, day by day, to our bodies is the most glorious healing of all.

Where are you staying—
in Christ or in illness?

O Healing Christ, lay your hands of healing upon my mind, my spirit, my body, for I turn them over to you. You have the whole me; then heal me wholly.

Affirmation: In Christ I am well and whole.

For further reading: Psalm 103:1-3; Isaiah 53:4-6; Exodus 15:26

WBF 381, CM 329

96 — My Code Is a Character

*All of us, with unveiled faces, seeing the glory of the Lord
as though reflected in a mirror, are being transformed
into the same image from one degree of glory to another.*
—2 Corinthians 3:18

The seventh thing Jesus Christ means to me is that my
code is a character. That Character is Jesus Christ himself.
You can outgrow a code but you never outgrow a character if that character is a Divine Character. The more you
see the more there is to be seen. He is an unfolding revelation—forever with you and forever beyond you. There is
a surprise around every corner. . . .

And he lets me see nothing less than my Heavenly
Father. When an H-bomb was exploded with its blinding
flash, a physicist said that it reminded him of a passage
from the Bhagavad-Gita: "If the radiance of a thousand
suns were burst into the sky, that would be like the splen-
dor of the Mighty One." But that is not the revelation of
God I get in Jesus. Jesus is God's Transformer, transforming
[God] from blinding light that would sear us into the glory
of God as seen in the face of Jesus Christ. That doesn't sear
us, it saves us.

We need light to grow.

O Lord Jesus, you do not blind me with your radiance, you
beckon me with your love. You do not deafen me with your
thunder, you speak in the still small voice. And God the
Eternal is in that still small voice.

Affirmation: I will walk with Christ in the glory of God's light.

For further reading: 2 Corinthians 3:12-18; 4:1-6; 1 John 1:5-9

WBF 381

106

In Christ I Have Everything

*"All authority in heaven and on
earth has been given to me."*
—Matthew 28:19

The eighth thing Jesus Christ means to me is the kingdom of God—God's total answer to our total need. Without this fact of the kingdom our faith would be a personal allegiance to a Person—it would lack total meaning, individual and corporate. But with Jesus and the kingdom one—he is the kingdom—then "all authority" is in him, both "in heaven and on earth." I belong to the sum total of Reality and the sum total of Reality belongs to me.

Ninth, Jesus Christ means to me eternal life. I don't get it hereafter, I have it now in him. I am sure of heaven, for I'm sure of him. To be in him is to be in heaven wherever you are. So whether I live or die, so-called, is a matter of comparative indifference.

Tenth, Jesus Christ means to me a divine-human fellowship in the church. . . . The church has been the mother of my spirit—at her altars I found Christ. When I found Christ I found the church. But I do not belong to the church, though I'm a member of it—I belong to Christ—the church belongs to me— a gift of Grace. The most precious fellowship the world holds.

Do you have everything you need?

O Redeemer, how much you have given me! Nothing less than your self, your All. And what an All! It fills heaven and earth and me—with Glory.

Affirmation: All authority in heaven and earth belongs to Christ, and Christ belongs to me.

For further reading: John 1:29-34; 3:1-8, 16; Colossians 1:9-19

WBF 382

98

I Am His

I regard everything as loss because of the surpassing value of knowing Christ Jesus my Lord.
—Philippians 3:8

Eleventh, Jesus Christ means to me self-surrender. Not a self-surrender once and for all—it is that—but a continuous moment-by-moment surrender of my self and my problems as they arise. I say to him, "I am yours and this problem is yours, tell me what to do about it."

One morning early at what I call my Listening Post, he said, "You are mine; life is yours." I saw its amazing sweep, so I asked him to repeat it. He did. I belong to him; life with all its problems and possibilities belongs to me; I can master it.

One morning as I got out of bed, I said to myself, "Stanley, how are you?" And I found myself replying, "Well, I am his." That settled everything. So when I have Jesus Christ—The Word become flesh—I have Everything. For it has me—has me with the consent of all my being....

I commend my Savior to you.

"Let those of us who are mature be of the same mind."
(Philippians 3:15)

O Redeemer, I cannot give you this, that, and the other, for nothing less than my very all is befitting. I am yours.

Affirmation: "All of us, with unveiled faces, seeing the glory of the Lord as though reflected in a mirror, are being transformed into the same image from one degree of glory to another; for this comes from the Lord, the Spirit" (2 Corinthians 3:18).

For further reading: 2 Corinthians 3:18-4:6; Philippians 3:7-15; Romans 12:1-2

WBF 382

108

ℒearning to Pray

Prayer Is Surrender

"Whoever does not abide in me is thrown away like a branch and withers.... If you abide in me, and my words abide in you, ask for whatever you wish, and it will be done for you."
—John 15:6-7

Prayer is fundamentally and essentially self-surrender ... [not] a method of obtaining from God your wishes. That idea is self-assertion. This is self-surrender.

Then is prayer passive submission? A denial of the will to live? Is it the will to die? Far from it. Prayer is a will to die on the level of a defeated, empty, ineffective, short-circuited life, and a will to live on the level of a victorious, full, effective, and cosmic-connected life. It is self-renunciation in order to find self-realization. Your petty self is renounced in order that your potential self might be realized....

A branch not surrendered to the vine, but cut off and on its own, is not free; it is dead. A person who doesn't pray isn't free but is futile—a blind person who won't surrender the blindness to the surgeon in order to see. Such a person is free—to remain blind.

Would you rather be cut off or connected?

God, my Father, forgive me that I fear to surrender to you. Help me, as I begin this adventure of prayer, that it may be no sideline activity. May it become *me*, that I may become you.

Affirmation: Surrendered to God I live.

For further reading: John 15:1-11; Romans 12:1-2

AL 225

109

100 — Prayer Is Alert Passivity

*Then Jesus told them a parable about their
need to pray always and not to lose heart.*
—Luke 18:1

Prayer is not a passive surrender. It is an alert passivity
...that awakens us to an amazing activity. The musician
listens in the silence to Music, surrenders to it, and then
pours it forth with complete abandon. He is creative
because he is receptive....

We must learn to live in the passive voice. Only those
who do so know what it means to live in the active voice.
The fussy activity of modern humans is not life; it is the
nervous twitching of disordered and starved nerves...
crying out for vitamins of real life.

Jesus put the alternatives this way, that we "ought
always to pray and not to faint" (Luke 18:1 KJV). It is pray
or faint—literally that. Those who pray do not faint, and
those who faint do not pray. You can become alive to your
finger tips—every cell in you body alert, active, creative—
provided you pray. Otherwise you faint.

You will learn to pray by praying.

Gracious Father, I do not want to be weak when I might be
strong. I will surrender to you, your power, your creativity,
your release.

Affirmation: Today I will spend time with God, being receptive.

For further reading: Luke 18:1-8; 21:36; John 15:7; Ephesians 6:10-11,
18

AL 226

110

101 — Is Prayer Autosuggestion?

*"Ask, and it will be given you; search, and you will find;
knock, and the door will be opened for you."*
—Matthew 7:7

Is . . . prayer "autosuggestion," "wishful thinking," "an echo of your own voice"? Suppose it were just autosuggestion; even on that level it would be a healthy thing, for you are suggesting to yourself the highest instead of the lowest. . . .

But how is it that those who use prayer most are convinced that it is Other-suggestion rather than autosuggestion? Only those who use it least, or not at all, claim that it is autosuggestion. . . . Prayer would never have survived had it been only autosuggestion, with no Voice answering our voice, no Heart answering ours. . . .

The sense of Otherness is in true prayer. Something answers—and answers in terms that are worthy: release, power, vitality, insight, heightened accomplishment.

We pray to Someone.

My God and my Father, I want the highest for my life, and I believe that you hear my prayer and will answer me.

Affirmation: Jesus promises that if I ask I will receive.

For further reading: Psalm 55:22; John 14:13-14

AL 227

111

102

Prayer Is the Perfect Instrument

Praise is due to you,
O God in Zion;
and to you shall vows be performed,
O you who answer prayer!
To you all flesh shall come.
—Psalm 65:1-2

Prayer is the perfect instrument of development and of doing—it is outgoing, it is incoming; it is faith in God and faith in oneself; it is active, it is passive; it is strenuous, it is calm; it works as if the whole thing depended on us, and trusts as if the whole thing depended on God.

Is such a faith, so sound and health-giving, itself a delusion? Like produces like. How is it that the bitter and disillusioned deride prayer, and the calm, the poised, the hopeful, the radiant delight in prayer? It was said of William Gladstone, "He lived from a great depth of being." Is it better to live from a great depth of being, or to live from the shallow life around us?

How would you describe your prayer life?

O God, my Father, I want to live in you and have you live in me. Then I, too, will live at a great depth of being. Teach me to pray, so that I may live abundantly.

Affirmation: I will pray strenuously and trust calmly.

For further reading: Psalms 55:1-2, 16-19, 22; 68:16-20

AL 227

Prayer Is a Fact, Not a Formula

*"So I say to you, Ask, and it will be given you . . .
For everyone who asks receives. . . ."*
—Luke 11:9-10

While prayer is life's most wonderful resource, it can be twisted and turned into all sorts of things. First, into a formula. A minister's wife expatiated on the beauty of the prayer book they used and then added: "Do you really think that God answers prayer?" She thought of prayer as a formula but not as a fact.

Does God answer prayer? The answer is that just as God has made an open universe contingent upon our action so that things won't be done unless we do them, so he has left certain things open to prayer, things that won't be done unless we pray. This is a universe of law and order, yet it is an open universe—things can happen within this universe if we decide to do them. So while the spiritual universe is one of law and order, it is an open universe—open to cooperation with God for new things to happen, things that God wants to happen, but can't let them without our cooperation.

**What difference does it make to you
that some things won't be done unless you pray?**

O Father, thank you that you have made the universe open to my actions and my prayer. Help me to take my responsibilities seriously.

Affirmation: I will pray because I believe God answers prayer.

For further reading: Acts 4:23-31

MAS 288

104 — Prayer Is Cooperation with God

"If you abide in me, and my words abide in you, ask for whatever you wish and it will be done for you."
—John 15:7

Prayer is cooperation with God—cooperation with him in carrying out unfinished creative purposes. God wants to make us in helping him to finish an unfinished universe. So in prayer we do not have to overcome God's reluctance; we only have to cooperate with his highest willingness.

Anything that ought to happen can happen to the person who prays. When we pray we have linked ourselves with Divine purposes, and we therefore have Divine power at our disposal for human living.

The person of prayer is a person of power.

Amazing, that God wants us to work with him!

Father, thank you that I am not at the mercy of a universe without heart and without purpose. I am aligned to you, and therefore anything right can happen.

Affirmation: I want to work with God for his purposes.

For further reading: John 15:1-11

MAS 288

105

They Did the Most Incredible Things

When they had prayed, the place in which they were
gathered together was shaken; and they were all filled with
the Holy Spirit and spoke the word of God with boldness.
—*Acts 4:31*

Laws govern prayer [just] as laws govern the universe. The people in the book of Acts were guided by them, for they did an incredible thing; and it was not telling lame men to walk and dead people to arise. It was infinitely more incredible. It was nothing less than accomplishing in a short space of thirty years something that philosophers and lawgivers and moralists had attempted for ages with little success—they lifted humanity onto a new plane of living and introduced into society the basic changes upon which humanity has lived ever since. They did the most difficult thing that has ever been done. And they did it with incredible ease, without strain and without drain; for they didn't do it—they let God do it through them. They did it through prayer.

... This didn't just happen. It happened because they put themselves in line with God's purposes.

Are you willing for God to work through you?

O God, I would work without strain and without drain, doing your work and your will. So I offer myself to you today.

Affirmation: I will put myself in line with God's purposes.

For further reading: Acts 10:9ff.; 12:12ff.

MAS 289

115

106 — Jesus Christ and Prayer

*When Jesus also had been baptized and was praying,
the heaven was opened, and the Holy Spirit descended
upon him in bodily form like a dove.*
—Luke 3:21-22

The Acts of the Apostles gives an account of the use of prayer that is the cleanest, the sanest, the wisest, and the most powerful ever seen on our planet—yes, ever. There isn't a misstep in regard to prayer in the whole account, not a misemphasis. It is all sound—as sound as a bell.

First, they had seen prayer in Jesus.... He used it and used it mightily. In three great crises he prayed. First at his baptism, and as a result the Spirit descended upon him "like a dove." Prayer brought the Holy Spirit. Second, he prayed at the Transfiguration, and as a result he stood transfigured. Prayer made him luminous—showed what the material can be. Third, he prayed when he was accomplishing the end for which he came—the atonement for sin. When he prayed, "Father, forgive them," God could forgive, for Jesus was dying for us humans that we might be forgiven. He answered his own prayer by making it possible for God to forgive.

When do you pray?

O Jesus, your life was behind your prayer—your life laid down. Therefore you did the incredible—you redeemed a race. We are at your feet—wholly yours.

Affirmation: I shall do incredible things through prayer, for I do not do them—God does.

For further study, look at the place of prayer in Christ's life as found in the Gospel of Luke: Luke 3:21-22; 4:40-42; 5:15-16; 6:12-16; 9:18-20, 28-35; 10:21-22; 11:1-4; 21:37-38; 22:31-32, 39-46; 23:32-34, 44; 24:30.

MAS 289

Praying for One Thing—
The Holy Spirit

*All [the disciples] were constantly devoting themselves
to prayer, together with certain women, including Mary
the mother of Jesus, as well as his brothers.*
                                                    —Acts 1:14

The people in Acts showed the sanest and most effective use of prayer that has ever been seen....

First of all, we find them starting out as a group in prayer and praying for one thing—the Holy Spirit.... They were not praying for their safety, for their loneliness now that Jesus was taken away, for revenge upon their enemies who had crucified Jesus, for their needs to be met; for the power to perform miracles—none of these. They were praying simply for the Holy Spirit. And for the Holy Spirit unconditionally. They weren't praying that he might ...make them a success or give them power to do miracles or even to witness—they prayed for him and him alone. And in order for him to take them over unconditionally, they surrendered to him unconditionally. They wanted him for nothing but himself.

What do you pray for?

O God, my Father, thank you that you have pointed me in the right direction—toward you. Give me yourself in your Holy Spirit, and I will have all I need.

Affirmation: I will pray today for the highest and best—for the Holy Spirit himself.

For further reading: John 14:25-26; Luke 24:45-49

MAS 290

Prayer Is Not
a Success Cult

*"You will receive power when
the Holy Spirit has come upon you."*
—*Acts 1:8*

[The disciples] didn't grow into this purified form of prayer—they began with it. That . . . set a standard. Prayer was not primarily for things, for success, for healing, for power—prayer was a person wanting a Person. And wanting that Person so much as to be willing to surrender everything, including self . . . , if only that Person would come in and take over. And he did—and how! "All of them were filled with the Holy Spirit" (Acts 2:4). The hands of God were untied—he could do anything, everything, for people who didn't want anything except for him to come in and take over.

What a corrective to a great deal of modern praying which makes prayer into a success cult, a healing cult, an ego-expanding cult! All this is making ourselves the center —we're using God. . . . Here God is the center. We are surrendered to God. That is the right relationship. Anything can now happen.

Do you have a secret agenda in prayer?

O God, I do want only you. I surrender everything, including myself, to you.

Affirmation: Today I will walk with God, asking for nothing.

For further reading: John 14:15-17, 23

MAS 290

The Holy Spirit and the Group

*When the day of Pentecost had come,
they were all together in one place.*
—Acts 2:1

[The disciples] prayed for the Spirit to come not upon each person alone but upon each one and the group. Had it been individual praying for an individual coming of the Holy Spirit, it might have been a coveted desire for uniqueness in spiritual power. In other words it might have been all in the service of the ego. But here they prayed for each and all—"with one accord" (Acts 1:14 KJV)....This canceled out egoism and socialized the experience of the Holy Spirit. Yet deeply individualized it. For we are more personalized when we transcend ourselves and think of others. We find ourselves when we lose ourselves.

What is your first concern in praying?

O Holy Spirit, I want you in my life—but I want you to be present in power in my place of worship as well.

Affirmation: I will pray today for the Spirit's coming upon my church.

For further reading: Acts 1:1-14; 2:1-4

MAS 291

119

110

The Kingdom First

Scripture

"Your Father knows what you need before you ask him."
—Matthew 6:8

Did the disciples' praying for the Holy Spirit preclude their praying for their own needs—material needs? On the contrary those needs were met—"there was not a needy person among them ... the proceeds of what was sold ... was distributed to each as any had need" (Acts 4:34-35). They fulfilled that saying of Jesus: "Seek ye first the kingdom of God ... and all these things shall be added unto you" (Matthew 6:33 KJV). They got the supreme value straight and sought it—the kingdom of God—and all their lesser needs were met. They found food and success and self-development added to them....

A great many use prayer as a means to their ends—if you pray, you'll get this, that, and the other. That is using God, making him a means to our ends.... Prayer in the Acts began with God and ended with everything.

Question

What are you looking for?

Prayer

O Holy Spirit, I want you and you alone—all else can wait, or never come at all. But I cannot do without you. In you I have everything and more than everything.

Affirmation: Today I am determined not to use Christ but to let him use me.

For further reading: Matthew 6:28-33; Luke 11:9-13

MAS 291

120

Not for Safety but for Boldness

"And now, Lord, ... grant to your servants to speak your word with all boldness."
—Acts 4:29

The next instance of specific praying in the Acts (4:29) . . . is significant. Here again prayer was not for their needs but for the needs of others—they prayed for boldness to witness to others. God was first, others were second, and they were third. Prayer breaks the tyranny of self-preoccupation, absorbs you with God, and makes you interested in others. It is freeing. . . .

Had their prayer been initially for their own needs and for self-development, they would have prayed for their safety in view of the threats. But they were afraid of safety. They were in an adventure with God—an adventure of love. God had loved them into loving, and their own safety was unimportant. They wanted not safety but souls. So the doors of prayer turned out, not in. . . . They were bearers of Good News, and the only thing that mattered was to bear it.

**Have you prayed about sharing
the Good News with others?**

O Christ, I have looked into your face in prayer, and now I cannot rest until I share the blessed vision of what I have seen.

Affirmation: I shall pray not for safety but for boldness in witnessing to my Lord.

For further reading: Philippians 1:12-20; Acts 4:23-24, 29-31

MAS 292

112

The Highest Prayer— for Others

Peter and John . . . went down [to Samaria] and prayed for them that they might receive the Holy Spirit.
—*Acts 8:14-15*

This instance of prayer is in the direct line of the kind of prayer that emerged in Acts—it was a prayer for others. And the highest prayer for others—that they might receive the highest gift God had—the gift of himself, the Holy Spirit. . . .

The next place prayer is mentioned is when Ananias goes in to the stricken Saul and lays hands on him and prays: "Brother Saul, the Lord Jesus . . . has sent me so that you may regain your sight and be filled with the Holy Spirit" (Acts 9:17). Again the same outgoing type of prayer for others and this for an enemy. Infinite compassion is in the prayer: *"Brother* Saul." Turning an enemy into a brother through love! Ananias went beyond the original commission of Jesus to him (v. 12) . . . and added on his own "and be filled with the Holy Spirit." He wanted his former enemy to share the highest he had—the Holy Spirit.

How do you pray for your "enemies"?

Father, thank you for giving yourself to me in your Holy Spirit. I would pass on the gift to others who need you, so that through your Spirit, my enemies may become brothers and sisters.

Affirmation: I shall touch everything redemptively through prayer this day.

For further reading: Acts 8:1-16; 9:1-19

MAS 293

122

118 — Prayer Can Do Anything

Peter... knelt down and prayed. He turned to
the body [of Dorcas] and said, "Tabitha, get up."
Then she opened her eyes, and seeing Peter, she sat up.
—Acts 9:40

When Peter went into the death chamber of Dorcas [and] ... prayed ... here was prayer reaching even beyond death to the spirit world. Prayer can do anything, anywhere, provided it is linked to the loving redemptive purpose of God. If it is linked to the self and its selfish purposes, it goes nowhere except in futile circles, round and round on itself....

[Other] instances of prayer in the Acts ... prayer was the instrument through which the Jewish prejudices of Peter were broken down and he saw there was no ceremonial cleanness or uncleanness of any person before God (Acts 10). Prayer here brought one of the most important revelations that ever came to humans....

"While Peter was kept in prison, the church prayed fervently to God for him" (Acts 12:5). Here prayer was not for the safety of those praying that the persecution might not strike them, but for him whom it had struck. It was outgoing and altruistic.

According to James,
"the prayer of faith" can also save the sick.
(James 5:15)

Father, thank you for the wonderful love and power that pulsates through all this praying. Turn my prayers from festering inwardness to healthy outgoingness, so that you may show your power.

Affirmation: My praying shall be the outgoing of my love to others and to God.

For further reading: Acts 9:36-42; 10:1-46; 12:1-12

MAS 294

Prayer and Victorious Joy

He put them in the innermost cell and fastened their feet in the stocks. About midnight Paul and Silas were praying and singing hymns to God, and the prisoners were listening to them.
—Acts 16:24-25

A striking instance of prayer going out to others is found in Acts 13:2-3. "While they were worshiping the Lord and fasting, the Holy Spirit said, 'Set apart for me Barnabas and Saul for the work to which I have called them.'" This was the mightiest outreach of prayer ever seen; for it touched the ends of the earth, even to us.

...In Acts 16:25, had Paul and Silas been praying for their own release, the prisoners would not have been listening to them—that would be what was expected. But here the prayer was so set to victorious joy—"singing hymns"—that the prisoners were drawn to it with amazement.

Another instance: When Paul's life was in danger, he remembered "the words of the Lord Jesus, how he said, 'It is more blessed to give than to receive.' And...he knelt down and prayed with them all" (Acts 20:35-36 RSV)....
He prayed that they might think more of giving than receiving. Prayer was outgoing still.

What power in prayer!
missionary outreach, victorious joy,
earthquakes and conversions!

My Father, thank you, too, for the joy that prayer can produce in the direst circumstances. I would experience that kind of joy through prayer.

Affirmation: "It is more blessed to give than to receive."

For further reading: Acts 13:1-5 (the rest of the book of Acts describes Paul's missionary journeys that brought him from Asia to Greece and eventually to Rome—to Europe); 16:11-40; 20:17-38

MAS 294

Prayer—Love in Action

*The father of Publius lay sick in bed with fever
and dysentery. Paul visited him and cured him
by praying and putting his hands on him.*
—Acts 28:7-8

In the Acts prayer had been redeemed. From being a self-concerned act of getting benefits for oneself, it became the agent of a glorious redemption. Everywhere prayer was love in action through God. People were reaching out through God to touch others redemptively. In the process prayer . . . was turned out instead of in. Except in one instance—when they prayed for the Holy Spirit for themselves. [So] we can pray all out for ourselves. For if [the Spirit] comes, he takes over the self. Prayer then is not for ourselves but for One to control and guide and use the self.

Then is there no place in prayer for our own personal needs? Is that ruled out? No, they are provided for but indirectly. Note that the last thing said about Paul praying for the sick of the island [Malta] was "they put on board all the provisions we needed" (Acts 28:10) . . . their needs were all met. That brought them out at the place Jesus had promised: "Seek ye first the kingdom . . . and all these things shall be added" (Matthew 6:33 KJV). But "all these things" come as a by-product of seeking the kingdom first.

The pattern of prayer is outgoing prayer.

O Jesus, you have guaranteed our needs if we seek the kingdom first. Then help me to get first things first, to focus on you and your kingdom.

Affirmation: I shall seek God's Spirit for my spirit, that my spirit may be given to others.

For further reading: Acts 27:21-44; 28:1-10

MAS 295

125

116

Prayer and Power

One day Peter and John were going up to the
temple at the hour of prayer. . . . [Peter took
the lame man] by the right hand and raised him up;
and immediately his feet and ankles were made strong.
—*Acts 3:1, 7*

Prayer in the Acts is psychologically sound. Instead of leaving them absorbed in their own mental and physical and spiritual states, it was continually pushing them out and making them absorbed in others. That made them healthy-minded. Moreover, it made it possible for God to guarantee their needs. . . . Prayer has therapeutic, or healing, value only if it looses you from self-preoccupation and gets you interested in something beyond yourself.

When Jesus spent all night in prayer to the Father, the next morning "the power of the Lord was with him to heal" (Luke 5:17). The all-night prayer meant the all-morning power. And power to heal in two directions—it kept him whole and made others whole. Our needs are automatically guaranteed if we let prayer carry us beyond ourselves. The self is lost in others and found in itself.

What place does praying for others have in your life?

O Jesus, thank you that the soundest psychology comes from knowing you, for you are mental soundness itself. Let me take your attitudes, and I will find wholeness.

Affirmation: With the Spirit's help I will gladly pray for others today.

For further reading: Acts 2:41-47; 3:1-10; James 4:3-6

MAS 296

126

Prayer—The Greatest Single Power

*The prayer of the righteous
is powerful and effective.*
—James 5:16

The psychiatrist Dr. William Sadler says that in neglecting prayer we are "neglecting the greatest single power in the healing of disease." He refuses to take a patient who does not believe in God—says it is impossible to get patients straightened out unless they have something to tie to and love beyond themselves. We are literally coming down to this alternative: meditation or medication. And even the latter is not effective unless linked with the former.

Then the art of prayer must be learned, for reservoirs of power are at our disposal if we can learn this art. If we learn it—that is the rub. People expect results without any practice of the art. We would deem a person foolish who stepped up to a musical instrument only occasionally, expecting to tune into Music and become the instrument of Music without long training and practice.... We just as foolishly believe we can get ready-made results without the practice of prayer....

How much time do you give to prayer?

Gracious Christ, teach me to pray. For if I fall down here I fall down everywhere—anemia spreads through my whole being. Give me the mind to pray, the love to pray, the will to pray.

Affirmation: Let prayer be the aroma of every act, the atmosphere of every thought, my native air.

For further reading: James 5:13-18; Psalms 30:2, 11-12; 28:6-7; Luke 6:12-13

AL 228

118 — The Art of Prayer

*I pray that, according to the riches of his glory,
he may grant that you may be strengthened
in your inner being with power through his Spirit.*
—Ephesians 4:16

If we know and practice the art of prayer, we know and practice the art of living; if we don't know that art, then we don't know the art of living. To pray is to penetrate—to penetrate through this physical encasement into the spiritual world of light and power and to live within this physical encasement by that spiritual light and power. We live in two worlds at once—the physical world interpenetrated by the spiritual and lifted to a new level of life. We can live literally by resources not our own—we can live by Another.

Prayer can be our access to God's power.

O Father, thank you that you have not abandoned me to mere physical existence. Help me to learn how to live in the world of spiritual light and power.

Affirmation: I am determined to learn the art of prayer, so I'll make prayer my life climate today.

For further reading: Luke 11:1-13; Ephesians 1:17-19; 3:14-19

MAS 288

The Art of Prayer: Decide What You Really Want

Ask in faith, never doubting.
—James 1:6

If we spent half the time in learning the art of prayer as we do in learning any other art we would get ten times the results. . . . There are nine specific steps in the art of prayer.

1. Decide what you really want. I would stress the "you"—not a part of you, a vagrant portion of you wandering into the prayer hour as a side adventure. It must be you, the whole "you." For prayer is not a luxury; it is a life. If you take things from God there will be one result: God will get you, or prayer will cease, blocked by the refusal of self-giving. The request must be backed by you, or the answer will not be backed by God. God cannot give things to you apart from himself, and you cannot take things from God apart from yourself. Prayer involves a mutual self-giving. Decide what you really want, for if the whole you does not really want it, the prayer is blocked.

What do you really want?

Patient Christ, help me over the hard places, as I learn to walk on this pathway of prayer. I want to want you with all my heart.

Affirmation: I can do anything in and with Christ.

For further reading: James 1:5-8; Matthew 6:5-15

AL 229

The Art of Prayer: Write It Down

Everyone who asks receives, and everyone who searches finds, and for everyone who knocks, the door will be opened.
—Luke 11:10

2. Decide whether the thing you want is a Christian thing. God is a Christlike God; his actions are Christlike actions; and he can answer prayer only if the thing desired is in accord with Christ. That is what Jesus meant when he said, "The Father will give you whatever you ask him in my name" (John 15:17)—in my character, according to my spirit. Don't try to get God to do something that isn't Christlike. He can't, for he can't do something against his own nature. Within that limit he gives you freedom to ask anything.

3. Write it down. . . . If you are willing to commit your prayer to paper, you probably really mean it. In writing it down you do two things: You write it more deeply on your own heart; you commit yourself more fully to a line of action. To write it down is one step in self-committal.

**Have you written down what you really want?
Is it Christlike?**

O Christ, I commit myself to live in your way. Help me to want only what is in line with your character.

Affirmation: The Father will give me whatever I ask in Christ's name.

For further reading: Luke 11:9-13; John 14:11-14; 15:12-17

AL 229

The Art of Prayer: Be Still

Scripture

"Be still, and know that I am God!"
—*Psalm 46:10*

4. *Still the mind.* Just as the moon cannot be reflected well on a restless sea, so God cannot get to an unquiet mind. "Be still, and know"; be unstill and you do not know—God cannot get to you. In the stillness the prayer itself may be corrected. For God does not only answer prayer; he also corrects prayer and makes it more answerable.

One night I bowed my head in silent prayer before a sermon and whispered to God, "O God, help me." Very quickly came back the reply: "I will do something better; I will use you."

That amendment was decidedly better. I was asking God to help me—I was the center; I was calling God in for my purposes. But "I will use you" meant I was not the center; something beyond me was the center, and I was only the instrument of that purpose beyond myself. God's answer shifted the whole center of gravity of the prayer.

Comment

God's changes are always for the better.

Prayer

O Father, help me to listen to you and to be responsive at the depth of your purposes. I would be used by you.

Affirmation: I am the instrument of God's purposes.

For further reading: Psalms 46; 55:22; 62:1, 5, 11-12

AL 230

The Art of Prayer:
Talk with God

*Eli said to Samuel, "Go lie down;
and if he calls you, you shall say,
'Speak, Lord, for your servant is listening.'"*
—1 Samuel 3:9

5. *Talk with God about it.* The order of steps 4 and 5 is important: Listen to God before you talk. For, as someone has said, "Instead of saying, 'Speak, Lord, for your servant is listening,' many say, 'Listen, Lord, for your servant is speaking.'" Let God have the first word and the last word—you take the middle word. Let your speaking with God be largely a turning over of the whole matter into his hands—you becoming the instrument of his purposes. Remember, the word is "Talk with God," and not "Talk to God." Make prayer a two-way conversation.

**Did you ever think
you were meant to help answer your own prayers?**

O Father, I begin to see what prayer is. I was asking for the little, you are giving the great, the permanent, the everlasting. You are involving me in the work of your kingdom.

Affirmation: Today I will listen more than I speak.

For further reading: 1 Samuel 3:1-11; Psalms 16:7; 40:6-8; 63:5-8; John 11:28-44

AL 230

The Art of Prayer: Promise God

"I delight to do your will, O my God;
your law is within my heart."
I have told the glad news of deliverance
in the great congregation.
—Psalm 40:9

6. *Promise God what you will do to make this prayer come true.*
As the conversation is a two-way affair, so the accomplishment is a double affair. God answers the prayer, not for you, but with you. The answering of prayer is a cooperative endeavor. God's interest is not to give you things, but to make you through the getting of those things. The end of the whole process of prayer is not the prayer but the person.

How does the idea of cooperating with God
change your idea of prayer?

O Father, I begin to see. My object has been things I thought I needed, and now I see that your object is to make me—make me by showing me how to work with you.

Affirmation: I will work with God today.

For further reading: Psalms 40:1-10; 56:12; 65:1-2

AL 230

133

124

The Art of Prayer: Do Everything Loving

Little children, let us love, not in word or speech, but in truth and action.
—1 John 3:18

7. Do everything loving that comes to your mind about it. That word *loving* is important. If the thing suggested to your mind is unloving, it is from below—perhaps from the depths of your subconscious mind; but if it is loving, it is from above. A discerning friend said: "The only thing the devil cannot get into is the love of Christ, for if he did, he wouldn't be the devil any longer." That word *do* is also important, for if you are unwilling to do, you have tied God's hands—he can't do if you won't.

Prayer is the working out of what God works in.

Gracious Spirit, I want to live a Spirit-inspired life and so a Spirit-empowered life, to do the loving thing in every situation.

Affirmation: I will look at life through the eyes of love.

For further reading: 1 John 3:14-22

AL 231

The Art of Prayer: Thank God

In everything by prayer and supplication with thanksgiving let your requests be made known to God.
—Philippians 4:6

8. *Thank God for answering in his own way.* Remember that *no* is an answer as well as *yes*. Sometimes God has to save us as Tagore says, "by hard refusals." But if he refuses on one level, he refuses only to make an offer on a higher level. His no is only in order to offer a higher yes. But the probabilities are that if the prayer has run the gauntlet of the previous steps and survived to this stage, it is a prayer that is answerable by yes. But that yes may be delayed—delayed in order to put persistence and toughened fiber in us. God often holds us off to deepen our characters, so that we won't be spiritual crybabies if we don't get everything at once.

**Thanking God in all circumstances
is God's will for us in Jesus Christ.
(1 Thessalonians 5:18)**

Loving Father, I cannot pray as I ought unless I am taught by your Spirit to pray according to your will—with faith and thanksgiving.

For further reading: 1 Thessalonians 5:16-24; Psalms 40:1-3; 56

AL 231

135

The Art of Prayer: Release

Cast all your anxiety on him, because he cares for you.
—1 Peter 5:7

9. Release the whole prayer from your conscious thinking. If the prayer is real and has hold of you, it will be at work in the subconscious mind—there will be an undertone of prayer in all you do. But it should be released from the conscious mind, lest it become an anxiety center and make you tense and wrought up. The very releasing of it from the conscious mind is an act of faith in God. You relax and trust God to do the right thing in the matter.

These nine steps are the ladder by which you climb from your emptiness to God's fullness. And prayer is just that—it is the opening of a channel from your emptiness to God's fullness.

Can you let go of your concern?

Gracious Spirit, inspire the prayers within me that I may pray according to your will, and hence be answered according to your power and in your time.

Affirmation: I trust God's power and God's presence—in me and for my request.

For further reading: Romans 5:11; Ephesians 3:14-20

AL 231

Discovering the Power of the Holy Spirit

Half-Souls Needing Transformation

"Why could we not cast it [the unclean spirit] out!" He said to them, "This kind can come out only through prayer."
—Mark 9:28

Up to a certain point [the disciples] were streaky in their allegiance and in their achievements.... Sometimes they could rejoice that the evil spirits were subject to them (Luke 10:17), and sometimes they had to ask with sinking hearts, "Why could we not cast it out?" They were ready to go to prison and to death with him (John 11:16; Mark 14:31), and on the way were ready to quarrel over first places (Luke 22:24). They could whip out a sword and strike off an ear and then could quail before the gaze of a serving maid (John 18:10, 15-17)....

The new life within them was functioning feebly and intermittently.... They were half-souls trying to produce a whole service. Then something happened. A divine reinforcement took place.

Streaky, spotty, intermittent:
do these words describe your life and work?

O God, I see that my life, too, is a feeble and flickering torch. I would be alight with you.

Affirmation: Transformation from the ordinary to the extraordinary is possible.

For further reading: Look up the references in today's reading.

WPP 27

128

The Secret of Power and Poise

Scripture

The doors of the house where the disciples had met were locked for fear of the Jews.
—John 20:19

What was the turning point in the lives of these very ordinary folk who became extraordinary folk doing extraordinary things in an extraordinary way?

Some would say that it was the fact of the resurrection of Jesus. . . . But while the fact of the resurrection did mentally reassure them, it did not cleanse away the emotions of fear and inferiority. It did not give them power and poise. . . . Something else was needed. What was it?

The answer is clear: *It was the coming of the Holy Spirit.* A new power moved into them; took over control; cleansed the depths of them from self-centeredness, fears, inferiorities; reinforced all their natural faculties, coordinated them; made them unified persons; and thus filled them with power and poise.

Are you looking for a complete transformation?

O Father, is it possible now for me to be changed? I come with eager expectancy, believing that it cannot be for some and not for others.

Affirmation: I open my heart to God's answer.

For further reading: John 20:19-23

WPP 27, 26

Dynamic

*He ordered them not to leave Jerusalem, but
to wait there for the promise of the Father.*
—Acts 1:4

The coming of the Holy Spirit into the inner lives of the disciples transformed them from timid believers into irresistible apostles. Draw a line through the pages of the New Testament. On one side you will find spiritual inadequacy and moral fumbling mixed with a good deal of moral and spiritual adequacy and certainty—it is all very sub-Christian. On the other side you will find spiritual adequacy, moral certainty, power of redemptive offense, contagion, healing love, personality a surprise to itself and others, a "plus"—it is all very Christian.

That line runs straight through an upper room where a group of people waited in simple confidence and prayer that the promise their Master made to them would be fulfilled, namely, that they would receive a divine reinforcement within the total person and the total group. "All of them were filled with the Holy Spirit" (Acts 2:4). That line was the dividing line in the moral and spiritual development of humanity.

Which side of the line are you on?

Gracious Father, I need power—power to live the thing I know. Give me this inner dynamic.

Affirmation: My resources are at hand—God has promised.

For further reading: Acts 1:1-5; Romans 8:9-17

WPP 28

130 — Contagious Goodness

The fruit of the Spirit is . . . goodness.
—Galatians 5:22 RSV

[The coming of the Holy Spirit] marked an era. Hitherto people thought that goodness was the exceptional achievement of the exceptional person; but here the ordinary garden variety of humanity found a contagious, powerful type of goodness that transformed the face of humanity. And they found it, not as the whipping up of the will in a strained effort at goodness, but as a relaxed spontaneity from within. Goodness became their native air, the natural output. They were naturalized in contagious goodness.

This opened up such an astonishing possibility to morally beaten humanity that multitudes flocked into this new Fellowship where anything that was right was possible. A strange, sober joy went across that sad and decaying world—joy that goodness was here for the asking, that moral victory was possible now, that guilt could be lifted from the conscience-stricken, that inner conflict could be resolved and inner unity found . . . and that a Fellowship of like-souled persons gave one a sense of belonging. It was Good News. And it worked.

It was the coming of the Spirit that wrought this momentous change.

What is your native air?

My Father, I want to be introduced to the secret of power, the secret of inner unity, the secret of contagious goodness.

Affirmation: I believe in the Holy Spirit, whose fruit is goodness—in my life.

For further reading: Galatians 5:22-26; Romans 8:1-8

WPP 28

From Imposition to Imitation to Indwelling

"Jesus... being exalted at the right hand of God, and having received from the Father the promise of the Holy Spirit, he has poured out this that you both see and hear."
—Acts 2:33

Since the coming of the Holy Spirit was the climaxing of redemption...Jesus took great pains to prepare [the disciples] for his—the Holy Spirit's coming.

I say "his," for the Holy Spirit is not just an impersonal influence, nor is he just a sense of fellowship when we are together, nor an enthusiasm over ideas or causes. The Holy Spirit is a Person with whom we can commune, from whom we can draw resources, who can be the Life of our life. The coming of the Holy Spirit inaugurates a new era in humanity—the era of the Spirit.

...In general the stages may be marked as (a) The Old Testament stage—the childhood stage. (b) The age of the Incarnation—the youth stage. (c) The age of the Spirit—the mature state. In the age of the Spirit the authority moves into the center of our beings, and we do from within what was demanded from without. We are not compelled but impelled. In the Old Testament stage religion was an imposition, a Law; in the Incarnation stage religion was an imitation, trying to do what Jesus was doing; in the age of the Spirit religion is an indwelling, a spontaneous imperative from within.

Who is the Holy Spirit to you?

O God, I want to enter the new era of the Spirit, to have your life be my life.

Affirmation: The Holy Spirit is God within me.

For further reading: Acts 2:29-26; Ephesians 3:16-19

WPP 32

141

Authority Within

I pray that, according to the riches of his glory,
he may grant that you may be strengthened
in your inner being with power through his Spirit.
—Ephesians 3:16

We can put the three stages another way: God the Father is God *for* us; God the Son is God *with* us; God the Spirit is God *in* us. I cannot be satisfied with *for*, nor with *with*, nor only with *in*. God the Father is the Creator; God the Son is the Redeemer; God the Spirit is the Creator-Redeemer within.

The Father's love, the divine intention; the Son's approach, the divine invasion; the Spirit's coming, the divine indwelling. God dwelt in a holy temple, then in a holy Person; now he dwells in us who want to be holy. God in the Old Testament is Light; God in Jesus is Life; God in us is Power. Each time God comes closer, until finally he comes to the ultimate place—within. Authority is never authority until it is within. But when the authority is within, and when that authority is the Holy Spirit, then it must be spelled Authority.

God within me—Authority within me. How amazing!

O Father, that is where I want you to be—within. I am grateful that you are above, that you are with me, but I can never rest until you are within me.

Affirmation: God in me is power.

For further reading: Ephesians 3:14-21

WPP 32

The Holy Spirit in Jesus' Life

Scripture

The Holy Spirit descended upon him [Jesus] in bodily form like a dove.
—Luke 3:22

The Christian faith is a religion of the Spirit.

Jesus was conceived by the Holy Spirit (Luke 1:35).

The Spirit descended on him at his baptism (Luke 3:21).

He was led by the Spirit into the wilderness, came out in the power of the Spirit, and he began his ministry by saying, "The Spirit of the Lord is upon me" (Luke 4:1, 14-19).

He cast out evil spirits by the Spirit of God (Matthew 12:28).

He was offered up as a sacrifice through the Eternal Spirit (Hebrews 9:14).

He was raised by the Spirit of holiness (Romans 1:4).

He issued commandments by the Holy Spirit after his resurrection, and said that John baptized with water but he would baptize with the Spirit (Acts 1:2 RSV; 1:5).

... Jesus reveals the nature of the Father; he also reveals the nature of the Spirit.

Question

If Jesus lived in the power of the Spirit, can you do less?

Prayer

O Jesus, you have purified my conception of the nature of the Spirit. The Spirit is the Holy Spirit—the nature of the holiness I see in you.

Affirmation: I will follow Jesus today, through his indwelling Spirit.

For further reading: Look up the passages listed in today's reading.

WPP 33

Led by the Spirit

For all who are led by the Spirit of God are children of God.
—Romans 8:16

We are in the era of the Spirit—the Law of the Old Testament became the Life in the Incarnation, which became the Liberty in the era of the Spirit. . . .

The church was born of the Spirit at Pentecost (Acts 2).

The whole of the Christian faith is a "dispensation of the Spirit" (2 Corinthians 3:8 NEB).

Only those led by the Spirit of God are the children of God (Romans 8:16).

We are made into Christ's image from glory to glory by the Spirit (2 Corinthians 3:18).

The group forms a habitation of God in the Spirit (Ephesians 2:22 RSV).

The Spirit guides us into all truth (John 16:12).

God gives us power by his Spirit in our inner being (Ephesians 3:16).

The fruits of our Christian lives are the fruit of the Spirit (Galatians 5:22-23).

Our mortal bodies are quickened by the Spirit of Christ dwelling in us (Romans 8:11).

The law of the Spirit of life delivers us from the law of sin and death (Romans 8:2).

We receive power to witness to Jesus when the Spirit comes upon us (Acts 1:9).

From first to last the Christian faith is a religion of the Spirit.

Have you been forgetting the Spirit?

O Christ, I claim your promise of the Spirit, to be made into your image.

Affirmation: With the Holy Spirit in my life I have all that I need.

For further reading: Look up the references mentioned in today's devotional.

WPP 33

The Content
of Divine Power

Scripture

Let the same mind be in you that was in Christ Jesus.
—*Philippians 2:5*

We have seen that the nature of the Spirit is determined by what we see in Jesus. The fact is that the Holy Spirit and the Spirit of Jesus are used interchangeably: "Having been forbidden by the Holy Spirit to speak the word in Asia...the Spirit of Jesus did not allow them [to go into Bithynia]" (Acts 16:6-7). The Holy Spirit seemed to the disciples to be the Spirit of Jesus within them—they were one.

...But the Spirit apart from the Spirit of Jesus is often the spirit of queerness, of unbalance, of the weird. Even today people are afraid of surrendering to the Spirit, for they are afraid that to do so will be to surrender to emotionalism, to get off balance. But not only was Jesus sanctity—he was sanity. There was nothing psychopathic about him. He never went off into visions or dreams. He got his guidance through prayer, as you and I get our guidance, and this always when in control of himself. He was always balanced, and sane, and poised. He was the most balanced character that ever moved down through human history. And if we are possessed of the Holy Spirit, we will be made like him.

The Spirit of Jesus is controlled power.

O Jesus, I am not afraid of being made like you—I am afraid I'll not be like you. For if I am not like you, I shall not live. If I am like you, I do.

Affirmation: "We will be like him.... All who have this hope in him purify themselves, just as he is pure" (1 John 3:2-3).

For further reading: 1 Peter 2:21; Colossians 1:27-28; 2:9-10

WPP 34

145

Jesus Was No Miracle-Monger

Christic Jesus . . . emptied himself, taking the form of a slave.
—*Philippians 2:5-7*

When the early Christians spoke of the Holy Spirit, the content of Jesus was in it. Paul puts them together in these phrases: "the help of the Spirit of Jesus Christ" (Philippians 1:19) and "the law of the Spirit of life in Christ Jesus" (Romans 8:2). . . . Jesus is the revelation of God's nature and also the revelation of God's power. Do not expect God to exercise any power that is not power that Jesus would exercise.

Jesus refused to exercise any magical power to impress people or to validate his claims; so the Holy Spirit will operate with you, not as magical power, but as moral power. Jesus used outer miracle sparingly. If he had power, he had power to restrain that power. He used outer miracle just enough to let us know God was ruler over the total life, and that the universe was not fixed but open; but he threw his emphasis upon God working in the moral and spiritual to produce changed lives. . . .

The emphasis in the power of the Holy Spirit is not on outer signs and wonders but on the inner signs of morally crooked men and women made straight, spiritually impotent and barren people being made victorious and fruitful. . . . The Holy Spirit is not a miracle-monger, but a moral manager.

The power to change lives is power indeed.

O God, I need a moral and spiritual cleansing and reinforcement that will make me all-glorious within and adequate for anything without.

Affirmation: I am determined to be God's moral miracle.

For further reading: John 14:15-17, 26; Philippians 2:5-11

WPP 35

Preparing for the Spirit

" 'He on whom you see the Spirit descend and remain is the one who baptizes with the Holy Spirit.' "
—*John 1:33*

Since the Holy Spirit is God in action, then we must expect Jesus to put his disciples through a deliberate course of moral and mental training for the reception of the Spirit. We find this course of training unfolded best in John's Gospel. . . . There are twelve steps.

1. *The revelation of One upon whom the Spirit descends and remains and One who imparts the Spirit* (John 1:33). This is our first necessity: to have One who, though divine, possessed the Spirit in human surroundings, demonstrated its meaning there, and who gives the Spirit to others in the same human surroundings and in the same moral and spiritual manifestations. . . .

John struck two vital notes about this One: "Here is the Lamb of God who takes away the sin of the world!" (1:29). And he "baptizes with the Holy Spirit" (1:33). Here are the two characteristic things in the Christian gospel: clearing the way between humans and God, by the atonement; clearing the way between humans and themselves by the Indwelling. One is atonement, the other is attunement. The Christian gospel makes it possible to live with God and to live with ourselves.

Jesus is a true leader.

Gracious Father, thank you that you are moving straight within me in the Spirit, the Spirit of Jesus.

Affirmation: The baptism of the Spirit—Jesus' baptism and mine.

For further reading: John 1:29-33

WPP 36

The Birth of the Spirit

"Very truly I tell you, no one can enter the kingdom of God without being born of water and Spirit." —John 3:5

2. *The birth of the Spirit....* The first step in imparting that fullness [of the Spirit] is to impart the new birth of the Spirit. You cannot know the meaning of the kingdom of God, nor receive its powers to live by, until you are born into it. And how are you born into it? By two things: "born of water and Spirit." Being born of water means an outer birth into a Christian fellowship—you join a community by an outer rite. Being born of the Spirit means an inner joining of the kingdom.

It is possible to be outwardly born of water but not born of the Spirit. You may join a community but not the kingdom. Simon Magus was baptized with water (Acts 8:13), but did not have the birth of the Spirit (8:21).... Without [the birth of the Spirit] the rest of the program is impossible....

We would define this birth of the Spirit as that change, gradual or sudden, by which we who are the children of the first birth, through a physical birth into a physical world, become children of the second birth, through a spiritual birth into a spiritual world, by the power of the Holy Spirit, who applies the grace of Christ to us within. Humanity is thus divided into the once-born and the twice-born.

Are you born of the Spirit?

O God, my Father, I see that without the birth of the Spirit I cannot have the blessings of the Spirit. Give me that birth.

Affirmation: I pass from the once-born to the twice-born.

For further reading: John 3:1-16; Acts 8:9-24

WPP 37

A Measureless Coming

*He whom God has sent speaks the words of
God, for he gives the Spirit without measure.*
—John 3:34

3. The coming of the Spirit without measure.... The last "he"
(in John 3:34) can refer either to God or to him "whom
God has sent." In the latter case it means that Jesus promises to give the Spirit without measure. That fits into
exactly what happened—Jesus did give the Spirit without
measure to those who sought.

In the new birth the Spirit's coming is by measure. But
it is a fact of experience that while new life is present in
the birth of the Spirit, it is limited—usually lacks an overflow, an abundance. Jesus said, "I came that they may
have life"—the first stage of his coming within us, the
stage where he imparts life—"and have it abundantly"
(John 10:10), "more abundantly" (KJV)—the next stage
where, having imparted life, he now inundates us with life.
In the new birth we had joy, now we have joy with a bub-
ble in it; we had peace, but it was measured, now it is like
a river; we possessed love, now it possesses us.

This living on overflow is what is so lacking in the
church of today.

**Overflow; abundantly; without measure:
what a bountiful promise!**

O God, I am so grateful that you have promised to enlarge
my margins. I have been living in skimpy resources. Now
give me life abundantly.

Affirmation: From life limited to life unlimited—that is my open door.

For further reading: John 1:11-13; 3:31-36; 10:7-11

WPP 38, 39

The Outflow
Without Measure

Scripture

"'Out of the believer's heart shall flow rivers of living water.'" Now he said this about the Spirit.
—John 7:38-39

We come now to the next step in the training of the disciples concerning the coming of the Holy Spirit.

4. The outflowing of the products of the Holy Spirit without measure. Step three told of the inflowing of the Spirit without measure. This step tells of the overflowing of the products of the Spirit without measure. One was intake—the other outgo. Both of them equal—without measure.

This is the rhythm of the life of the Spirit—intake and outflow. If there is more intake than outflow, then the intake stops. If there is more outflow than intake, then the outflow stops—exhausted. The doors open inward to receive only to open outward to give.

Life is no longer a reservoir with only so much resources that if we draw on them we have only so much left, so that therefore we must husband our resources. Life is now a channel, a channel attached to infinite resources. The more we draw upon those resources the more we have.

What is the rhythm of your life?

O Spirit divine, come within this being of mine, fill me to overflowing with the living waters.

Affirmation: I am a channel of infinite blessings.

For further reading: John 4:7-14; 7:37-39

WPP 40

To Be Really Free

*Now the Lord is the Spirit, and where the
Spirit of the Lord is, there is freedom.
—2 Corinthians 3:17*

The Spirit's rivers of living water (John 7:38-39) are nine:
"The fruit of the Spirit is love, joy, peace, patience, kindness, goodness, faithfulness, gentleness, self-control"
(Galatians 5:22-23 RSV). They begin with love and end
with self-control. The Christian method of self-control is
not to sit on yourself in a vain endeavor to keep yourself
under control, but to express yourself under the law of
love—you love God supremely, and then every other lesser love falls into its place naturally and normally. You are
only self-controlled when you are Spirit-controlled. . . .

Paul adds: "There is no law against such things"
(Galatians 5:23). There is no law, there is only a liberty—
a liberty to express yourself. . . . And yet while we are free,
we are under the deepest exactions ever laid upon the
human spirit; for you cannot think a thought, resolve a
thing, or even long for anything without the Spirit's intimate approval or disapproval. What bondage! And yet
what freedom!

**"Make me a captive, Lord,
And then I shall be free."
(George Matheson)**

O Spirit Divine, I thank you that the moment of your coming within me is the birthday of my freedom. Then I begin
to live—fully and freely.

Affirmation: In myself—bound; in the Spirit—free.

For further reading: John 7:37-39; 2 Corinthians 3:17-18; Galatians
5:16, 22-26

WPP 41

151

The Pattern
of Triumph

*Now he said this about the Spirit, which believers
in him were to receive; for as yet there was
no Spirit, because Jesus was not yet glorified.
—John 7:39*

Why couldn't the Spirit be given until Jesus was glorified?
Apparently for two reasons.

1. If the power of the Spirit was to be Christlike power, then
it was necessary to see that power manifested through the
whole gamut of life, from a carpenter's bench to the throne
of the universe. . . . We had to see this power manifested on a
cross as forgiveness of enemies; and . . . as supreme modesty
and humility which, when he triumphed over his enemies in
the resurrection, made him refuse to appear in his triumph
before them to cow and overwhelm them. . . .

2. . . . The disciples had to see that this power manifested
in Jesus was the ultimate power—it took its place at the center of the universe when Jesus went to the right hand of the
Father. . . . In Jesus love was overcoming evil with good, hate
by love, and he would overcome the world by a cross. . . . The
disciples had to see this power face everything, overcome
everything, and go to the place of ultimate power. Then they
knew that when this Spirit which was in Jesus came into
them, it was ultimate Spirit, with ultimate power.

Power for anything, at any time, in any place.

O God, my Father, thank you that the Spirit within me is
the Spirit of triumph. I would live the life of the Spirit, live
the life of triumph.

Affirmation: The Power at work in me is Final Power.
For further reading: Acts 3:1-16; Romans 8:1-4, 9-11

WPP 42

The Spirit of Grace

"I will ask the Father, and he will give you another Advocate, to be with you forever. This is the Spirit of truth.... You know him, because he abides with you, and he will be in you." —John 14:16-17

Here is the fifth step in Jesus' preparation for the coming of the Holy Spirit.

5. *The Spirit's coming would not be a temporary coming ... he would abide in them forever.* The pattern the disciples had of the coming of the Holy Spirit ... was that of temporary afflations of power for temporary tasks. Jesus reversed this and gave them the breathtaking news that the Holy Spirit's coming would be a permanent coming. We see it intimated in the Spirit's coming upon Jesus: " 'He on whom you see the Spirit descend *and* remain is the one who baptizes with the Holy Spirit' " (John 1:33, italics added)....

The Holy Spirit would not come and go.... He would move within the recesses of the inner being and stay there forever. The only way he would leave would be by being sinned out by conscious, purposeful, continuous sin. An occasional fall that brought contrition and repentance would not break the relationship. It might cloud it, but he would still be there, ready to restore and heal and reestablish the interrupted intimacy. He is "the Spirit of grace" (Hebrews 10:29)....

**The Holy Ghost is the Holy Guest,
and a permanent Guest.**

Gracious Spirit, with you taking up your permanent abode in me, I lack for nothing, shrink from no task.

Affirmation: The Spirit is as permanent within me as my choices—and beyond.

For further reading: 1 Samuel 10:9-13; 16:13; John 14:12-17; 1 Thessalonians 5:19; Ephesians 4:30–5:2

WPP 43

The Strengthener

"I will pray the Father, and he will give you another Counselor, to be with you for ever, even the Spirit of truth."
—John 14:16-17 RSV

The Holy Spirit is more than an influence—an impersonal entity. He is a person who counsels, guides, cleanses, empowers, and most of all, just abides with us and in us. Here he is called the "Counselor" ("Advocate" NRSV). The translators were all scholars and would therefore lean toward a word having a content of advice, of verbal direction but the Greek is *para* (beside), *kaleo* (call)—one who is called beside us. For counsel? Yes! For strength? Yes! For everything? Yes! There isn't a single thing needed for life that he isn't there to provide. The word used in older translations, "Comforter," is nearer to it if you take the literal meaning of the word—*con* (with) and *fortis* (strength)—one who strengthens you by being with you. . . .

The Strengthener is called "the Spirit of truth." He not only brings truths to you, but he himself is the essence of truth. . . . The Spirit of truth doesn't free us by magic—he frees us by making us be identified with truth, and then "the truth" makes us free. . . .

The Holy Spirit will make you Christlike.

**Not a single thing lacking—
do we really believe it?**

O Spirit of truth, make me so truthful that I become truth, so pure that I become purity, so loving that I become love. I cannot do this—you can.

Affirmation: Identified with truth, I become truth.

For further reading: Luke 2:25-26; John 8:31-32; Ephesians 5:20-25

WPP 45, 28

God's Complete
Self-Disclosure

*"The Counselor, the Holy Spirit, whom the Father will
send in my name, he will teach you all things, and bring
to your remembrance all that I have said to you."*
—*John 14:26 RSV*

6. The Holy Spirit would become Teacher and Remembrancer.
This is an important step. A prominent agnostic said that
there is an irreconcilable conflict between science and religion for science is never fixed—it is open and progressive;
religion, on the other hand, becomes fixed in absolutes and
non-open dogmas. This observation is true of some inter-
pretations of Christianity. But it is not true of the
Christianity of Christ. For in it he provides for a continuing
revelation—"the Holy Spirit . . . will teach you all things."

It is true that . . . in Jesus we have God's final—because
of God's complete—self-disclosure. [Not God's total omnipotence or omniscience. That] would not be redemptive—
it would be paralyzing. What we do want to know is:
What is God like in character? For what he is like in character we must be like. God's character we have seen in
Jesus. . . . Jesus is God's final unfolding of himself.

But if this revelation is final, it is unfolding. The Holy
Spirit continues the revelation. . . . [It is] unfolding according to what we see in Jesus.

Jesus is the content of God's self-disclosure.

O God, I have just what I want: something fixed and yet
something unfolding. For I want to rest in something and
yet be spurred to more by that very assured rest.

Affirmation: The one point of my compass is fixed on Christ, the
other sweeps the horizon of reality.

For further reading: John 14:25-27; Hebrews 1:1-4

WPP 49

Becoming Creative and Contagious

Scripture

*"When the Counselor comes, whom I shall send
to you from the Father, even the Spirit of truth,
who proceeds from the Father, he will bear witness to
me, and you also are witnesses."*
—John 15:36-37 RSV

Here is a step further. *7. The Spirit is the Witness to Jesus and the creator of witnesses to Jesus.* He not only unfolds truth—he unfolds persons. He makes them creative and contagious. Wherever the Spirit is, there creation continues.

This verse was fulfilled after the Holy Spirit came upon the disciples. (See Acts 5:32.) Here were human spirits and the divine Spirit working together for the same purposes, witnesses to the same Person and with the same power. The creative Spirit makes creative persons who in turn make creative persons.

This is the line of apostolic succession. Those who have the apostolic success are in line with the apostolic succession. They transmit not merely truth but the very Spirit of truth—the creative activity of God.

Do you long to be creative?

O Creator Spirit, live within me and make me creative. I cannot rest until I am outgoing and creative. I surrender all my dead powers to your Life. Make them live.

Affirmation: I am made for creative activity, to be a witness to the Truth.

For further reading: Acts 1:8; 5:27-32

Convincing Witnesses

"It is to your advantage that I go away, for if I do not go away, the Counselor will not come to you; but if I go, I will send him to you. And when he comes, he will convince the world concerning sin and righteousness and judgment."
—*John 16:7-8 RSV*

8. *The Holy Spirit not only makes us witnesses but convincing witnesses to Jesus....* Two people speak the same thing: the words of the one fall upon the heart and mind but leave little or no impression; the words of the other are not only convincing but creative—newborn souls and new impulses and movements arise.

Before there is a coming to newness, there must be a break with the old. The Holy Spirit precipitates a crisis. Sin must be faced and effaced. Sin is what you have done wrong; righteousness is what you might have done right if you had not done wrong; judgment is in regard to both....

The very center of evil has been judged. Evil has met its match, has been defeated, and now we face no evil that hasn't the footprint of the Son of God on its neck.

**Through the Spirit
we can recover what might have been.**

Jesus, thank you that I face nothing that you haven't faced and conquered. That gives me a glorious sense of victory as I go into life.

Affirmation: I am afraid of nothing, for I've bowed to Christ, and I will witness to his saving power.

For further reading: John 16:4-11; Acts 14:3

WPP 52

148

Good News or Musty Views?

Scripture

*"When the Spirit of truth comes,
he will guide you into all the truth."*
—John 16:13

Across the street on a third-rate hotel is a sign with letters washed out and made dim with age: "Newly Furnished Rooms." It isn't convincing! There is no sign of newness. [Just so] the average church makes you think, not of good news, but of musty views. . . . There is no unexplainable Plus. It is the human spirit instead of the Holy Spirit. It is not convincing. . . .

9. *The Holy Spirit guides us into all the truth*. This is a step beyond the stage of John 14:26 (RSV) where "he will teach you all things." Here he not only teaches you the truth, he guides you into the truth, guides you into the possession of it. In the first stage you see; in this you seek—and find! The one is illumination and the other is illustration; one is the word, the other the word made flesh.

Here is the weak place in contemporary religious life—it is informed but not inspired; it knows all about life but doesn't possess it. . . . The Holy Spirit is not in control. For he guides you—takes you by the hand and guides you—in the possession of all the truth. He turns the ideal into the real, aspiration into acceptance, and makes the whole operative now. As in Jesus through the Holy Spirit the Word became flesh, so in us the Word again becomes flesh.

Is your life convincing?

O Holy Spirit, this is what I want. I want to have all my longings become actuality. So I surrender to your guidance now.

Affirmation: Today, illumination becomes illustration.
For further reading: John 14:7-11, 25-28; 16:12-15

WPP 53

149 — Destiny in Directions

"When the Spirit of truth comes . . . he will declare to you the things that are to come."
—John 16:13-14

10. The Holy Spirit will give you the prophetic spirit.

. . . Jesus determines destiny—whatever fits with him lives, and whatever goes in opposition to him perishes. "For the testimony of Jesus is the spirit of prophecy" (Revelation 19:10). If you testify to Jesus and point people to Jesus as having the final word, then you have the spirit of prophecy. You are forecasting the future, for you see the present. You see that the way of Jesus is the Way . . . the way to think, to act, to be, in every conceivable circumstance. . . . The Way of Jesus is always the Way, and every other way is not-the-way. Therefore you can write the destiny of everything . . . now. Everything that fits in with Jesus is destined to rule, and everything that does not fit in is doomed to ruin. . . .

So those who possess the Spirit of God . . . see the future in the past—see it in the revelation of Jesus. They know that he is the Alpha, the Christ of the Beginning; and he is the Omega, the Christ of the Final Word.

Insight is a gift of God.

O Jesus, I know that you are the Way and that in you the past, present, and future are unfolded. Help me to boldly testify to you.

Affirmation: I follow the Christ of the Final Word.

For further reading: Luke 1:67-73; John 3:16-23; Revelation 22:12

WPP 54

Light Up the Face of Jesus

"He [the Spirit of truth] will glorify me; because he will take what is mine and declare it to you."
—John 16:14

11. The Holy Spirit will glorify Jesus. The whole purpose ... of the coming of the Holy Spirit is not to glorify the person who receives, nor the Person who is received, but to glorify Jesus. ... If it glorified those receiving, making them seven-day wonders in spiritual things, that would make religion egocentric—the wrong center. ... If it glorified the Holy Spirit, that would glorify something without character content, for it would be cut loose from the Incarnation. It is the Incarnation that gives character content to God, to the Holy Spirit, and defines what we must be like. Hence the final emphasis is on Jesus, the Incarnate.

In India in a marriage procession the people often walk alongside the bridegroom, seated on a horse, and hold up torches to light up the face of the bridegroom. The work of the Holy Spirit is to light up the face of Jesus. "No one can say 'Jesus is Lord' except by the Holy Spirit" (1 Corinthians 12:2).

Jesus is the center of our lives.

O God, my Father, give me the clear vision of Jesus so that I shall always make my decisions according to him.

Affirmation: Today, none of my light shall turn to darkness.

For further reading: John 16:12-15; 2 Corinthians 3:17-18; Ephesians 4:4-13

WPP 55

Take the Holy Spirit

Scripture

[Jesus] breathed on them and said to them,
"Receive the Holy Spirit."
—John 20:22

12. Receive the Holy Spirit.

[The last of Jesus' twelve steps was] the reception of the Holy Spirit as a personal gift. The quest ended in finding. ...But the finding did not take place when he breathed on them....It did not take place for nearly fifty days afterward.

Then where is the reality of the saying "Receive the Holy Spirit" when they did not receive? It is in the fact of Jesus' character. When he says "Receive," then you have received, even though the manifestation does not take place till later. The space in between is the space where you rest on him, not on your subjective realization. It is the period of intensive schooling, teaching us that faith and not feeling is the basis of the life of the Spirit. For him to say "Receive" is to receive. His word is our sufficient assurance....

But note that the word "Receive" is not passive but active. It could be translated, "Take the Holy Spirit." Here was active receptivity, a reaching out by faith in the character of the One who invites us to take.

How often we prefer feeling to faith!

O Jesus, when you speak, it is done then and there. Help me to accept it and to walk in it, even though I walk by dry faith. For I know that faith will turn to fact and fact to feeling.

Affirmation: My soul, accept the Holy Spirit and live by him.

For further reading: John 20:19-23; Acts 15:6-11; 19:1-7

WPP 56

The Pulse Beat
of All We Do

*They returned to Jerusalem . . . and . . . went up
to the upper room, where they were staying.*
—Acts 1:12-13 RSV

We come now to the holy place of the Christian faith—the
Upper Room. . . . The Upper Room was the birthplace of
the Church. It was there that power was loosed that
changed the world.

But the Upper Room has often become in our present-
day Christianity the Supper Room. . . . The Supper Room is
all right, provided it is second and the Upper Room is first.
For Jesus was "eating" with them in Jerusalem (Acts 1:4,
margin) when he charged them to "wait there for the
promise of the Father." The Holy Spirit was to be associated with the commonplace happenings of life—like eating. He was going to make every meal sacramental and
every place "where they were staying" into a shrine.

. . . The Holy Spirit came in the most common place—
the home. Therefore he is to be given not for special "spiritual" occasions, but for all occasions, for all life. . . . [He]
is not a spiritual luxury to be imported into the unusual,
but a spiritual necessity for the usual. He is to be the pulse
beat of all we do—the Life of our living.

How might this truth change your mealtimes?

O God, I thank you that I do not have to wander from
sacred place to sacred place in search of you. You come into
me, into my life, and fill me with your glory.

Affirmation: Today the Holy Spirit turns all my seculars into sacreds.

For further reading: Luke 22:7-13; Acts 1:1-9; 2:1-4

WPP 78

158

The Significance of the Upper Room

"This is my body, which is given for you."
—Luke 22:19

The Upper Room...was associated in [the disciples']
minds with the Last Supper, for in this same room Jesus
sat with them and unfolded the redemption he would
make in the self-giving on the cross.... Now this same
place would find them confronted with the same necessity
of their self-giving. The divine Self-giving—the coming of
the Holy Spirit—would mean their initial self-giving as a
preparation for the Spirit's coming....

So in the Christian faith the Upper Room has a double
content—the Cross and the Spirit.... If you do not bear
within you the spirit of the Cross, you will not bear within you the Spirit of God. You must die to live. We are crucified followers of a crucified Lord and yet by that very fact
are risen followers of a risen Lord and "endued with power
from on high" (Luke 24:49 KJV).

Are you ready for the coming of the Spirit?

O God, in this Upper Room where I am today, I offer my
little all, and I take the great All. I exchange my poverty for
your riches, my emptiness for your fullness.

Affirmation: Today, my all on the altar, and my all on fire with the
fire of that altar.

For further reading: Luke 22:14-20; Romans 5:6-11

WPP 79

Pentecost— the Firstfruits

When the day of Pentecost had come, they were all together in one place. And suddenly from heaven there came a sound like the rush of a violent wind....
—*Acts 2:1-2*

Pentecost was . . . the festival when the firstfruits were offered to God in thanksgiving and prayer for the rest of the harvest.

As the nation was offering the firstfruits of the harvest, so . . . the firstfruits of the harvest which Christ would reap from the whole world was there in that little company of a hundred and twenty men and women.

Five hundred disciples saw Jesus after his resurrection (1 Corinthians 15:6), and yet only a hundred and twenty obeyed his charge for them to tarry for the Spirit. Three hundred and eighty . . . dropped out, victims of arrested development. They probably excused themselves from the waiting for the ten days to be endued with power by saying that they were too busy. They were the practical minded.

But no amount of fussy busyness can atone for [neglecting] the first business of the Christian: namely to be the kind of person God can use. Time spent in seeking the Holy Spirit is the most fruitful time of one's life. It saves one from needless repentances, inward preoccupation with inner unsolved problems.

Are you too busy?

O God, I give you the one thing I have—I give myself. Let this day be my Pentecost, for I want to take from you your All in exchange for my little all.

Affirmation: All I have and am belongs to God.

For further reading: 1 Corinthians 15:3-10; Acts 1:12-15

WPP 80

The Phenomena
of Pentecost

*Suddenly from heaven there came a sound
like the rush of a violent wind, and it filled
the entire house where they were sitting.*
—*Acts 2:2*

A great deal of the phenomena surrounding Pentecost was temporary scaffolding which was taken down when the building emerged. That scaffolding had its use for that time—it served a needed purpose. God was teaching certain principles with kindergarten methods, but the kindergarten method was laid aside when the principle was established.

For instance, what was the use of the phenomena of the "sound like the rush of a violent wind" except to arouse in them a general expectancy that the group as a whole was going to receive the Spirit? And what was the meaning of the "divided tongues, as of fire," sitting upon the heads of each of them, except to arouse in each individual the expectancy that each as a person was to receive the Spirit? When the principle had been established that the group and the individual would both receive the Spirit, then the outer scaffolding of events could be removed. . . . Thus collectivism and individualism came together in one experience of the Holy Spirit.

What is the place of the Holy Spirit in your life?

O God, I am grateful that in the coming of the Spirit you have harmonized both collectivism and individualism. Let me be the meeting place of that harmony.

Affirmation: In me and in my group the Spirit will work today.

For further reading: Acts 2:1-4; Ephesians 4:7-13

WPP 81

Speaking in Other Languages

*All of them were filled with the Holy Spirit and
began to speak in other languages . . . each one
heard them speaking in the native language of each.*
—Acts 2:4-6

There is another temporary phenomenon which we must face—the speaking directly in the languages of the people who heard—the speaking "in other tongues" (KJV). . . . Without this there would have been the tendency to insist that those who received the gospel through the Jews would have to adopt the Jewish language and culture— Christianity would be identified with the medium through which it came. That had to be scotched at once. The crowd heard in their native languages "about God's deeds of power" (Acts 2:11). That meant that God was going to use every language and every culture to be the medium through which the universal gospel would come. There would be no imposing of a foreign culture and language on people. . . . The universal gospel would be expressed in local forms and local cultures, and thus a rich variety would be brought into the kingdom of God. It would be a unity of diversity instead of a unity of uniformity.

**What might learning to speak another language do
for you and your faith?**

O God, I am grateful that the miracle of Pentecost paved the way for me to hear the gospel in my own language.

Affirmation: I rejoice in the infinite variety in God's kingdom.

For further reading: Acts 2:5-13; Colossians 3:9-11

WPP 82

An Unknown Tongue

Pursue love and strive for the spiritual gifts, and especially that you may prophesy. For those who speak in a tongue do not speak to other people but to God; for nobody understands them.
—*1 Corinthians 14:1-2*

Three times the coming of the Spirit in Acts was accompanied by speaking in tongues: at Jerusalem, Caesarea, and Ephesus.... The universalizing [of the message] was needed in those three strategic places—the seat of Jewish nationalism, Jerusalem; the seat of Roman authority, Caesarea; and the seat of Asiatic paganism, Ephesus.[1] ... Once the lesson was learned, this temporary phenomenon disappeared.

...At Corinth there appeared a different type of tongues—unknown tongues—needing an interpreter. At Pentecost no interpreter was needed, for people heard in their own languages the wonderful works of God. At Corinth the type of tongues that appeared was one of the gifts of the Spirit. "To each is given the manifestation of the Spirit for the common good" (1 Corinthians 12:7)... The gift of the Spirit is for all, but the gifts of the Spirit he "allots to each one individually just as the Spirit chooses."

Have you thanked God for the gift of the Holy Spirit?

O God, I thank you that you have made us of one blood but of many cultures and languages. Help me to be tolerant of differences and yet one among them.

Affirmation: My tongue will be God's tongue today.

For further reading: 1 Corinthians 14:1-19

WPP 82, MAS 79

---

[1]See Acts 2:1-21; 10:23-48; 19:1-7.

158   All Places Sacred

"The hour is coming when you will worship the Father neither on this mountain nor in Jerusalem . . . when the true worshipers will worship the Father in spirit and truth."
—John 4:21, 23

At Pentecost the barriers went down and a universal faith and movement emerged.

1. The Holy Spirit makes all places sacred. . . . God's most precious promise, the promise of himself, was given in the most commonplace place, a home (Acts 1:13).

That lifted religion out of the tyranny of sacred places where God is said to be found especially. . . . Millions in money, years in time, are spent in various lands to get to sacred places—all to get a special touch with God through a touch with a sacred place. . . . God cannot approve of giving himself in some specially sacred place; for if he did, how would the poor, those who are tied up in families, the busy, find him? . . .

It lifted God's availability out of the hands of priests, places, and the paraphernalia of organized religion. . . . God will use any person, any building, any rite or ceremony that looks beyond itself and is the instrument of the Divine; but he has not confined himself to anything except two—He comes through Christ and he comes to a person, whoever and wherever that person may be, provided that person lifts up a surrendered, trusting heart to God through Christ.

Is your home a sacred place?

O God, thank you that I need not move from where I am, except in attitude, to find you coming in your fullness and power. Here, where I am, I offer you my all, and I take your all.

Affirmation: My attitudes alone determine my altitudes.

For further reading: John 4:19-26; Acts 1:12-14; 2:1-4; 10:44-48   WPP 85

All Persons Sacred

159

When the day of Pentecost had come, they
were all together in one place. . . . All of them
were filled with the Holy Spirit.
—Acts 2:1, 4

2. The Holy Spirit makes all persons sacred. . . .

The Spirit came upon the disciples while they were in a home. . . . That naturalized the Christian faith within the natural. The Holy Spirit was given to live life out in the ordinary relations. He is power for life and not power for special occasions connected with special places. . . .

The Holy Spirit came, not on the Twelve, but upon the one hundred and twenty (Acts 1:15). Suppose the Spirit had come [only] on the Twelve . . . what would that have done to religion? It would have tied up the Spirit's presence and power to people specially called to specially sacred tasks. The addition of zero to twelve making the hundred and twenty was one of the most important additions in human history. It lifted the gifts of God from priests and prophets and put them on people. The prophets and priests could have them too, but not as prophets and priests—only as people. All distinctions based on sacred class were gone. Sacredness attaches to persons and not to their duties. . . . Sacredness is found in character, not collars; in value, not vestments. . . .

"God is no respecter of persons."
(Acts 10:34 KJV)

O Divine Spirit, I thank you that I as a person, apart from everything else, can receive you and live out your life in my vocation.

Affirmation: I take the Spirit everywhere.

For further reading: 1 Corinthians 3:5-9; Acts 10:1-8, 34-48

WPP 87

The Highest Open to Woman

All [the disciples] were constantly devoting themselves to prayer, together with certain women, including Mary the mother of Jesus. . . . All of them were filled with the Holy Spirit.
—Acts 1:14; 2:4

3. *The Holy Spirit makes both sexes equal.* There had been a specially sacred sex—the male sex. " 'The firstborn of your sons you shall give to me. . . . You shall be men consecrated to me" (Exodus 22:29, 31 RSV). That was as far as Judaism went. But the Christian faith went beyond this: a woman as a woman received the highest gift of God— the Holy Spirit. And if this is true, then all the lesser gifts must be open to her. . . .

The Holy Spirit came upon women equally with men. . . . This outflanked all the arguments of antiquity about man's superiority and placed men and women on the basis of equality before God and hence in all the rest of life. No wonder Paul sums up the Christian attitude in these words: "There is no longer Jew or Greek, there is no longer slave or free, there is no longer male and female; for all of you are one in Christ Jesus" (Galatians 3:28).

**Mary, the mother of Jesus,
was twice filled with the Holy Spirit!**

O Gracious God, you are wiping out our barriers and making us see life through your eyes. Help us to be true to the heavenly vision and act upon it in all relationships.

Affirmation: Thank God for the equality of the Spirit!

For further reading: Luke 1:26-38; Matthew 1:18-24; Acts 21:8-9

WPP 88

161

The Conservative
and the Radical

"God declares
that I will pour out my Spirit upon all flesh,
and your sons and your daughters shall prophesy,
and your young men shall see visions,
and your old men shall dream dreams."
—Acts 2:17

4. *The Holy Spirit made both ages—youth and old age—equal.*
There has always been a sacred age, and it has always
been old age. In every religion power and sanctity have
gravitated toward old age. It has therefore tended to
become conservative.

But the Christian faith is so dynamic that it cannot be
expressed by conservatism alone. . . . Not only does
Christian faith conserve values; it pushes those values into
more and more realms of life and makes them operative
there. Hence it demands a radicalism as well as a conservatism to fully express itself. Both old age and youth must
combine to show its true nature. The Christian faith as
conservatism is weak; the Christian faith as radicalism is
also weak—but as both conservatism and radicalism it is
a living blend, and then it is truly strong. . . .

The Holy Spirit is the redemptive Spirit, pushing upon
more and more areas of life to redeem them. Hence the
young shall see visions and the old dream dreams—both
radical because both redemptive.

The Holy Spirit
breaks down the divisions and limitations of ageism.

O God, you are the ceaseless urge within me toward the
new. Keep me forever responding to you and to that urge.

Affirmation: I will dream dreams with the Spirit's help.

For further reading: 1 John 2:12-14; 1 Timothy 4:12   WPP 89

$\mathcal{L}$iving Under God's Guidance

162 — **God Has a Plan for You**

"The shepherd of the sheep . . . calls his own sheep by name and leads them out." —John 10:2-3

God has a plan for every life. When he made you, he made you different. He has not made anyone like you and never will again. He destroyed the pattern. You are unique and have a unique contribution to make. You are important in the scheme of things. The one supreme business of life is to find God's plan for your life and live it. Having a life plan from God gives you a backbone upon which all the bones of your life are fastened—all cohering in the central plan that holds them all together in meaning and purpose.

Most people go through life spineless and disjointed. No central plan organizes their life and directs it toward a single goal. They live a hand-to-mouth existence of opportunism. Hence they leave nothing but a blur. They live aimlessly and then stumble into the arms of death, and it is all over—tragedy.

Do you have a backbone for your life?

O Father, teach me to know your will, your plan for my life, so that I don't live an aimless life but one focused on you.

Affirmation: I am important to God and I will follow God's plan.

For further reading: Isaiah 26:7-9; Psalm 23:1-2; John 10:1-5, 11-15

MAS 242

The Mastery
of Guidance

Live by the Spirit, I say, and do not gratify
the desires of the flesh....If we live by the
Spirit, let us also be guided by the Spirit.
—Galatians 5:16, 25

Guidance is at once the most precarious and the most precious thing in the Christian life. I say "precarious," for you can go wrong following "guidance." Some do. A pastor's life was a wreck, his credentials surrendered and his home life broken, because he followed a "guidance," a wrong relationship with a woman. He got his wires crossed, mistaking the voice of his sex emotions for the voice of God.

While there are casualties now and then in guidance, and its direction and fruit must be carefully watched and scrutinized, nevertheless the casualties of living unguided lives are infinitely greater. The wreckage of not living by God's guidance is so fast that we scarcely notice it, for it is commonplace. All the troubles and wreckages in the world have one root—not living under God's guidance. So the occasional wreck that takes place in mistaking God's guidance should not scare us away from the infinite possibilities of life under God's guidance.

Why do we think we know better than God?

O Father, I do not want to mistake your will for mine. Help me not only to know your will but also to work it out with all my powers for your glory.

Affirmation: When God guides, God provides—provides everything I need for carrying out that guidance.

For further reading: Galatians 5:16-26; James 4:2-3

MAS 242

173

164 — Listen, Learn, Obey

"Take my yoke upon you and learn from me;
for I am gentle and humble in heart,
and you will find rest for your souls."
—Matthew 11:29

Since God has a plan for every life, then we must become skilled in the art of knowing and working out that plan. . . . When we come to prayer we should have three attitudes: listen, learn, obey. Some of us listen but won't learn, and some of us learn but won't obey. The Christian is one who listens, who learns, who obeys. If we do not approach God in all three attitudes, then there will soon be nothing to listen to, or to learn, or to obey. The Voice will grow silent. Only to the degree that we do all three will there be something speaking.

Guidance involves surrender.

Forgive me, O God, that I sometimes refuse to listen to you, and other times refuse to follow the directions you give me. I do want to hear your Voice speaking to me.

Affirmation: I will obey the directions I get from God today.

For further reading: Matthew 11:28-30; Deuteronomy 31:10-12; Acts 5:17-32

AL 252, 251

165

Guidance Doesn't Just Happen

Scripture

*"Then I said, 'See, God, I have
come to do your will, O God.'"*
—Hebrews 10:7

If we do not have guidance, then it is probably withheld
for one of two reasons: we are untrained, or we are
unwilling. Guidance doesn't just happen. It is a result of
placing oneself in the way of being guided. A radio doesn't
just happen to pick up messages; it is tuned in by deliberate intention, and then it receives. Receptivity is necessary
to perceptivity—you perceive only as you receive. To this
psychology agrees when it explains life as "instrumenta-
tion." When the king [of France] complained to Joan of Arc
that he never heard the voice of God, she replied, "You
must listen, and then you will hear."

You can learn to listen.

O Jesus, help me to learn to hear you calling me by name.
Help me to recognize your voice as you speak to me—
through the Scriptures, through prayer, in my thoughts.

Affirmation: Jesus is my shepherd, who calls me by name.

For further reading: Hebrews 10:5-10; Psalm 40:6-8; John 10:1-5, 27-28

AL 252

Receptivity

"Abide in me as I abide in you. Just as the branch cannot bear fruit by itself unless it abides in the vine, neither can you unless you abide in me."
—John 15:4

The first law of life is receptivity. The first act of a child is to receive. Instinct provides that the child turn to its mother's breast—to receive. That first law of life—receptivity— begins there and goes through life. We can expend only what we receive and no more. . . .

Jesus said, "Consider the lilies of the field, how they grow" (Matthew 6:28). How do they grow? by striving, getting into an agony of desire to grow, by working hard? No, the lilies grow by receptivity. They take in from the soil and sun and atmosphere and they give back in beauty. They grow effortlessly without strain and without drain. So Jesus points us to the lilies and asks us to grow by receptivity.

Do you have the art of being quiet?

O Spirit Divine, teach me how to relax, to receive, to take from you what you have in abundance for me, so that I may follow your guidance.

Affirmation: If the first law of life is receptivity, it shall be my first emphasis.

For further reading: Matthew 6:25-33; John 15:1-11

CM 316

Listening

"When you are praying, do not heap up empty phrases as the Gentiles do; for they think that they will be heard because of their many words."
—Matthew 6:7

The nervous, pushing, active type of modern living has lost the art of receptivity, of being quiet, of listening. It pushes itself against the problems of living and exhausts itself upon those problems. Hence our mental institutions are filled with disrupted, exhausted persons. . . . And think of those who never get to institutions or psychiatric offices, but who are a problem to themselves and to others. . . . They bring themselves to this state by pushing, by pulling, by tense striving—all outgo and no income. When they get to the state of being neurotics they continue this meaningless outgo. They talk interminably and write long and exhausting letters, going round and round on the same things and getting nowhere. They have acquired the habit of outgo and they can't stop it. . . . If they should learn how to listen, to receive, they would be well.

And many semiexhausted souls would be well and whole and adequate for living if they should learn the art of receptivity, of lowly listening, of the Great Intake.

Talking can be a way of not dealing with our problems.

O Jesus, my hands are so full of problems that I have no room to receive. Help me to empty them, turn them up to you, and then receive, receive—to overflowing.

Affirmation: I will listen twice as much today as I talk—whether to others or to God.

For further reading: Psalms 37:1-7; 46:10; Isaiah 55:1-2; Matthew 6:7-8

CM 316

177

Is God's Will Disagreeable?

*Be transformed by the renewing of your minds,
so that you may discern what is the will of God—
what is good and acceptable and perfect.*
—Romans 12:2

Many of us don't want to listen to God, for we are afraid that if God reveals his will to us it will be along the line of the disagreeable. The fact that we have changed "Thy will be done" into "Thy will be borne"—something hard and disagreeable to be borne—shows that we look on the will of God as something that mortals must accept with a sigh, like the death of a loved one.

That view of the will of God...must be completely reversed, or we shall get nowhere with guidance. Jesus reverses that view when he says, "My food is to do the will of him who sent me and to complete his work" (John 4:34)....The will of God is food—food to every tissue, every brain cell, to everything that is good for us. My will is my poison when it conflicts with God's will. To real living the will of God is reinforcement, not restriction.

There are none so deaf as those who refuse to hear.

Forgive me, O God, that I hesitate to throw down every barrier to your guidance. Why should my eye be afraid of light, my stomach afraid of food? No more should I be afraid of your will. I will not be.

Affirmation: Every faculty is sensitive and open to God's suggestions.

For further reading: Romans 12:1-2; Ephesians 1:3-14

AL 252

169 Be Silent to God

"Be still, and know that I am God.
I am exalted among the nations,
I am exalted in the earth!"
—Psalm 46:10

Many of us talk fast in the presence of God, afraid that if we keep quiet God will say something unpleasant to us. We must learn to listen, to live in the passive voice....

One translator interprets the command, "Be still, and know that I am God," this way: "Be silent to God and He will mold you."...An almighty Will will reinforce your weak will, but only when that weak will is aligned to the purposes of that almighty Will. An all-wise Mind will brood over your mind, awakening it, stimulating it, and making it creative. An all-embracing Love will quicken your love into world-sensitivity until "he will set the world into your heart."

God has three things in mind in reference to you: purpose, plan, person. He has a purpose to make you the best that you can be. He has a plan which embodies that purpose. God has a plan for every life. The next step is for you to be the person for the carrying out of that purpose and that plan. In the silence you listen for the unfolding of that purpose and that plan.

What a reward for receptive silence!

O God, alone, I am a dead wire; but attached to you I am full of energy and light. Make my connection with you sure, so that I will not periodically go dead and lightless.

Affirmation: I will maintain my spiritual connection so that I will keep my spiritual glow.

For further reading: Jeremiah 1:4-10; Ephesians 5:7-20

AL 253

First, Last, and Always

Hebron became the inheritance of Caleb the son of Jephunneh the Kenizzite to this day, because he wholly followed the Lord.
—Joshua 14:14 RSV

We must be willing to be guided of God, not merely now and then, but as a life proposition. You cannot get light in a crisis unless you are willing to get light in the continuous. God must not be called in to get you out of scrapes in which you have entangled yourself by continuous self-will.

A Swedish literary woman wanted God to tell her what the next step in her career was to be. At length, in a surge of abandon that broke through all her reserves, she seemed to hear God saying, "How could you expect me to speak when you have gagged me so long?" Don't gag God in the continuous and expect him to speak in the crisis.

In the beginning of guidance, then, make a decision that decides all decisions down the line—the decision that the will of God is first, last, and always in your life. Nail that down. Let there be no loophole of exceptions. Make it absolute.

What is your decision about the will of God?

Gracious Father, help me to seek your way and your will with my whole being and without reservations. I would be like Caleb who wholly followed you.

Affirmation: I will make God's will my primary goal—first, last, and always.

For further reading: Joshua 14:6-14; John 5:19, 30; 8:28; Acts 26:19-23

AL 254, 255

Gradual or Sudden

The plan of your life may be unfolded in a moment of sudden insight, or it may be a gradual unfoldment. The gradual unfoldment may be the highest form of guidance. "The steps of a good man are ordered by the Lord" (Psalm 37:23 KJV)—every two and a half feet. "Thy word is a lamp unto my feet" (Psalm 119:105 KJV). Note "unto my feet"—just enough light by which the next step can be taken and then the next. That puts adventure into life and a moment-by-moment trust. There is a surprise around every corner.

But the life guidance may be a sudden insight. One day, as a young man, I placed a letter on a chair and knelt before it. The answer to that letter would determine my lifework. The Inner Voice said, "It's India." I arose and said, "Then, it's India." That clear moment was a real moment, and has held me steady amid low moments of discouragement about the details in India.

The Inner Voice brings inner unity.

O God, help me to build according to the pattern I see and the word I hear when your voice is clear and I am receptive and responsive. For I want to live not on a surmise, but on a summons; not on a guess, but on a goal.

Affirmation: I will wait for God's bidding and God's blessing—listening with all my heart.

For further reading: Acts 9:1-19; 1 Thessalonians 5:16-18

AL 254

God Guides
in Many Ways

And the Lord will guide you continually,
and satisfy your needs in parched places,
and make your bones strong;
and you shall be like a watered garden.
—Isaiah 58:11

I suppose the great problem to God is how to guide us and not override us. He must guide us and develop us as persons at the same time. To lead us and at the same time produce initiative in us is a task worthy of divine wisdom. That task is the problem of every thinking parent. Many parents are benevolent tyrants, snuffing out initiative and personality. Guidance must be such that each person is guided into a free-self-choosing, creative personality.

To do this God will guide in many ways, awakening the personality to aliveness and alertness of mind and spirit to his hidden leadings. God's leadings should be sufficiently obvious to be found, but not so obvious as to do away with the necessity of thought and discriminating insight. They must be "an open secret"—open, yet sufficiently secret to make us dig.

How does this fit with your picture of God?

Gracious Father, I know that your way is really my way—the way I am made in my inner structure to obey. Help me to find it and follow it wholeheartedly.

Affirmation: God's way is the best way—for me.

For further reading: Psalms 25:8-10; 32:8-9; 73:24-25

AL 255

Guidance Through the Revelation in Christ

"When the Spirit of truth comes, he will guide you into all the truth.... He will glorify me."
—John 16:13-14

(1) God gives general guidance through the character and person of Christ.

Christ has revealed to us the nature of God—has shown us what God is like. He has lifted up into bold relief the laws that underlie our moral universe, and the laws that underlie our own spiritual, intellectual, and physical beings. In short, he has revealed to us the nature of Reality. Then Christ is our "general guidance." If we want to live according to the nature of Reality, we must live according to Christ.

...To be an example is to live in such a way that one's life in a particular situation is lived on universal principles, so that the spirit of these principles can be applied anywhere. Jesus took [this] method. There is no situation conceivable where his spirit is not the norm for that situation. He is the universal conscience of humanity.

...Ask the question in any situation, "What is the Christlike thing to do?" And if you do it you will not go wrong.

**Think of having guidance
along the line of the Christlike!**

O God, I see I am predestined to be conformed to the image of your Son, for the nature of reality is Christlike, and if I live according to it I will come out there. What a destiny awaits me! Help me to be willing to be thus predestined.

Affirmation: I will live today with my eyes always on Jesus Christ.

For further reading: John 13:12-15; 16:12-15; 1 Peter 2:20-25

AL 256

Guidance Through the Wisdom of the Church

...so that through the church the wisdom of God in its rich variety might now be made known....
—Ephesians 3:10

(2) God guides us through the collective experience of the Church—the corporate wisdom gathered through the ages.

The importance of this method is seen when we look at the use the great Roman Catholic Church makes of this corporate wisdom. We cannot accept this as the sole method of guidance for the individual, but certainly as one of the chief methods. The accumulated experiences of the ages are at the disposal of the individual.

The Church has been the mother of my spirit; and just as a child turns to its mother for guidance in crises, so I can turn to the Church for direction. Pastors are the mouthpiece of that collective wisdom. They should therefore not seek to be novel, but to interpret the wisdom of the ages to the people before them.

What do you know about the Church's thinking and history in the past two thousand years?

Lord Jesus Christ, thank you for your hand on your Church through the years and your continuing refining of her life, her thinking, her teaching. Help me to appreciate my heritage.

Affirmation: I will honor the Church—and study to discern Christ's words through the Church's words.

For further reading: Matthew 18:15-17; Acts 13:1-3; 15:1-32

AL 257, TW 301

Guidance
Through Counsel

Ananias . . . laid his hands on Saul and said, "Brother Saul, the Lord Jesus . . . has sent me so that you may regain your sight and be filled with the Holy Spirit."
—Acts 9:17

(3) God guides through the counsel of good people.

As we look back across the years we find that a word here, a phrase there, a conversation yonder with a friend, has lifted horizons, untangled snarled-up situations, and has sent us on our way rejoicing, with clarified minds and purposes.

Counseling is no longer a hit-and-miss affair; it is becoming an art and a science. The minister who cannot combine public utterance with private counsel is "out" as a safe guide to his or her people.

The Orientals have a saying that you don't drop eye medicine from a third-story window into a person's eye. Guidance must be intimate and personal and confidential. Counseling is a heavy responsibility. "Should I marry this man?" asked a girl after describing him. When I told her I thought not, she replied, "There, that settles it. I promised God last night that I would take your answer for his answer." I held my breath. What a responsibility!

God has many ways of getting his message across.

Gracious Father, thank you for those who have come into my life with kindly word and deep insight. Help me this day to be the agent of your mind to some other person, to speak that word which will lift the darkness for some fumbling soul.

Affirmation: "Lord, speak to me, that I may speak \ In living echoes of Thy tone" (Frances Ridley Havergal).

For further reading: 2 Timothy 2:1-2; 3:10–4:2

AL 257

Guidance Through Opportunity or Need

"I have set before you an open door, which no one is able to shut."
—Revelation 3:8

(4) *God guides through opening providences—matching us against some opening opportunity or need.*

A little waif boy of the streets of London sidled up to a doctor and said, "Do youse want to see where wese live?" He took the doctor by the hand and led him into alleyways where boys slept in boxes and under steps, huddled together to keep one another warm. Before morning that doctor knew he belonged to those boys. He went out and set up Dr. Barnardo's Homes, through which thousands of boys have been blessed. God's guidance was the opening of the doctor's eyes to see a need.

If God lets you see a need, the seeing of it is his invitation for you to meet that need. . . . Don't wait for specific guidance when there is specific need at hand. Here is a passage to the point: "Do whatever your hands find to do, for God is with you" (1 Samuel 10:7 RSV).

**When God is with you,
then everything is an open opportunity.**

O Father, help me to be willing to meet the needs I see—with your help and your resources, and in the power of your Spirit.

Affirmation: "I can do all things through him who strengthens me" (Philippians 4:13).

For further reading: Acts 16:9-10; 1 Corinthians 16:8-9

AL 258, CM 319

Guidance Through Natural Law

*The heavens are telling the glory of God;
and the firmament proclaims his handiwork.*
—Psalm 19:1

(5) *God guides through natural law and its discoveries through science.*

We have a primary faith in revelation and a secondary faith in science. But in a sense science is revelation—God speaking to us through the natural order. That natural order is God's order. It is dependable because God is dependable. He works by law and order rather than by whim and notion and fancy.

There was a time when we tried to put God in the unexplained gaps in nature . . . for these gaps are mysterious and unexplainable. But when science began to fill up these gaps, God was pushed out. To have relegated God to those gaps was a mistake, for God reveals himself in the very law and order and the explainable facts of nature, not merely in the unexplainable and the mysterious. The law and order express God far more than the unexplainable and mysterious. For this very law and order is of God—he is in it, is the author of it, works through it, but is not straitjacketed by it. For this law and order is full of surprises and of freedoms. A closed system of nature is now unscientific.

God guides through science. Accept that fact.

O God, your will is wrought into the natural order, and by that very order you discipline us to lawful, orderly living. Help us to accept and rejoice in that discipline, for your disciplines are our freedoms.

Affirmation: Guided by the revelations of science, I will be open-minded to life around me as well as to life above me.

For further reading: Psalms 8; 19; 65:8; 104

AL 258

187

Guidance Through Moral Intelligence

*I pray that the God of our Lord Jesus Christ,
the Father of glory, may give you a spirit of
wisdom and revelation as you come to know
him... with the eyes of your heart enlightened.*
                        —Ephesians 1:17-18

(6) God guides through a heightened moral intelligence and insight—we become persons who are capable of exercising sound moral judgments.

This is the usual and perhaps the most dependable form of guidance. I should think it would be the form that God most delights in. It is certainly the form discerning parents delight in, when they see their children now no longer leaning parasitically on them, but capable of exercising sound moral judgments of their own. That is the sign of a free personality. The Parent God must love that. Jesus loved it—"Why do you not judge for yourselves what is right?" (Luke 12:57). Fellowship with Christ stimulates and heightens our moral insights and judgments.

Jesus makes us fully adult human beings.

O God, you guide us through conscience, and yet beyond conscience, when choosing is not so much a question of right and wrong but perhaps of good and best. Continue to enlighten my mind and heart by your Spirit.

Affirmation: I will spend time with Jesus Christ today.

For further reading: Ephesians 1:15-19; 1 Corinthians 14:13-20; Romans 12:1-2; Hebrews 5:11-14

AL 259

Guidance Through the Inner Voice

For all who are led by the Spirit of God are children of God.
—Romans 8:14

(7) God guides through the direct voice of the Spirit within us.

That [this method of guidance] is capable of being abused is not to be denied. Thoughts may arise from our subconscious which we mistake for the voice of the Spirit. Any suggestion that speaks to us must be tested, particularly as to whether or not it fits in with the guidance we receive through the person and teaching of Christ. If the guidance is not in thorough accord with that, then suspect it and reject it. And don't depend on the Inner Voice as the usual method of guidance, for if we do we may be tempted to manufacture guidance through our own desires when no Inner Voice comes.

The guidance of the Inner Voice comes, at least to me, when none of the other steps in guidance can meet my particular need. I need a special word for that special crisis. Then the Inner Voice speaks. And it is distinguishable as something self-authenticating and authoritative. When a voice rises from my subconscious it argues with me. The Voice doesn't argue; it is self-authenticating.

"That very Spirit [bears] witness with our spirit
that we are children of God."
(Romans 8:16)

O God, help me not to be led astray by my own desires, but to be sensitive to the Inner Voice, your Spirit. And help me to obey at any cost. For your leadings are my enablings.

Affirmation: Today I shall listen to the internal testimony of the Holy Spirit.

For further reading: Romans 8:1-17; 1 Thessalonians 5:19-21; 1 John 4:1-6

AL 259, TW 304

180 — Power and Guidance

"Repent and be baptized everyone of you in the name of Jesus Christ so that your sins may be forgiven; and you will receive the gift of the Holy Spirit."
—Acts 2:38

The secret of power [as seen] in the book of Acts is twofold: first, these Christians fully surrendered to God and through that surrender were enabled to accept the gift of the Holy Spirit. That enabled the Holy Spirit to come into immediate contact with the human spirit, heightening all its powers and adding a plus to everything.

Second these heightened powers were under divine control and were working out a plan—a life plan. Without this following out of divine guidance the Holy Spirit's power in their lives would have been canceled or frustrated. Without this divine guidance life is like a hose with the water running to waste. Guidance directs the water of the hose where it is needed.

With God's guidance, we don't have to worry about wasted efforts.

O God, I surrender my life to you. I need your Holy Spirit to direct me in all that I do.

Affirmation: God's guidance is always into greater character and greater effectiveness.

For further reading: Acts 2; 8:14-40

MAS 243

Some Mistakes

They cast lots for them, and the lot fell on Matthias;
and he was added to the eleven apostles.
—Acts 1:26

The disciples made some mistakes in guidance, but the mistakes taught them to turn to truer guidance and over-rule their mistakes. They made a mistake, I believe, in deciding on a successor to Judas. First, they put forth two men and asked God to choose between them. They gave God no leeway; they tried to tie his hands. He didn't want either of them—he wanted Paul.

Second, they took a wrong method of guidance—they cast lots. That was the first and last time they used that method. The God of law and order can't be made into a Cosmic Juggler making chance lots fall in the right way. . . .

The disciples learned their lessons; guidance moved from the outward to the inward, from chance events to obedience to the voice of God under moral law.

Lotteries are a waste of time, money, and character.

O Holy Spirit, teach me to hear your voice and to distinguish between it and the voice of my desires. And help me to obey when I know, risking my all.

Affirmation: I will listen today for the Spirit's inward leading.

For further reading: Acts 1:15-26; Isaiah 30:20-21

MAS 243

Inner Guidance

"For it has seemed good to the Holy Spirit and to us to impose on you no further burden than these essentials...."
—Acts 15:28a

In the book of Acts guidance moves from the outer guidance of events [as seen in the Old Testament]—wet fleece, lots, fire on sacrifice—to the voice of God within the soul. But that voice was not independent of or apart from human intelligence. Sometimes where the intelligence could not be a part of the decision, the voice was direct and immediate and imperative [see, for example, 9:10-12, 10:19-20, 13:3]. But mostly the Holy Spirit's voice and the human intelligence coincided and were one. The statement, " 'It has seemed good to the Holy Spirit and to us,' " is the high watermark of guidance.

God wants us to think as well as trust and listen.

O God, cleanse my mind and heart so that I may think your thoughts after you and not be led astray by ideas and desires that do not glorify you.

Affirmation: I will test my desires and ideas by the standard of Jesus Christ.

For further study: Acts 9, 10

MAS 244

183 — Marginal Irrelevances

"For it has seemed good to the Holy Spirit and to us to impose on you no further burden than these essentials: that you abstain from what has been sacrificed to idols and from blood and from what is strangled and from fornication."
—Acts 15:28b-29

[This high watermark of guidance], however, was not free from marginal irrelevance. . . . The two items "from blood" and "from what is strangled" were practices of the Jews which [the Jewish Christians] tried to pass over into the Gentile world as universal practices. They failed. A marginal reading says: "Other ancient authorities lack *and from what is strangled.*" It was quietly dropped out. It was local and temporary and not universal. Yet the guidance not to put the Jewish yoke of circumcision on the Gentile Christians was right. It was so right it could stand the marginal irrelevance introduced and still be right.

Thankfully, God is greater than our cultural prejudices.

O God, continue to teach me your ways through your Holy Spirit so that I will not hinder your work by trying to make it conform to my prejudices.

Affirmation: I will do God's will today, trusting him to renew my mind and my thinking.

For further reading: Acts 15:4-29

MAS 244

Sometimes a No

*When they had come opposite Mysia, they attempted
to go into Bithynia, but the Spirit of Jesus did not
allow them; so...they went down to Troas.*
—Acts 16:7

Sometimes the guidance of the Spirit was a No! [Paul, Silas, and Timothy] were "forbidden by the Holy Spirit to speak the word in Asia" (Acts 16:6). Then they tried "to go into Bithynia" but were stopped.[1] But that No was in order to guide them to a larger Yes. For the closed doors into Asia meant an open door into Europe—the man of Macedonia called them to Europe and to us.

God never closes one door without opening a bigger one.

"I just love red lights," said [an overflowing Christian]. Why?

"Because he gives me a red light in order to give me a bigger green."

God's blockings are God's blessings
—always—
if we know how to take them.

O Father, I know that your red lights are only in order to guide me to a more glorious green. Help me to take gladly your prohibitions in order to take your possibilities.

Affirmation: If I am blocked today, I shall look around to find the larger open door.

For further reading: Acts 17:1-15

MAS 244

---

[1]The Roman province of Asia was at the western end of Asia Minor, which is present-day Turkey. Mysia and Bithynia were small provinces in the same area.

Guidance in the Story of Philip

"It is not right that we should neglect the word of God in order to wait on tables. Therefore . . . select seven men of good standing, full of the Spirit and of wisdom, whom we may appoint to this task."
. . . They chose . . . Philip . . . .Philip the evangelist.
—Acts 6:2-5; 21:8

[From] the very creative story of Philip [in Acts 6:1-6; 8:1-40], we can gather up some lessons . . . on guidance.

1. Philip, to whom a secular task was assigned, made the secular and the sacred part of one whole. For he put evangelism through the tableserving, and made tableserving a part of evangelism. All life spoke one message—the good news. . . . He got his guidance through the implications of his own gospel. His gospel was founded on bringing the spiritual and the material together and making them one— "the Word became flesh" (John 1:14). Out of that basic fact he worked out particular guidance regarding his applying it to a so-called secular job. He spiritualized it. Deduction: Our most general guidance will be to work out the implications of our gospel as seen in the person of Jesus.

All of life is sacred.

O Christ, you are calling us to make our Christian calling a life calling—the whole of life expressing one thing, the good news of the gospel.

Affirmation: Today, I will consider everything I do as a sacred calling.

For further reading: Acts 6:1-6; 8:4-8; 1 Corinthians 12:15-21

HBTP 290, 295

Guidance Through Circumstances

A severe persecution began against the church in Jerusalem, and all except the apostles were scattered.... Philip went down to the city of Samaria and proclaimed the Messiah to them.
—*Acts 8:1, 5*

Philip got his guidance through a set of circumstances not of his choosing.... He didn't complain about being "scattered" by persecution—he used it.

...Why weren't the apostles scattered? Were they braver? Or did the authorities see that the apostles were not the dangerous element—they would probably fit in and become a Christian sect among Jews? It was these laymen, represented by Stephen and Philip, the dangerous innovators and radicals, who must be suppressed. The apostles played safe—the laymen played Christian!... The leaven of Christianity passed from the hierarchy of apostles to the lay group.... Philip began a revival in Samaria....

Evil became the instrument of the good. Deduction: Much of our guidance will be to use opportunities which we didn't plan. They may come through evil; we turn them to good.

**"All things work together for good
for those who love God."
(Romans 8:28)**

O Spirit of God, teach me how to transform difficulties and problems into opportunities for the gospel.

Affirmation: Today I will not use the word *problem*—only the word *possibility.*

For further reading: Acts 8:1-13; 14:1-7; Isaiah 30:20-21

HBTP 295, 291

Direct Guidance

Then an angel of the Lord said to Philip, "Get up and go toward the south." ... Then the Spirit said ... "Go over to this chariot and join it."
—Acts 8:26, 29

Some of our guidance will come very directly. . . .

After the amazing revival in Samaria . . . [Philip] felt guided to leave it all and to leave it at high tide and go into a desert. . . . There time (noon), place (the desert road), and the person (the Ethiopian) converged with Philip at one of the most important moments in history. The Christian missionary enterprise through the centuries was bound up in that moment. This was a seed moment.

. . . That Spirit-guided moment resulted in a far-reaching movement. A person as a person was to be the field of the gospel. Special privileges and class and race and color were all canceled. . . . Tradition says that this Ethiopian minister-treasurer became the founder of the Abyssinian Church. . . . Often when God guides us to break with some developed situation and go into a seeming desert, he is really germinating one of those seed situations that may change the face of history. Philip did more in Ethiopia through one man than he did in Samaria. . . .

**Is anything preventing you
from hearing the Spirit's voice?**

O Spirit of God, help me to be sensitive at the moment when your impulses are within me. And teach me the difference between my impulses and yours.

Affirmation: Perhaps the Spirit will say to me today, "Go over to this chariot and join it"—contact that person—and I shall obey.

For further reading: Acts 8; 21:7-9; Psalm 25:8-9, 12

HBTP 295, 293

188

Corrected by Group Guidance

Now when the apostles at Jerusalem heard that Samaria had accepted the word of God, they sent Peter and John to them.
—Acts 8:14

There is one further lesson we must gather from the guidance of Philip.... At one point the insight and guidance of Philip needed correction by a group. In the enthusiasm of the revival in Samaria, Simon Magus, a sorcerer, was converted and baptized. It was a big fish Philip had caught, and he and the city were impressed—elated. But it took the impact of the Jerusalem group and their insights to show that Simon Magus, for all his superficial change, was as Peter said, "a bitter poison and a pack of evil" (Acts 8:23 Moffatt). It took corporate guidance to correct the movement of Philip at that point.... If individual guidance is uncorrected and unchecked by group guidance, it may go off on a tangent and get tangled up in its own subjective states.

... God guides through the group—and guides especially. But the group not only corrects you—it contributes to you as well. The partial idea is filled out by the idea of another. The sparks that fly from the clash of thought upon thought illuminate a subject—and you.

Can you accept godly criticism?

O God, you have made us for corporate living, so help us to accept and rejoice in that possibility and to submit to group guidance.

Affirmation: "Whoever reverences the Eternal, learns what is the right course to take" (Psalm 25:12 Moffatt).

For further reading: Acts 8:14-24; 13:2-3

HBTP 296

Three Stages
in Group Guidance

*Be of the same mind, having the same love, being
in full accord and of one mind. . . . Let the same
mind be in you that was in Christ Jesus.*
—Philippians 2:2, 5

There are three stages in group guidance as seen in Acts 15.

(a) "The apostles and the elders, with the consent of the whole church, decided . . . " (v. 22). . . . Obviously the decision was made by the apostles and the elders. This is oligarchy.

(b) "We have decided unanimously" (v. 25)—the decision of the total body of believers. This is democracy.

(c) "It has seemed good to the Holy Spirit and to us" (v. 28) —the decision of God and humans working together. This is the highest Christian guidance. . . . It is not God dictating or merely humans deciding—it is a combination of listening to God and of thinking too. Here God is not dictator and humans a blank sheet. Nor is it the grouping of human wisdom without any sense of being guided. It is a group surrendering their thoughts to God and then thinking too and finding that they and God were thinking the same thoughts. They arose convinced that they had found God's mind.

When we think God's thoughts, those thoughts stand.

O Spirit of Truth, we think truth and become truth when we think your thoughts, will your purposes, and feel your feelings. Help us this day.

Affirmation: May all my decisions today seem good to the Holy Spirit and to me.

For further reading: Revelation 2:7, 17, 29; Philippians 2:1-15

HBTP 297

Living with Health

Disease Is Not the Will of God

"I came that they may have life, and have it abundantly."
—John 10:10

God does not will disease. God wills health. Disease is an enemy which Jesus fought against and healed whenever he could get cooperation. He never once told people to bear disease as the will of God. "I have come that they may have life, and that they may have it more abundantly" (NKJV). This is the Christian note. It is true that disease comes from breaking the laws of God which he has written into the constitution of things, but God does not send it; we break his law and they break us. But that makes us, not God, the author of that disease. God has provided for health, not disease.

A friend once said to Dr. W. B. Cannon, the great Harvard physiologist: "When you know all the diseases it is possible to have...you wonder how anyone is ever well." To which Dr. Cannon replied: "When you know a great deal about the human body, you wonder why anyone is sick."[1]

Have you discovered why you get sick?

O God, you have wrought possibilities for health and rhythm into the structure of my being. Help me to cooperate with you so that no crippling disease shall mar the efficiency of my work for the kingdom.

Affirmation: I truly want life and health.

For further reading: Matthew 9:1-7; Psalms 6; 103:1-5

AL 169

---

[1]Quoted by Dr. Russell L. Dicks, *Religion in Life*, 1941, Vol. X, No. 4, p. 515.

Segregating Our Enemies

191

*What the flesh desires is opposed to the Spirit, and what the
Spirit desires is opposed to the flesh; for these are opposed
to each other, to prevent you from doing what you want.*
—Galatians 5:17

The way to fight disease germs is to raise the tone of health
in the total organism, and the fact of health throws off the
disease germs as they come—expelled by health. When
disease germs do get a footing, then nature sends up the
temperature into fever in order to get rid of the germs. . . .

There is a par life, but many of us are living below par.
When we do, disease germs rush in and gain a footing.
We must examine specifically some of the mental and
spiritual disease germs that throw disruption and disease
into human living. . . .

These enemies are [not] merely spiritual, throwing disruption only into the soul; they are enemies of the total
life, causing physical disease, mental disruption, and spiritual disharmony and decay. They attack the total person.
They may begin in one portion, but in the end they extend
their effects to all.

Are you living below par?

Help me, God, to see my enemies and face them all. They
attack me in subtle ways, but I am not dismayed. If sin
abounds, your grace abounds much more.

Affirmation: I will face all my enemies with courage and strength in
the confidence of God's presence.

For further reading: Matthew 15:10-11, 15-20; Galatians 5:19-21;
2 Timothy 3:2-5

AL 37, 36

You Are Made for Loyalty to God

*"What must I do to inherit eternal life?"... [Jesus]
answered, "You shall love the Lord your God with all your
heart, and with all your soul, and with all your strength,
and with all your mind; and your neighbor as yourself."*
—Luke 10:25-27

The first enemy is *the lack of a faith in and loyalty to
Something beyond oneself—a Something that gives ultimate
meaning, coherence, and goal to life.* We, of course, believe
that Something is a Someone—God....

In order to be well, in order to be the kind of person you
ought to be, you must believe in something beyond yourself
and be loyal to it. Why? The answer is that you are made
that way.... That way is stamped into your being.... Take
the statement of Dr. Jung, who certainly was not prejudiced
in a religious direction. Dr. Jung (to a patient): "You are suffering from loss of faith in God and in a future life." Patient:
"But, Dr. Jung, do you believe these doctrines are true?" Dr.
Jung: "That is no business of mine. I am a doctor, not a
priest. I can only tell you that if you recover your faith you
will get well. If you don't you won't."

Why did this famous psychiatrist say that?... He had
found by experience that life works that way. Life needs
something outside oneself to fasten its love and loyalty to,
or it will break down.

Does your life have meaning and coherence?

O God, can my lungs do without air, my eyes do without
light, my heart do without love, my aesthetic nature do
without beauty, my conscience do without truth? No more
can I do without you. You are the Life of my life.

Affirmation: I belong to God as glove to hand.

For further reading: Mark 10:49-52; Romans 8:10-11; Colossians
1:15-50, 2:6

AL 38

Substitutes for God

You were dead through the trespasses and sins in which you once lived, following the course of this world.
—Ephesians 2:1

[Perhaps] faith in anything beyond oneself can be a substitute for God. Art, music, patriotism, causes of various kinds—will these not take the place of God? Why is God necessary?

There is no doubt whatever that all these interests will help to lift you out of yourself and are thereby real helps, but they do not ultimately hit the spot.... Do the things mentioned as substitutes give *ultimate* meaning, coherence, and goal to life? They may give local and temporary meaning to portions of life...but if they lack total meaning and ultimate goal, then the meaning and the coherence drop to pieces. None of these things give ultimate meaning and goal to life, except God; therefore only God can make life cohere. Paul says of Christ, "In him all things hold together" (Colossians 1:17)—"all coheres in him" (Moffatt). They do, for he is ultimate Being, the human life of God....

Everything less than God...not rooted in eternal reality ...will let you down.

Ultimate significance only comes from the Ultimate.

O God, only those rooted in you, the Eternal, can stand up under life. I would be one of them. Then let all my being be rooted in you—my thoughts rooted in your thoughts, my emotions rooted in your love, my will rooted in your will. Then I shall live.

Affirmation: I am rooted in the Eternal.

For further reading: Colossians 1:15-20; 2:6-7; Ephesians 2:12-22

AL 39

194 — Having Our Being in God

" 'In him we live and move and have our being.' "
—Acts 17:28

Life is a restless, disrupted thing until we give ourselves to Something beyond ourselves. . . . A doctor said to me, "If three quarters of my patients found God, they would be well." A psychiatrist in Hollywood, who is paid handsomely by his disrupted patients of filmdom, said to a friend, "Most of my patients do not need me; they need a mourner's bench; they need God."

. . . Then why do not more of us find him and live by him? Here is one reason: The harboring of moral wrong makes God unreal. We will know as much of God as we are willing to put into practice, and no more.

Another reason is a lack of appropriating faith. . . . We live and move in God, for he is the inescapable. We can only deny him with the very powers he gives us. . . . And yet we do not "have our being" in him. We live on surface roots—the taproot has not gone down into God. . . . We fail to appropriate his amazing resources. And we fail because we do not take.

**Whether we like it or not,
we live in and through God.**

O God, you are the source of my life. From this moment I not only live and move in you—I have my being in you as well.

Affirmation: I am living with God's resources today.

For further reading: Hebrews 4:14-16; 6:9-12

AL 42

When We Become God

Scripture

> *In the last days distressing times will come.*
> *For people will be lovers of themselves . . .*
> —2 Timothy 3:1-2

The second major enemy of healthy living is *self-centeredness.* . . . When God is no longer the center, then we become the center—we become God. . . . But this centering on ourselves works badly; in fact, it works havoc to the very self upon which we are centering. . . . Every self-centered person is a self-disrupted person. . . .

Those who center upon themselves and have their way don't like their way; they do as they like, and then don't like what they do; they express themselves, and then find the self that is expressed souring on their hands. And this . . . doesn't merely stop with the soul; it extends straight out into the nerves and tissues, and poisons them with disease, functional and structural. Apparently they are running against a fundamental law of life, deeply imbedded in the constitution of things. More people are being broken by that law than by any other one single thing in life.

Perhaps my problem is myself?

Father God, I see that when I am adjusted only to myself I am not adjusted to life. Teach me how to make the right adjustment.

Affirmation: I will live fully, abundantly, overflowingly by centering on God.

For further study: 2 Timothy 3:1-5; Romans 15:1; 1 Corinthians 10:24

AL 43

Living in a State of Self-Reference

They are darkened in their understanding, alienated from the life of God because of their ignorance and hardness of heart.
—*Ephesians 5:18*

All self-centered persons when self-frustration begins to set in will probably turn toward themselves in self-pity. They will feel that life is hard on them. They will blame everything except themselves. . . .

Such self-centered persons usually draw disease to themselves as a magnet draws iron filings to itself. . . . I know a girl who has had thrown into her lap everything that civilization can offer—money, opportunity, etc. But since she is self-centered, she can enjoy none of them. Every sickness that comes into her neighborhood visits her. She draws sickness and melancholy to herself like a magnet; for that is the end of the egocentric. They start out to draw life to themselves—its joys, its thrills—and all they succeed in drawing to themselves is sadness and disillusionment and sickness—spiritual, mental, and physical.

How sad to live in such total disruption!

O God, I see I cannot center on myself without that self going to rack and ruin. Here is this self of mine. Lift me out of myself into yourself, where I may find my freedom and my true self.

Affirmation: God's will is my home, my center.

For further reading: Ephesians 5:17-24; Romans 12:1-3, 10; James 2:8-9

AL 45

Stress and Disease

*But understand this, that in the last days
there will come times of stress.*
—2 Timothy 3:1 RSV

A Montreal doctor . . . has propounded the thesis that stress is the cause of all diseases. He says that the pituitary and the adrenal glands keep the body in balance when stress comes upon one. They can succeed if the stress is not too great, but if it becomes too great than the defenses break down, the body is thrown out of balance, and we may develop any kind of disease to which we are prone. . . .

Paul has something to say on this subject: ". . . in the last days there will come times of stress" (1 Timothy 3:1 RSV)—"distressing times" (NRSV).

For people will be lovers of themselves, lovers of money, boasters, arrogant, abusive, disobedient to their parents, ungrateful, unholy, inhuman, implacable, slanderers, profligates, brutes, haters of good, treacherous, reckless, swollen with conceit, lovers of pleasure rather than lovers of God, holding to the outward form of godliness but denying its power (vv. 2-5).

Here are nineteen things that produce stress. We would have expected them to be from without—wars, famines, earthquakes, tornadoes—but they are not mentioned; all these nineteen things are from within.

**Paul's cure for stress:
prayer and thanks resulting in peace.
(Philippians 4:6-7)**

O God, help me not to dodge the fact that most of the stress in my life comes from within.

Affirmation: Calm and joy are inside jobs.

For further reading: Philippians 4:6-9; Ephesians 1:17-19

CM 243

Self-Centered Love

198

For people will be lovers of themselves, lovers of money,...lovers of pleasure rather than lovers of God.
—2 Timothy 3:2-4

Paul puts his finger on the first cause of stress: love of self. Self-centered love is the primary cause of stress. When you are a self-centered and self-preoccupied person, you are off-center, for the universe does not back your being God. You feel that nothing is backing you except yourself; hence you are uneasy.

The second cause of stress is love of money. People who put their whole weight down on loving money are uneasy and at stress because they are afraid that money might slip away from them and leave them with nothing but emptiness....

The third "love" among the nineteen mentioned...is love of pleasure. A person who loves pleasure is always uneasy and at stress if nothing is taking place in the form of entertainment. For the pleasure distracts them from their own inner emptiness.

These three...loves have gone astray and...need to be redeemed. Until they are [redeemed] they are causes of stress, hence of personality disruption and disease. And these are found in religious people, "holding the form of religion" (v. 5 RSV).

Who is responsible for the stress in your life?

O Jesus, Master, teach me how to let my faith in you release my tensions and make me free. Teach me the power of your Spirit to untie my knots and loose me from my inner conflicts.

Affirmation: I love my Savior, Jesus Christ, above all else.

For further reading: James 4:1-10; 2 Timothy 3:1-7

CM 244

Self-Centeredness in Religion

"Do not be astonished that I said to you, 'You must be born from above.'... Are you a teacher of Israel, and yet you do not understand these things?"
—*John 3:7, 10*

Self-centeredness—egocentricity—may be very religious, may be occupied in an attempt to save one's soul, or the souls of others. But it will still be egocentric, and as such destructive.

A very religious woman was suffering from arthritis. It was discovered that her anxiety to dominate her family... was at the basis of this arthritis. She surrendered this anxiety to God, ceased to desire to dominate the family, even though it was for their supposed good, and both her spiritual life and her physical life cleared up—the arthritis disappeared.

[After a businessman ended five years of psychoanalysis, when] he saw that all this self-probing was ending in futility,... a sense of infinite sadness and loneliness came over him.... Suddenly a Voice seemed to say, "Look this way." It was the Voice of Christ saying, "Look away from yourself, your misery, your fear, and your failures! Look to Me." He looked.... That look was followed by a lift that took him out of himself.

**Trying on our own to make life
—our own or others'—
turn out our way doesn't work.**

Living Christ, I do look to you. To whom else can I go, for you have the words of eternal life—you are the Life.

Affirmation: I take from Christ the power, the release, the harmony I so deeply need.

For further reading: Matthew 7:1-5; John 3:1-10; 1 John 3:17-21

AL 49

200 — Unchristian Emotions

*When we came into Macedonia our bodies
had no rest, but we were afflicted in every
way—disputes without and fears within.*
—2 Corinthians 7:8

[Another enemy of human personality is *unchristian emotions.*]

We often create our own sickness. T. E. Murphy says: "Physicians have come to a realization that worry, fear, anger, and hatred are poisons that can cripple and destroy the body as well as the mind; grudges can bring arthritis, rage can bring about the need for surgery. A man's thoughts are the theater of his soul." Christian attitudes toward life would clear up a great many physical illnesses....

Every emotion that upsets the body is an unchristian emotion. Every emotion that sets up the body is a Christian emotion. An eminent doctor, Charles T. Bingham, says: "Worry, fear, and anger are the greatest disease causers. If we had perfect faith, we wouldn't worry. Faith is the great healer."... God wills health. For salvation is wholeness—wholeness to the total person, including the body.

**Not a single cell of our body
is removed from the effects of our emotional states.**

O God, I owe it to you and to myself to make every emotion contribute to health. Help me to give up all disease-producing emotions.

Affirmation: All my emotions today will produce health, not disease.

For further reading: 2 Corinthians 2:8-11; 7:5-7, 13; Philippians 4:5-8.

HBTP 323

Unresolved Guilt

Have mercy on me, O God,
according to your steadfast love;
according to your abundant mercy
blot out my transgressions.
—Psalm 51:1

Another enemy of the human personality is *a sense of unre-solved guilt.* . . .

A good many ideas in reference to guilt [have had] to be thrown into the wastebasket. They were false guilts which needlessly tormented many sincere people. . . . We know now that sex feelings are not sin; they are part of normal, healthy life—everybody has them, saint and sinner. We also know that a normal self-love is right and natural; to act as if you had none is to end in hypocrisy. Every normal person has self-love, and ought to have it. The fear of having committed the "unpardonable sin" is usually a false fear, for the unpardonable sin of which Jesus spoke was saying that Jesus had "an unclean spirit," that the Spirit within him—the Holy Spirit—was unclean. Seldom is that sin committed. Therefore do not fear that you have committed the unpardonable sin.

The conscience should be trained at the feet of Christ;
only then is it a safe guide.

O God, if I have built up within me false guilts which hide my real guilt, forgive me, for I want to be inwardly absolved from all haunting guilts that rob me of my confidence and power.

Affirmation: I will look to Christ for reconciliation and cleansing and health.

For further reading: Psalms 19:12; 51; 103

AL 92, 93

202

Reconciliation, Forgiveness, Assurance

...our great God and Savior, Jesus Christ. He it is who gave himself for us that he might redeem us from all iniquity and purify for himself a people of his own.
—*Titus 2:13-14*

The human heart will not be put off with subterfuges. It needs reconciliation, forgiveness, assurance.

"Is this the place where they heal broken hearts?" asked a Korean girl of a mission station. Whether that broken heart comes from outer sorrow or inner guilt, the need is the same. . . . Dr. Howard Kelly, the great surgeon, said to a patient, "What you need is a New Testament." And the healing in that New Testament which the patient needed was the certainty of forgiveness, of grace, of reconciliation. We need a forgiving God. . . .

We are children of the Father, and our spirits will never rest until they see his face; but when we see it, we must read in that face reconciliation and forgiveness.

Do you believe God can meet your need?

O God, cleanse the depths of my soul, for I cannot live with guilt. I can live only with fellowship and reconciliation.

Affirmation: Bless the Lord, O my soul, who forgives all my iniquities and heals all my diseases (Psalm 103:2-3).

For further reading: Psalms 51; 103; Luke 15:11-24

AL 92, 94

Relax in the Presence of God

*For once you were darkness, but now in the
Lord you are light. Live as children of light.*
—Ephesians 5:8

How can we be assured [of God's love and forgiveness]?
First, *relax*. Recline in some semidarkened room with a
towel over your eyes. Talk about yourself, letting your mind
free to roam across your life as it will. Do not debate with
yourself, but in a calm, detached way bring to the surface
anything to which the mind returns again and again . . . a
sore point, a buried fear, a hidden guilt. At first you may
not even want to acknowledge that there is any sore point
in your life . . . but now you are resolved to be perfectly
honest and perfectly frank, even with yourself. . . .

Second: *Anything that appears touchy bring up gently but
decisively.* Perhaps this sensitive spot is your difficulty. If
so, segregate it and see what is to be done about it. Don't
push it down out of sight and try to forget it. . . . Perhaps
your difficulty is a hidden resentment, something you had
pushed down into the subconscious mind and put the lid
on. Now it is up, and you are looking at it frankly.
. . . Perhaps it is guilt . . . or fear . . . or emotional conflict. . . .
Look to . . . God as the way out. There is no other way.

**It is better to face problems
than run away and hide.**

O God, I want to live a life of complete frankness and open
honesty, to have no hidden, closed caverns in the depths of
me. I will face all my sore points with your help.

Affirmation: Believing in God's forgiveness, I am from now on a child
of light.

For further study: Psalms 4:4-5; 36:4-9; 38:4; 1 John 1:5-10

AL 95, 96, 97

Turn from Yourself to Christ

*Let us . . . lay aside every weight and the sin that
clings so closely, and let us run with perseverance
the race that is set before us, looking to Jesus. . . .*
—Hebrews 12:1-2

The third step in finding assurance of God's love and forgiveness: . . . *Turn your attention and your loyalty from yourself to Christ.* The bringing up of all these conflicts and fears and guilt will leave a vacuum which only Christ can fill. When he comes in and takes possession, then as you turn your attention within, you are not turning your attention to yourself, but to the Christ who is within you. . . .

A very intelligent woman, of excellent character and ability, loved her father devotedly. When he died she had no one she really loved, so her frustrated love turned upon herself. This upset her nerves and ended in further frustration. That frustrated love could be released and satisfied only as it centered on Christ, the Eternal. . . . Our love, fastened supremely on Christ, will give all lesser, legitimate loves their meaning and their place. They are hallowed by that supreme love. You dare love yourself if you love Christ supremely.

Jesus Christ is the love of God demonstrated.

Jesus, my Lord and Master, I see that I can be free only when I am in love with you, for love of you is love of myself. I am beginning to understand what Jesus' promise means, "If the Son makes you free, you will be free indeed" (John 8:36).

Affirmation: Thank God, I am free.

For further reading: John 3:14-16; Philippians 2:1-11; Ephesians 3:14-10

AL 98

205

Bodily Harmony
and Disease

Scripture

"...a body you have prepared for me."
—Hebrews 10:5

Another major enemy of the personality [is] *bodily dishar-mony and disease....* Body and mind are intertwined until one can scarcely say body and mind, but body-mind. If the soul and mind pass on their sickness to the body, then just as definitely does the body pass on its sickness to the mind and soul. The whole person becomes sick.... There are many people who are castigating their souls and loading them with guilt when they should attend to their nutrition or have out an infected tonsil. If the nerves are starved on account of the lack of vitamins, they will kick back in spiritual depression in exactly the same way that a starved soul will kick back in bodily depression.

Therefore Christianity shows its absolute sanity by taking the body seriously. It is the only one of the great faiths that does so. It is founded on an Incarnation.

Do you take your body seriously?

O God of my body, you have made me for health. Help me to present this body of mine for you to make out of it the very finest instrument for your purposes. Help every brain cell and every tissue and every nerve to be the string upon which your creative fingers will play and bring out undreamed-of harmony.

Affirmation: I want my body to be at God's best.

For further reading: Hebrews 10:5-7; John 1:14; Galatians 6:17; Romans 12:1-2

AL 165

The Moral and
Spiritual Bases of Disease

*If the Spirit of him who raised Jesus from the
dead dwells in you, he who raised Christ from
the dead will give life to your mortal bodies
also through his Spirit that dwells in you.*
—Romans 8:11

The physical basis of disease is so obvious and insistent
that we need not emphasize it. . . . Nor need we emphasize
its effect upon the spiritual condition. The idea that you
can be more spiritual if your body is mortified is false. If
that is tried, the body kicks back and clouds the soul. . . .

The other truth—the effect of the mental and spiritual
upon the physical—is insufficiently emphasized. . . . Many
bodies . . . harbor death cells of anger, fear, self-centeredness, and guilt. Many a person, instead of having a living
vibrant body, awake in every cell and harmonious in every
relationship, has a body of death. That body of death can
become a sanctuary. "The first concept I had that God could
heal a body wrung dry of all ability to resist disease, came
from your book, *The Christ of the Indian Road*," a reader confesses. "The leaven of your ideas was responsible for the
metamorphosis of a lump of clay to a seeker after truth."

**"A body wrung dry of all ability to resist disease"—
a Christian has no business with that kind of body.**

O God, if my mind and my body are wrung dry of the ability to resist disease, then give to me what Paul meant
when he said that our mortal bodies would be given life
through the Spirit that dwells within us.

Affirmation: I give myself, body and soul, to the Spirit of God for his life.

For further study: Romans 8:9-16; Psalms 31:9-10; 32:1-5; Isaiah 1:4-6

AL 168

The Sources of Disease

Scripture

Jesus ... said to the paralytic, "Take heart, son; your sins are forgiven."
—Matthew 9:2

If disease and physical disharmony are ours it is probably that they are from one or more of four causes: (1) actual structural disease, brought about by heredity, accident, contagion, ignorance, or willful abuse; (2) functional disease, which may pass into structural disease, brought about by wrong mental, moral, and spiritual attitudes; (3) lack of, or unbalanced, nutrition, brought about by poverty, ignorance, or willful neglect; (4) environmental factors which directly produce disease, or wrong mental and spiritual attitudes, which in turn produce disease.

Note that in the four sources of disease and disharmony I do not mention the will of God.

**How easy it is to have wrong thinking
and wrong actions about disease.**

O God, help me to give up all disease-producing attitudes, emotions and thoughts, since disease is not your will.

Affirmation: I will educate myself as to the true sources of disease—my own and in general.

For further reading: Matthew 9:1-7; Psalms 6:1-7; 19:7

AL 169, HBTP 323

Salvation Is Wholeness

Scripture

[Jesus] said to the woman, "Your faith has saved you; go in peace."...He said to [the leper], "Get up and go on your way; your faith has made you well."
—Luke 8:50; 17:19

Health . . . is written into the constitution of things. God wills it. If we do not have health, then some law has been broken somewhere, either by our ancestors, or by ourselves, or by society, or by environmental factors. We cannot be responsible for the body we begin life with, but are responsible for the one we die with. For the body can be improved no matter how handicapped it may have been in the beginning. I have lived for thirty-five years in one of the worst climates of the world—India, a land poverty-stricken and disease-ridden. . . . Yet I have come out of it at the end of these years with a better body than I had when I went in. . . . I was interested in the linking of real religion with health and vitality. . . .

Jesus defined salvation as health. Wherever he used the word *saved* ("Your faith has saved you" Luke 18:42) the word is also translated "made you whole" (see ASV) or "made you well" (RSV). Salvation is wholeness, health—health in total personality, body, mind, and soul.

Have you paid attention to your whole health?

Healing Father, I come to you with this body of mine. Forgive me for the sins I have committed against it and so against you, its Creator. Help me to work with you to make it the perfect expression of your will. Give me insight into the law of my body.

Affirmation: I will obey the laws of health, physical, mental, spiritual.

For further study: Compare Luke 7:50 and 18:42 with Luke 8:48 and 17:19—all passages use the same Greek word. Read Luke 13:11-17.

AL 170

Some Steps Toward Physical Health

*[Jesus] spat on the ground and made mud with the
saliva and spread the mud on the man's eyes,
saying to him, "Go, wash in the pool of Siloam."
...Then he went and washed and came back able to see.*
—John 9:6-7

If we are not at our best physically...the following steps
may help.

(1) Get a thorough physical examination by a competent
doctor, preferably one who is not a materialist, but one who
sees the interlocking of body and spirit....On the other
hand, don't go to one who says that disease is only of mental or spiritual origin. He is equally dangerous and equally
liable to write you a pass to a graveyard or...to an infirmary.

(2) If there are physical weaknesses...ask whether
they are of physical or spiritual origin...and [whether] an
operation or medication may correct them. Don't hesitate
to let God heal you through the surgeon or physician. Real
surgeons or physicians recognize that they do not heal. As
one doctor says: "I only clear the way; Nature or God does
the healing." Jesus did not hesitate to use physical remedies; he made clay and anointed the eyes of the blind
man. Don't be more spiritual than God, who has planted
in nature physical remedies for physical disease.

It is good to be discriminating about our doctors.

God, my Father, help me to face my physical being with
complete honesty and a willingness to know the truth
about my body which alone can make me free. Save me
from all self-deception and subterfuges.

Affirmation: I want to be a fit instrument for God's use.

For further reading: John 9:1-17; Matthew 6:32

AL 171

Pay Attention to Nutrition

Scripture

*So whether you eat or drink, or whatever you do,
do everything for the glory of God.*
—1 Corinthians 10:31

(3) A third important origin of disease or health is . . . nutrition. . . . According to Dr. James S. McLester . . . "those . . . who will take advantage of the new knowledge of nutrition [will have] . . . greater vigor, increased longevity, and a higher level of cultural development.". . .

(4) When eating start by thinking on your food. Bid the gastric juices attend the feast. For if they don't come . . . [the forces] of death will.

I was once in a restaurant, absorbed in thought and paying no attention to my eating, when a waitress came up to me and said, "Sir, do you know that you are just gulping your food down?" I've always been grateful for that motherly soul, and while I've not always obeyed her, I often feel her shadow over my shoulder in gentle rebuke when I am wolfing it.

(5) See that you are getting a minimum vitamin requirement. "Life's chemical reactions are disturbed more frequently by a deficiency of vitamins than by any other cause."[2] . . . Vitamins are necessary to vitality.

Your body is the temple of the Holy Spirit.

O God, you have hidden in the heart of food the germs of vitality and health. Thank you. Help me now to hunt them out and utilize them to the full.

Affirmation: Christ is my unseen guest at every meal today.

For further reading: Romans 14:6-9; Mark 7:14-20 (in a modern translation); 1 Corinthians 6:12-14, 19-20

AL 171, 172

---

[2]Dr. R. L. Greene, professor of chemistry, specializing in nutrition.

Check Your Attitudes

Scripture

[Jesus] said to him, "I will come and cure him."
—*Matthew 8:7*

Some of our lack of physical victory may result from actual structural disease; some of it may result from inadequate vitamin supply—but some of it may result from wrong mental and spiritual attitudes. (6) Go over your mental and spiritual attitudes and ask for the answer to the password: "Do you contribute to physical health?" If [your attitudes] do not, then in all probability they contribute to disease and disruption. For, according to high British medical authority, "there is not a tissue or organ in the body not influenced by the attitude of mind and spirit."

One doctor told a patient that he would remit her fee if she would come and listen to what I was saying on the relationship between mental and spiritual states and health, for the doctor couldn't find a physical basis for the pains she described. The pains were real; she was not malingering; but their origin was in her mental and spiritual condition. She passed on her mental and spiritual sickness to her body.

**Are your attitudes contributing to health
or to illness?**

O God, I see I must be healthy-minded if I am to be healthy-bodied. Purge my mind from all fears and worries and resentment, so that my body will be purged from all crippling disease and weakness. Make me the best that I can be.

Affirmation: I want to be strong and full of health—for God.

For further reading: Matthew 8:1-17; Psalm 103:1-5

AL 174

212 — The Whole Person Becomes Sick

Beloved, I pray that all may go well with you and that you may be in good health, just as it is well with your soul.
—3 John 2

Dr. Frank Hutchins, a nerve specialist, said "Seventy percent of the medical cases need new mental and spiritual attitudes for health." The powerful influence of mind over body is illustrated by Dr. Adelaide Woodard, a medical missionary to India, who had a finger amputated after a painful infection. She still has the pain in her finger, though the finger is amputated. . . . An elderly woman had vomiting spells, and the cause was found to be worry, brought on by financial insecurity. The worry threw functional disturbance into her digestive tract. . . .

Each of us is a unit. We cannot be sick in one part without passing on the sickness to the other parts. The entire person must be redeemed. The gospel provides for that total redemption. It provides healing for the body, cleansing for the mind from all conflicts and divisions, forgiveness and fellowship for the soul—the whole person unified and coordinated and made effective.

This is full salvation!

You cannot separate the physical and the spiritual.

O God, give me radiant health in every part of my being. Body and soul, I need you, and I yield every part of myself to you for your healing.

Affirmation: Body and soul, I belong to God.

For further reading: Proverbs 4:20-23; 16:21-24; Matthew 4:23

AL 175

Will to Be Well

*When Jesus saw him lying there and knew
that he had been there a long time, he said
to him, "Do you want to be made well?"*
—John 5:6

We may subconsciously desire the attention and sympathy which our maladies bring. . . . Talking about them focuses attention on one's self—even though that self is a shabby, shattered self. . . . When we are self-centered, we will use any means to gain attention. Jesus went straight to the heart of self-centeredness when he confronted the sick man with this question: "Do you want to be made well?" "Do you really want to be made well? If not, I cannot do a thing for you." The will to be well had to be there.

Will to be well. Throw your will on the side of deliverance. Just as there is a will to believe, so there is a will to be well.

[Whatever] you seek deliverance from . . . will to be well.

What do you really want?

My Father, I cannot will to be well unless I am reinforced at the center of my being. Help me to take the strength of your will into the weakness of my own.

Affirmation: I will to be well.

For further reading: Luke 8:50; 18:35-43; John 5:1-9

AL 72

223

Your Foes
Are Defeated Foes

This is the victory that conquers the world, our faith.
—*1 John 5:4*

When you will to be well, the whole of the universe of reality is then behind your will, ... wills your release and provides for that release. This fact is summed up in the words of Jesus: "In the world you have tribulation; but be of good cheer, I have overcome the world" (John 16:33 RSV). . . .

Remember that every . . . trouble, every sickness, every sin you may face has been and is defeated and overcome by the One you follow—Christ. When fears and sicknesses and sins come upon you to overwhelm you and to beat you into submission . . . just calmly look each one in the eye and say: "I am not afraid of you. You have been and are decisively beaten by my Lord. Will you bend your neck? There, I knew it! The footprint of the Son of God is upon your neck."

This confidence is your starting point: nothing can touch you that hasn't touched him, and that hasn't been defeated by him; and if you open your life to his power every ill can be defeated again by you through his grace. . . . You are caught up in a tide of victory, and nothing can stop it except your refusal to cooperate.

**Are you fighting against Christ and the universe
by refusing to accept his victory?**

O God, my Father, I have often closed my heart to your healing and to your deliverance. Forgive me. I open my life to your power.

Affirmation: Today I throw my will on the side of victory.

For further reading: John 16:33; 1 John 5:3-5; James 5:13-16

AL 73

Lack of a Creative, Outgoing Love

We know that we have passed from death to life because we love one another.
—1 John 3:14

If you were able to conquer the major enemies [of the human personality], you would still lack the one thing needful if you lacked an outgoing love. For life is not built for negative achievement—it is made for positive contribution, for outgoing love. The one who loves not, lives not; and the one who loves most, lives most. . . .

You can never get rid of your own troubles unless you take upon yourself the troubles of others. . . . As someone has put it: "When I dig a man out of trouble, the hole which is left behind is the grave where I bury my own sorrow." Then go out each day and do something that nobody but a Christian would do.

"Love ever gives,
Forgives, outlives,
And ever stands with open hands. . . ."
(Author unknown)

O God, I see that you have fashioned me in my inmost being for creative love. You, the Creator God, have made me to be a creator too, to share your power to make and to remake. Thank you.

Affirmation: I am no more a negative being—I am positive and outgoing and creative.

For further reading: 1 John 3:11-24; 4:7-21; 5:2-4

AL 180

The Miracle
Starts from Within

Scripture

You have ... clothed yourselves with the new self,
which is being renewed in knowledge according
to the image of its creator.
—Colossians 3:9-10

Leslie B. Salter says: "Every normal man or woman longs more keenly for love, for warm friendship, admiration and human responsiveness ... than for anything else in life. ... Wouldst thou love life? Then start giving those about you the feeling they long for. Start passing out good cheer and ... love, and you will receive in return a personal friendliness and genuine happiness you never dreamed possible and which will revolutionize your whole life."

Don't wait for some miracle to be performed on you from without, lifting you above your fears and doubts and self-centeredness.... All the medicine you can take, all the advice you can receive, all the praying you can do, will do you no good unless you throw your will on the side of outgoing love....

You help God from within by turning in outgoing love to others, and miraculously your fears and doubts and self-centeredness will vanish. The miracle starts from within, not from without. Throw your will on the side of outgoing love, and all the healing resources of the universe will be behind you.

"Loving our enemies because we first love God
is better treatment for nervous indigestion
than an operation or an analysis."
(Allan Hunter)

O God, you are always reaching out after me in love and awakening me. Help me this day to do the same, to quicken and awaken some life by the touch of my friendliness and love.

Affirmation: I cannot be too loving.

For further reading: Romans 12:9-13; 13-8-10; Galatians 6:7-10; 1 Peter 3:8-12

Health and Healing

Jesus came ... proclaiming the good news of God, and saying, "The time is fulfilled, and the kingdom of God has come near; repent, and believe in the good news."
—*Mark 1:14-15*

Someone has defined the Christian Ashram[3] in this way: "The Ashram is a positive healing of Christian love to mind, spirit, and body." Is that the right order? ... Yes. For if you put the body first, as some do, then you make Christianity a healing cult. That puts us at the center— God our servant. The first thing in Christianity is reconciliation with God—God is the center. When you are reconciled to God you become reconciled to yourself and hence reconciled to your body. The healing of that reconciliation with God is passed on to the body....

The mind ... is where Jesus began.... Repentance was his first emphasis—literally, a change of mind. For that which is in the mind as thought will pass into the emotions as feeling, then into the will as action, then into the body as result.

**Do you need to repent—
to change your thinking about yourself and God?**

O Christ, my Savior, save me from any lingering wrong viewpoint or thought. May my inmost thought be your thought; then I shall be yours in all I do and am.

Affirmation: I belong to God, mind, soul, and body, for loving, healthful service.

For further reading: Mark 12:28-31; Romans 12:1-2

CM 323, 324

---

[3]Ashram—a place of spiritual retreat. Several were created in the United States by E. Stanley Jones.

Conquering Anger and Anxiety

218 — Untransformed Emotions

*The heart knows its own bitterness,
and no stranger shares its joy.*
—Proverbs 14:10

Resentments, anger, and hate...are enemies of the human personality....

Some people are converted in mind—they accept the Christian faith in their way of life; and they are converted in their wills—they try to live the Christian way but their emotions are not converted. Their emotions are still filled with fears, griefs, resentments, self-pity.... Their emotional life has not been cleansed and coordinated and Christianized. Hence they are canceled-out Christians—canceled out by untransformed emotions. The emotions are the driving force of the personality, and if they drive in wrong or contrary directions, then the personality is a battleground instead of a smoothly working whole.... If properly harnessed, they can drive you to great goals, or if loose and unharnessed, can drive you "nuts."

What is driving you?

O God, my Father, if I'm to be straightened out, my emotions must be straightened out too. So I come for emotional transformation.

Affirmation: I acknowledge my emotions and look to God for transformation.

For further reading: Proverbs 14:10-24; Romans 12:1-2, 9-21

AL 50, HBTP 148

228

219 — Anger and Resentments

*Those conflicts and disputes among you,
where do they come from? Do they not come
from your cravings that are at war within you?*
—James 4:1

The emotions are a part of us and cannot be eliminated. All attempts at elimination end in complexes. They are pushed into the subconscious, and there they become a festering point. We cannot set aside the emotions; we can only direct them, sometimes redirect them to great aims and purposes....

Take anger, for instance. It is an instinct of self-protection, and for the protection of others. It causes us to stand up and fight against harmful enemies of the human personality. We are angry with evil, and therefore we stiffen ourselves against it and oppose it. Otherwise we would allow it to invade us and others....Our capacity to love the good determines our capacity to hate the evil. But note that it is our virtue that is to be lashed into a rage, not our pride, our hurt egoism, our fears....one is harnessed to higher ends, hence constructive; the other is harnessed to the ends of a wounded self, and hence destructive. The one is a righteous anger, and the other is unrighteous.

Anger is a powerful and dangerous tool.

O God, I am driven by tempests of emotion. Help me to harness them to the purposes of your kingdom.

Affirmation: I surrender myself and my emotions to God.

For further reading: Mark 9:33-35; James 3:13–4:3; Psalm 34:5; Isaiah 43:22

AL 50

220 —

A Good Anger

*[Jesus] looked around at them with anger;
he was grieved at their hardness of heart.*
—Mark 3:5

If anger is to be constructive, it must be harnessed to great causes.... Jesus was an example of controlled anger. When he was about to heal the man with the withered arm, he saw the hard faces of religious men who opposed the act because it was being done on the Sabbath. "He looked around at them with anger." Here his anger was not personal pique, a wounded egotism—it was grief at the hardness of people's hearts that could block the healing of a poor unfortunate. His anger drove him to oppose these men on behalf of the under-privileged. It was therefore a righteous anger.

Anger is righteous if it has in it grief on account of what is happening to others, and not a grudge on account of what is happening to oneself. But one must be careful at this point, for the mind plays tricks on itself: it will dress up its personal resentments in garments of righteous and religious indignation so that they will pass muster before our religious self....

But righteous indignation, even when it is simon-pure righteous, should not be kept overnight ... lest it corrode the soul into bitterness.

How clear-eyed are you about yourself?

O God, give me clear insight and courage to see myself truly, for I may be cloaking my resentments with garments of piety, and I know they are deadly in whatever form they gain a footing in my life.

Affirmation: With God's help I will be completely honest with myself and with God.

For further reading: Mark 3:1-5; Psalm 97:10; Ephesians 4:25-32

AL 51

The Disruptive Effects of Anger

Put away from you all bitterness and wrath and anger and wrangling and slander, together with all malice.
—Ephesians 5:31

The body is made for goodwill, not for ill will. . . .

A doctor could not find any physical basis for the constant vomiting of one of his patients. One day she incidentally remarked that her mother-in-law was coming to visit her at Thanksgiving. Taking this chance remark as a clue, he sent for the husband, persuaded him to wire his mother suggesting the postponement of her visit, told the wife that the mother-in-law was not coming, and the vomiting stopped. The resentments had upset her digestion.

The doctors tell us that stomach ulcers can be caused by anger and resentments, and that they will return even after they are cut out by operation, the edges of the wound becoming ulcerated again, if the resentments are not eliminated.

Such scientific revelation makes it quite clear that the stomach in its very constitution is made for goodwill and not for ill will.

Body, soul, and spirit are inextricably entwined.

O God, my Father, I see that ill will lays a paralyzing hand on soul and body, making for disharmony, upset and ineffectiveness. Save me from any clinging resentments.

Affirmation: Goodwill brings harmony and peace and effectiveness.

For further reading: Ecclesiastes 7:9; Genesis 49:7; Ephesians 4:25-27

AL 52, TW 120

Anger Is Poison

*But now you must get rid of...
anger, wrath, malice, slander.*
—Colossians 3:8

A counselor tells me that he knows of no single thing that causes more havoc in the human body than resentments. For resentment is poison.

A doctor was baffled over the cause of sickness in a baby. One day in visiting the child he came into the home while the parents were quarreling and saw the mother suckling the baby meanwhile. The doctor threw up his hands and said, "Now I know what is the matter with your baby—you are poisoning it by this ill will.". . .

A doctor in the Mayo Clinic told me that he could see a stomach ulcer healing before his very eyes on the X-ray pictures when a patient surrendered her resentments. . . .

A very able minister grasped my hand and said, "Teach me how to overcome my resentments." His large-domed forehead with blood vessels distended showed the tension he was under. Resentments were draining him mentally, spiritually, physically.

**We pass on to our bodies
the health and unhealth of our minds and souls.**

O God, I want to be healthy in soul and in mind. Therefore I would take into my very being the health of your mind. Let me be saturated with your ways and your thoughts so that I may live in radiant health.

Affirmation: I will stay in perfect peace because my mind rests on God (Isaiah 26:3).

For further reading: Colossians 3:7-10; Psalm 37:8; Proverbs 16:32

AL 53, HBTP 172

Subconscious Resentments

And the Lord said, "Do you do well to be angry?"
—Jonah 4:4

We think we are harming others in holding . . . spites and hates, but the deepest harm is to ourselves; for many times these resentments are dropped into the unconscious, the lid is shut down on them, and there they work their unconscious havoc. Unconscious resentments are often just as potent for disruption as conscious ones. . . . As one doctor put it, "It is very difficult to get people to see that illness is the price they pay for their unconscious resentments toward the very things they protest they love.". . .

A young woman could not raise her arm, which seemed paralyzed. It was found that, when angry, she had a secret desire to strike her mother. When the reason for the paralysis was shown and she gave up her resentments against her mother, the arm was restored to normal health again.

A similar case was that of a man who was constantly falling from his horse. He wondered why he couldn't stay on. It was discovered that he had a secret desire to commit suicide, and this falling was the outer sign of that secret desire.

**How important it is
to have unconscious resentment brought into the light.**

O Christ, you have urged us to get rid of anger and resentments. Your penetrating eye sees the havoc worked in us by our hates. Forgive us for not seeing—and for not surrendering them after seeing them.

Affirmation: I will live in Christ's light—without my resentments.

For further reading: The book of Jonah

AL 54, HBTP 176

Anger Dims the Vision

Scripture

"The hand of the Lord is against you, and you will be blind for awhile, unable to see the sun."
—Acts 13:11

Resentments and anger not only dim the spiritual vision so that the inner life becomes blurred; but they also literally dim the physical vision. Some doctors experimented with rats and found that after the rats had been kept angry for an extended period of time, opaque films came over their eyes. The report continues: "One realizes the picturesqueness and accuracy of the old expression 'blind with rage,' and the lesson to be learned is to avoid being angry. As the children say, 'One might freeze that way.' "[1]

An optometrist tells me that he can never examine the eyes of an angry person—such a person literally cannot see straight. As Dante puts it, describing the wrathful, their "hearts poured \ a bitter smoke."[2]

Neither spiritually, mentally, nor physically can those who hold resentments and angers see straight. Their outlook on life is distorted because their inner condition is out of joint through hate.

Comment

"Consider whether the light in you is not darkness."
(Luke 11:35)

Prayer

O God, you have made us for love. Forgive us for having introduced into the delicate fabric of our inner being the havoc of hate. Help us to live in your way.

Affirmation: I am made for God and God's way is love.

For further reading: Acts 13:4-11; Psalm 34:21

AL 55

---

[1] *Southern Medical Journal*, November 1940, p. 1237
[2] Dante, *The Divine Comedy, The Inferno,* translated by John Ciardi (New York: New American Library, Mentor Edition, 1954), Canto VII, lines 122-23.

Self-Pity

"Daughters of Jerusalem, do not weep for me...."
—Luke 23:18

It is obvious that to hold hate and resentments is to throw a monkey wrench into the machinery of life. Structurally you are made for positive goodwill, in other words, for the Christian way of life....

A woman involved in an automobile accident suffered a broken neck.... She is doomed to a wheelchair the balance of her days. But she has met the whole tragedy in a spirit of faith, confidence, and goodwill. Hence she is radiant—in spite of!... Depressed patients are assigned to her table so that her very presence may cheer them up.... But her husband reacted differently. He was unhurt by the accident, except in soul. He became embittered, held resentments against the man who was driving. The resentments have spoiled his lifework....

Hate is sand in the machinery of life; love is oil—and life works better with oil than with sand.

Self-pity seems to make resentment even more dangerous.

O God, I see the necessity of getting rid of all resentments. If I live with my hates, I will not be able to live with myself. I need your help to get rid of these things which have become rooted in me.

Affirmation: Today, with God's help, I will apply the oil of love to the machinery of life.

For further reading: Acts 21:13; Philippians 1:12-20

AL 56

Don't Suppress or Express Resentments

Scripture

Put away from you all bitterness and wrath and anger.
—Ephesians 4:31

If we are to live abundantly, we must get rid of resentments and hate at all costs. But how?

First of all, we must look at some of the ways we are *not* to use. . . .

We must not suppress them into forgetfulness and try to act as though we no longer have them. This treatment drives them only into the subconscious mind where they work as unconscious resentments. There they will produce conflict and disturbance . . . [and] work their havoc at deeper and more dangerous levels. . . . We must bring the resentments to the surface and face them honestly with no subterfuges, no evasions, no suppressions.

We must not try the contrary method—that of expressing our hatreds and resentments. . . . There is no doubt that we can get temporary relief by giving the other person "a piece of our mind." . . . But the resentments would fill up again and be ready for another spill-over. Expression is not the remedy —it is merely dealing with a symptom instead of with the disease.

How powerful the subconscious mind is!

O God, my heavenly Father, I am dealing with something too devastating to try to heal it lightly or to temporize. Help me to go to the roots and find release there. I need your grace for this task.

Affirmation: I want to let God into my subconscious mind.

For further study: Ephesians 4:31-32; Colossians 3:8, 13; 1 Timothy 2:8

AL 57

Don't Run Away from or Nurse Resentments

Sarai dealt harshly with [Hagar], and she ran away from her.... The angel of the Lord said to her, "Return to your mistress, and submit to her."
—Genesis 16:8-9

There [is not] much use in trying to run away from circumstances which give rise to resentments. A doctor found a patient nervous, unable to sleep [and] asked if his home relations were adjusted and happy. The patient replied that he and his mother-in-law didn't get on.... The doctor sent him and his wife off for a vacation, away from the mother-in-law. Good, but not good enough; for while there would be temporary respite and a letting down of tensions, yet they would tighten up again as the prospect loomed up of having to meet the same situation....

Nor will it do to nurse our resentments in our minds. That only makes them worse. They will carry over into the whole of life and spoil it.

All of these methods are attempts to heal over a boil. And to heal over a boil is a dangerous act—it may drive the poison in. The poison must be drawn up and out.

How easy it is to poison ourselves.

O Father, I am tempted to do everything about these resentments—except the one thing I must do: get them up and out. I need your help, for I cannot get them up alone. The roots have gone deep. Help me.

Affirmation: With God's help I will be honest with myself—and with God.

For further reading: Genesis 16:1-9; Titus 3:1-7; 1 Peter 3:8-9

AL 58

Forgiving for Christ's Sake

Be kind to one another, tenderhearted, forgiving one another, as God in Christ has forgiven you.
—Ephesians 4:32

No one has ever treated you worse than you have treated God, and yet God forgives and forgets. When he asks you to forgive, he isn't asking you to do something he himself is not doing. Here is one of the most wonderful passages in literature: "Treat one another with the same spirit as you experience in Christ Jesus" (Philippians 2:5 Moffatt). He forgives you, graciously and without reservation. You must do the same.

If not? Jesus tells what happened to the man in the parable who was forgiven a debt of "three million pounds" and then went out and refused to forgive a fellow servant who owed him "twenty pounds"—he was handed "over to the torturers, till he should pay him all the debt. My heavenly Father will do the same to you, unless you each forgive your brother from the heart" (Matthew 18:21-35 Moffatt).

The "torturers"? They are within you—resentments mean inner conflict, division, unhappiness, torture.

Are you experiencing the tortures of resentment?

O God, the wrong has entered deep into my spirit. In my own strength I cannot forgive. But I am willing to be made willing. Take my willingness and add your power, and then I shall be able to forgive.

Affirmation: Through God I can do anything—yes, anything; even forgive.

For further reading: Romans 12:14-21; Matthew 5:38-48; 18:21-25

TW 124, AL 59

229 An Unsurrendered Self

See to it that no root of bitterness springs up and causes trouble, and through it many become defiled.
—Hebrews 12:15

While the central and fundamental motive for forgiving injuries against us is that God forgives us, and we therefore copy God as his children, nevertheless there are minor motives and techniques which we can use in dealing with resentments.

Remember that at the basis of most resentments is a touchy, unsurrendered self. The fact that we have been able to hold the resentment shows that there is a self that is oversensitive because unsurrendered to the will of God. When surrendered to the will of God we throw off resentments as a healthy skin throws off disease germs unless there is inner disease or an abrasion of the skin.... So when resentments have gained a footing, it shows that there is a raw, sensitive self underneath.... Suspect a self that can grow resentments—it is probably diseased with self-centeredness.

Ask yourself whether your resentments aren't rooted in imaginary slights, insults, and wrongs. Self-centered people can imagine a group is talking about them when that group is talking about everything else but....

Are you holding on to resentments?

O God, my Father, help me to see myself clearly, for I gather self-defensive arguments around myself as a magnet. Let me then lay this resentment-gathering self at your feet for cleansing and release.

Affirmation: Today I will let go of my resentments.

For further reading: Acts 7:54-60; Psalm 37:8; Hebrews 12:14-15

AL 60

280 — Dissolve Resentments Through Prayer and Appreciation

Scripture

*"I say to you, Love your enemies
and pray for those who persecute you."*
—Matthew 5:44

*Every time the name of persons against whom you are tempted
to hold a resentment is presented to your mind, breathe a prayer
for them.* . . . Make the rule in your mind that, invariably, all
your thoughts of your enemies, real or imaginary, are to
become prayers for them. . . . Soon you will have no enemies, for you will have no enmity. . . .

A woman told how she got rid of her resentments: Every
time she thought of the person who had done her wrong, she
then and there said inwardly, "I bless you—in his name.". . .

*Say everything good you can about the person or persons
with whom you are unfriendly.* The probabilities are there are
many fine things in them. Fasten your mind on those fine
points instead of on the resentment points. . . .

*When you do have to speak of the faults of a person, don't
say, "I don't like that person."* Rather, say, "I don't like certain things in that person." After stating those faults, proceed to say, "But I do like these things," and name them.
End on the positive note.

Comment

How easy it is to be negative about other people.

Prayer

God, my Father, I want to be rid of all that corrodes my
soul. I know that my attitudes of resentment and criticism
eat like acid into my moral nature. Deliver me completely
from the last tiny root of resentment.

Affirmation: Today I will pray positively for everyone who crosses my
mind.

For further reading: Matthew 5:38-48: Romans 12:14-21

AL 61, TW 127

Love People for What They May Become

"You are Simon son of John. You are to be called Cephas" (which is translated Peter).[3]
—John 1:42

If you find little to love or admire in those persons against whom you hold resentments, then love and admire them for what they may be. You do not have to be dishonest...and like the things a person does. But you are now committed as a Christian, and you love people as Christ does. He loves them not for what they have been, or are, but for what they can be. Your love then becomes real and redemptive....

See if there isn't a reason in the other person for the things you resent. An outstanding surgeon would see red every time he saw W.P.A. workers.[4] Their slowness got on his nerves; and he was fast developing a complex....Then one day he noticed them at quitting time, putting away their tools with the same slowness. "Why," he said, "these men are sick from undernourishment, from lack of vitamins...." He set himself to rehabilitate them, and in doing so helped himself—he lost his own complex.

What we don't know *can* hurt us!

O God, give me clear insight and sympathy when I see in the lives of others the things that make them unattractive to me. And when I understand, help me to forgive.

Affirmation: Today I will look at people from Christ's point of view—and love them for what they can be.

For further study: John 1:35-42; Luke 22:31-32; Galatians 6:1-2

AL 62

---

[3]From the word for *rock* in Aramaic *(kepha)* and Greek *(petra)*, respectively (NRSV marginal note).
[4]W.P.A.: Works Progress Administration, a public works program set up in the 1930s, under Franklin Roosevelt's New Deal, to provide for those who became unemployed because of the Great Depression.

Use Only Redemptive Goodwill

232

Scripture

*"Forgive, and you will be forgiven; give,
and it will be given to you."*
—Luke 6:37-38

*Go out each day to do some positive good to those against whom
you hold resentments....* A Japanese student and a Chinese
student were in the same university, and the Japanese disliked the Chinese intensely. But when the Japanese was ill,
the Chinese brought food to him every day. This kind attention broke down the enmity, and they became fast friends....

*Be inwardly "too glad and too great to be the enemy of any
man" (Martin Luther).* Be so preoccupied with goodwill that
you haven't room for ill will....

The temptation will be to descend from the Christian
level of returning good for evil to the lower level of returning evil for evil.... Since God forgives you, you can forgive
others. But if you shut off others from your forgiveness,
then you shut off yourself from God's forgiveness....

When Jesus announced his program at Nazareth, he
read from Isaiah (61:1-2) until he came to the words, "the
day of vengeance of our God." Then he closed the book.
You do the same. Leave vengeance to God—use only
redemptive goodwill.

**The actions of love and forgiveness
can produce the feelings of love and forgiveness.**

O God, my Father, nothing that anyone can do against me
compares with what I have done against you. You have forgiv-
en me—help me to forgive others—graciously, not grudgingly.

Affirmation: With God's help I will actively demonstrate goodwill.

For further reading: Luke 4:16-21; 6:32-38; 17:3-4

AL 63, TW 130

288 — Fear vs. Intelligent Planning

*I believe that I shall see the goodness of the Lord
in the land of the living.*
—Psalm 27:13

Another major enemy of the human personality is the area of worry, anxiety, fear.

Almost every evil is some perverted good. Worry, anxiety, and fear are perverted good. There is an instinct within us to look ahead, to plan, to think about meeting possible situations before they come.... This capacity to foresee and foreplan and forestall is the power that lifts us out of the "is" into the "can be"—it is the secret of progress. And as such it must be cultivated.... We must master today, and we must master tomorrow. Jesus commended this: "Well, the master praised the dishonest factor for looking ahead; for the children of this world look further ahead, in dealing with their own generation, than the children of Light" (Luke 16:8 Moffatt).

Christians above all others are people of the long view, the long purpose, and the long plan. They plan how to live today, how to live tomorrow, how to live forever.... We are to love God "with all your mind" (Luke 10:27), and a part of the mind is foresight.

Fear distorts the long view.

O God, help us to catch the sweep of your mind and the glory of your purposes, as we study your working in history, so that we can become a part of them.

Affirmation: My future is secure in God's hands.

For further reading: Ephesians 1:1-10; Romans 8:28-30; Psalm 27

AL 64

Anxiety as Asset and Liability

Do not fret—it leads only to evil.
—*Psalm 37:8*

Christians are those who care about the past, the present, and the future.... But if this awareness is our greatest asset, it may also become our greatest liability. The fact that we are sensitive and aware . . . may make us worry. If so, then our light has turned to darkness. For worry and anxiety and fear can block the whole process of progress and paralyze and disrupt the personality....

There is a healthy fear that gives us skill and drive. There is an unhealthy fear that takes away both skill and drive—it inhibits us. "The fear of the Lord is the beginning of wisdom" (Psalm 111:10), but "I was afraid, and I went and hid your talent in the ground" (Matthew 25:25). Both are profoundly true. There is a fear that is wisdom, and a fear that makes us bury our life talents.

Fear, like any other drive, has to be brought under control and used for constructive purposes. Out of control it turns into worry and anxiety and becomes destructive to itself and others.

Can you distinguish between caring and worry?

O God, I fear the fear that gets rootage in my life; I am anxious about the anxiety that infects me. I am worried about the worry. Give me deliverance from them and bring me to complete freedom.

Affirmation: I will cast all my cares and anxieties upon God, because he cares for me (1 Peter 5:7).

For further reading: Psalm 37:1-9; Proverbs 19:23; Luke 21:25-28

AL 65

Fear and Disease

*"Do not let your hearts be troubled.
Believe in God, believe also in me."*
—John 14:1

A doctor said to me, "Fears are the most disruptive thing we can have." And all life bears this out. . . .

A teacher had a basic fear which brought on a stomach ulcer. When she got rid of the fear, she got rid of the ulcer. Doctors wanted to operate on a friend of mine for cancer or ulcer of the stomach. The facts were these: After he had failed in business, worry had stopped the gastric juices. When he saw the cause and surrendered his worries to God, he gained thirty pounds in two months. A YMCA secretary came up to me at the close of an address and said, "I am an illustration of what you have said. I'm tense and worried and bear on my mind all the troubles of the world. Hence I am fighting stomach ulcers all the time." He will never be well until he relaxes and surrenders all those strained worries to God.

The ancient writer saw the connection between worry and disease: "Banish all worries from your mind, and keep your body free from pain" (Ecclesiastes 11:10 Moffatt).

Worry and fear are corrosive.

O God, my Father, you have fashioned me for faith and trust, not for fear and anxiety. Help me then to surrender to what I am made for—faith.

Affirmation: This day I will walk in confident faith, afraid of nothing.

For further reading: John 14:1, 27; Psalm 37:1-8; Job 3:25-26

AL 66

Fear Is Costly

*For you did not receive a spirit of slavery to fall back
into fear, but you have received a spirit of adoption.*
—Romans 8:15

Sometimes fears are not basic but marginal. Even so they can upset the rest of the life. A woman went through surgical operations, a fire, even chased out a burglar from her house with a gun, and yet her life was tormented with the fear of what her neighbors might say of her. Here was a marginal fear which pushed out a basic courage. . . .

A young minister began to complain of tightness in his chest and developed a hacking cough. The doctors found no physical reason. Then he began to complain of severe pain in the lower bowel, saying he had a cancer there. Examinations . . . found nothing physically wrong. He resigned the ministry and sits around moping and groaning most of the time. . . . He is basically sound. It is the fear that is upsetting him. The fear itself is the disease. For fear is sand in the machinery of life. . . . Fear is costly!

What are your fears?

My Father, I see that fear is indeed costly—so costly I cannot keep it. But I cannot easily get rid of it. Help me tear it up root and branch.

Affirmation: Christ has not given me a spirit of fear.

For further reading: Proverbs 29:25; John 7:13, 9:22; 20:19; 2 Timothy 1:7

AL 68

Climbing Out of Fear: Be Honest

I sought the Lord, and he answered me,
and delivered me from all my fears.
—Psalm 34:4

The first step in deliverance from fear is *complete honesty.* There will be no attempt to deceive the mind, no effort to entice it into entering a fool's paradise of make-believe. No one can play tricks on the universe—least of all on the universe of mind. . . . The Christian way is the way of complete honesty.

The verse that most clearly expresses the spirit of this way is "See and do *not* be alarmed" (Matthew 24:6 Moffatt). Jesus did not try to teach his hearers to win release from alarms by refusing to see them. He told them to see—to look fears straight in the face and yet not to be alarmed. His way is the way of open-eyed honesty. . . .

[If you will] write down precisely what it is you are worrying about you will find that . . . about half of your fear will be seen to be baseless. . . . Many fears would drop away if we simply said to ourselves: "Well, suppose the worst should come to the worst and that thing should happen to me—so what?" Nothing that can happen to you—absolutely nothing—can ever be as bad as the fear itself.

A clear-eyed look will distinguish
between real and imaginary fears.

O God, I know that you are the answer and that these real fears are no longer real when I face them honestly with your help.

Affirmation: I will not worry about tomorrow, for tomorrow will bring worries of its own (Matthew 6:34).

For further reading: Luke 12:22-28; Psalm 34:4-10

AL 71, WPP 229

238 — Climbing Out of Fear: Want to Be Free

Scripture

*Truly the thing that I fear comes upon me,
and what I dread befalls me.*
—Job 3:25

The second step to climbing out of fear: *Be sure you want to give up the thing you are afraid of.* Very often your fears produce bodily ills which in turn determine your life strategy. Some people use their illnesses to gain attention or to gain power over others. A young girl had a large purple lump on her forehead [which] had come as the result of a great fear. When counseled . . . she surrendered the fear, and the lump disappeared. . . . [Later, the counselor] remarked about the lump being gone. "But," said the girl, grabbing her middle, "I've got terrible pains in my stomach." She was afraid to let go of her fears, for she lived by the attention which these illnesses brought her. . . . She "enjoyed" bad health!

I know a family that lived by recounting to one another their various ailments, each bidding for sympathy from the others. They nearly all died before their time. The one member that survived found interests outside that circle of self-commiseration.

Question

**What would you do
if you were completely free of fear
and completely well?**

Prayer

O God, I want to be completely delivered from fear and from the results of fear. My subconscious mind plays tricks on me. Save me to complete honesty.

Affirmation: Today I will honestly look my fears in the face—and then look in the face of Christ.

For further reading: Matthew 24:3-8; Acts 5:1-11; Philippians 4:6-7

AL 71

Worry Is Atheism

"Can any of you by worrying add a single hour to your span of life? If then you are not able to do so small a thing as that, why do you worry about the rest?"
—Luke 12:25-26

The next step: *Remember that worry or fear is a kind of atheism.* A person who worries says, "I cannot trust God; I'll take things in my own hands." Result? Worry, frustration, incapacity to meet the dreaded thing when it does come. With God, you can meet it, overcome it, assimilate it into the purpose of your life. Alone, you fuss and fume and are frustrated. Worry says, "God doesn't care, and so he won't do anything—I'll have to worry it through." Faith says, "God does care, and he and I will work it out together. I'll supply the willingness, and he will supply the power—with that combination we can do anything."

You remember the story of Martin Luther? One morning, when he was blue and discouraged, his wife appeared in black. At Luther's inquiry as to what the mourning meant, she replied, "Haven't you heard? God is dead." Luther saw the absurdity—and so should you. God lives—so will you!

How much energy do you spend on worry?

O God, as long as you live, I too shall live. Nothing can shake the rock of your existence on which I stand. As long as that fact continues, I shall not worry nor be afraid.

Affirmation: I believe God not only cares but is able to care for me.

For further reading: Luke 12:22-32; Ephesians 3:20; Hebrews 13:6; 1 Peter 5:7

AL 74

Fear—The Inner Enemy

There is no fear in love, but perfect love casts out fear.
—1 John 4:18

A further step: *Hold in mind that nothing that you fear is as bad as the fear itself.* I mean that seriously: nothing that can happen to you is, or can be, as disastrous and disruptive as the entrance of fear and worry into your life. If you keep the center of life intact, then you can come back from anything. Healed at the heart, you can say, "Let the world come on"; but, hurt at the heart by fear and worry, you are knocked down by happenings—real and imaginary.

The people who fight life's battles without fear fight one enemy—the real thing confronting them. But those who fight with fears within themselves fight three enemies—the real thing to fight, plus the imaginary things built up by fear, plus the fear itself. And the greatest of these is fear. . . .

How does fear go away? By fastening our attention not on the thing to be feared, or on the fear of this fear, but on Christ, the Savior from fear.

What are the fears in your life?

O Christ, my Savior, you know everything that causes me fear—you have gone through it all. And yet no fears or worries rooted themselves in you. Teach me your secret. I obey completely and fully.

Affirmation: I will focus on Christ, not my fears, today.

For further reading: 1 Peter 3:12-14; 1 John 3:18-22; 4:16-18

AL 75

250

Relax in His Presence

241

Thou dost keep him in perfect peace,
whose mind is stayed on thee,
because he trusts in thee.
—Isaiah 26:3 RSV

Attention must be fastened on Christ—the Man who met everything we meet and more, and didn't worry. Fasten your attention on him; for it is a law of the mind that whatever gets your attention gets you. If your worries get your attention, they will get you. If Christ gets your attention, he will get you.

How can you fasten your attention on him? . . . Take the next step. *Relax in his presence.* His power cannot get across to you unless you learn to relax. Fear and worry tighten you up. Faith relaxes you. Often fear and worry keep the motor running even after you are parked. You are worn out even when sitting still. . . . When you work, work hard; but when you stop working, then stop working—relax. You cannot repeat to yourself too frequently the oft-repeated, and yet always healing, statement: "Let go; let God." Let go your inward fears and worries, and let God absorb them in his grace and love. Let God replace the false energy of fear and worry with the true energy of faith working through love.

Have you learned to relax?

Father God, I've burned up my soul and body and mind energy in the false energy of fear and worry. Help me this day to link all my energies to the calm of your purposes and to the peace of your power.

Affirmation: I will stay my mind on God and relax in his perfect peace.

For further reading: Psalms 16:11; 23; 27:1; Zephaniah 3:17; Philippians 4:6-7

AL 76

Take One Day at a Time

"So never be troubled about tomorrow;
tomorrow will take care of itself. The day's
own trouble is enough for the day."
—Matthew 6:34 Moffatt

Worry is a useless expenditure of energy. In India we have a bird called "Pity-to-do-it." It goes around all day saying "Pity-to-do-it." And they say that at night it sleeps with its feet in the air to keep the sky from falling! . . .

Some of us are like that bird. But we do not have to be. . . .

We must learn to *meet today, today.* Jesus showed very penetrating insight when he told us not to worry or be troubled about tomorrow. He was not saying there were no troubles to be met. There are. Life is bound to bring trouble. It is made that way. But don't telescope the troubles of tomorrow and of the next day into today. Meet today, today; for if you put the troubles of next week into today by anticipation through worry, then you spoil today. . . . You are meeting . . . your troubles twice—once before they come, and once when they are actually here . . . a double expenditure of energy and needless. Worry is the advance interest you pay on troubles that never come. Some of them do come, and you can meet and conquer them separately. But tomorrow's troubles plus today's break you.

Worry is heavy burden—and a blinding one.

O God, you give me a sufficient load for today and you help me bear it. But I see that I add to my burden and so diminish my strength for legitimate tasks. Forgive me.

Affirmation: I will trust God and not be afraid.

For further reading: Luke 11:3; Psalms 27; 91

AL 77

In Quietness
and Confidence

For thus saith the Lord God, the Holy One of Israel:
In returning and rest shall ye be saved;
in quietness and in confidence shall be your strength.
—Isaiah 30:15 KJV

Today is the tomorrow we worried about yesterday. [Looked at that way] today isn't so bad, is it? It has its troubles, but they are bearable. . . .

Even if the whole day seems too difficult, then divide it up into hours. You are meeting this hour now with your full resources. Pack it with God and his resources. Throw all your energies into meeting the enemies as they come one by one. . . . Fight them, not by strained endeavor, but by quiet faith. That leads to the next step: *Say over and over: "In quietness and confidence shall be my strength."* . . .

Quietness: You must quiet everything in the presence of God. . . . Let his healing quiet get into every pore of your being, bathing the tired and restless nerve cells with his healing.

Confidence: Quietness alone will not be enough—confidence is necessary. Quietness is passive, and we must be passive to God; but confidence is active, and we must be active to God. Confidence is *con*, "with," and *fideo*, "faith." . . . It is a faith with God's faith. Your faith and God's faith flow together and hence can do anything.

Can you quietly trust God?

My Father, I see I am not left alone to battle trouble and fear. I have a faith—plus yours. I will work life on your cooperative plan.

Affirmation: I am no longer afraid—God is with me.

For further reading: Isaiah 26:2-4; Proverbs 3:21-26; Hebrews 12:5-6, 8

AL 78

253

244 — Faith in His Faith

Scripture

The Lord is my shepherd, I shall not want.
—Psalm 23:1

If confidence is having faith with God, then the Christian life is not lifting oneself by the bootstraps. It is linking our littleness with God's greatness, our incompleteness with his completeness. It is doing what the little boy did when he offered his five loaves and two fishes to Christ. That multitude could not be fed without his cooperation, and the feeding couldn't be done with his five loaves and fishes alone. He and Christ together did everything necessary.

Very often when I haven't faith in my faith, I have to have faith in his faith. He makes me believe in myself and my possibilities, when I simply can't.... "For the Eternal...will not let you go" (Deuteronomy 4:31 Moffatt). Faith is not merely your holding on to God—it is God holding on to you. He will not let you go!...Keep saying to your soul, "Your strength is quiet faith" (Isaiah 30:15 Moffatt)....Say to yourself, "What ought to be can be, and I will make it so." And you will. You will go beyond yourself.

"With God all things are possible."
(Mark 10:27 KJV)

O living Christ, I now see that I can be the happy warrior, for I am drawing heavily on your power and going forth in your confidence.

Affirmation: With Christ I can actually do what I can't.

For further reading: Psalm 23; Romans 8:9-17; Philippians 4:11-13

AL 79

245 Surrendering Our Fears

There is no fear in love, but perfect love casts out fear.
—1 John 4:18

The next step is to *surrender the thing you fear into the hands of God.* Turn it right over to God and ask him to solve it with you. Fear is keeping things in your own hands; faith is turning them over into the hands of God—and leaving them there.

...Sorrow and pain had left Mrs. ____ with an upset heart. She was on her bed for a year....She came to a gathering some distance away and told me she was afraid she would die on the way, as her heart began behaving very badly indeed....

After a talk with her I saw that anxiety and worry were causing the functional disturbance of the heart....I got her to surrender the whole matter to God. She did. The strained lines on her face relaxed, and she began to act like a normal person.

"...I was very much alive, and scarcely tired," [she wrote me] "when I reached home after a 550-mile drive in one day! And there has been no relapse since coming home. This recovery is so real it is not neurotic, for my nerves are becoming steady, and my heart is beginning to act like a normal heart should. It is wonderful."

Will you let go of your fears?

My Father, forgive me that I hold my worries, my troubles, my fears in my own incompetent hands and do not turn them over into your competent hands. So now I do turn them over to you. They are yours—not for an hour but forever.

Affirmation: I accept my release from fear—with grateful thanks.

For further reading: Matthew 8:23-27; 1 John 4:17-19; Isaiah 43:1-2

AL 80

Learning to Live Positively

246

Negativism and Inferiority Attitudes

For if the eagerness is there, the gift is acceptable according to what one has—not according to what one does not have.
—2 Corinthians 8:12

One of the outstanding enemies of human living is negativism and inferiority attitudes.... This enemy is all the more dangerous because it is often manifested as its opposite—superiority attitudes. Those who are not sure of themselves talk loud, boast and swagger to impress others....

Jesus saw small people trying to be big, so he said, "Which of you by taking thought can add one cubit unto his stature?" (Matthew 7:27 KJV). We try to add cubits to our stature by taking thought of outer decorations to make up for inner inferiorities.... A psychologist says that "there are a million chances to one that those who claim superiority are unpopular." They defeat their own purpose. "Those who want to save their life" by concentrating on it, dressing it up to appear bigger than it is, are bound to defeat their own purpose—in the words of Jesus, they "will lose it" (Mark 8:25).

**What is your reaction
when someone tries so hard to impress you?**

O God, I want to be what I am without any sham. But more, I want to be the person you intend me to be. For everything in your will is great.

Affirmation: I will live with simplicity and dignity in God's will and purpose.

For further reading: 1 Corinthians 1:26-29; 3:21-23

AL 99

Touchy People

Live in harmony with one another; do not be haughty, but associate with the lowly; do not claim to be wiser than you are.
—Romans 12:16

Sometimes there is an alternation between aggressive attitudes and periods of discouragement and self-depreciation ...resulting in moodiness. Such a person ranges in temperament from very high mountains to very low valleys. But often the attitudes of retreat and defeat result not in mood depression but in the "tic."

Professor David Eitzen says, "Slamming the door, walking rapidly, stamping the floor, arguing with one's associates, spanking the children—these are manifestations of a difficulty not faced and intelligently approached." Whether manifested as moodiness and sulkiness or as an outburst of temper with surroundings or with others, the difficulty is the same sense of inward inferiority. Those who behave in this way are out of sorts with themselves, so they vent their ill-humor on their surroundings. They create outer earthquakes usually in order to hide their own inner soul-quakes. . . . The person who is inwardly slipping takes to outer shouting. This is the law of overcompensation at work.

Have you ever traced your moodiness to its source?

O God, I come to you to find power to be really strong. Save me from these make-believe strengths that leave me weak. Fortify me inwardly by your strength.

Affirmation: I want to be the kind of person nothing without can upset because, with God's power, I am so sure within.

For further reading: Romans 12:3-4, 9-10; 14:1-15

AL 100

We Are Made for Positive Achievement

Scripture

We are not among those who shrink back.
—Hebrews 10:39

You and I are made in our inmost being for positive achievement—to be outgoing, to master our circumstances, to create. If we are not positively creating and producing, the machinery of life will get out of gear; for we are geared to creation. Negativism, therefore, not only keeps us from achieving; it also keeps us from being. The personality breaks down under negative attitudes. We are not made for them.

I know a person whose first attitude toward everything new that is presented is "No!" She lives in the objective mood. And hence her life is frustrated, when, with her powers, it might be fruitful. A more dramatic illustration is that of a woman of intellectual ability who became afraid of life, pulled in, and made retreat her life strategy. When she pulled in on herself and refused to be outgoing, Nature began to take her toll—her knees began to stiffen. She became a confirmed invalid. . . . As the doctors put it, "Her brain cells are rotten with fear.". . .

Retreatism and negativism are infections that corrupt the brain cells, make flabby the tissues, and poison the spirit. You must decide that they will have no part nor lot within you, since you want to live abundantly.

How terrible to be so negative!

My God and Father, I want to link myself with your creative Spirit and become creative and positive and victorious.

Affirmation: I do not belong to a willful sighing over a dead past, nor to a fear of today—I belong to victory!

For further reading: Hebrews 10:35-39; 11:1-7

AL 101

249 Negativism Is Not a Friend

For freedom Christ has set us free. Stand firm, therefore, and do not submit again to a yoke of slavery.
—Galatians 5:1

If we are to get out of negativism and inferiority attitudes, we must take certain positive steps. Our getting out will not just happen. No startling miracle of deliverance will happen unless we cooperate. The miracle of deliverance will work as we work, but only as we work. . . .

The first step to take is to *recognize negativism and inferiority attitudes as enemies. Do not try to dress them up as friends.* You will be tempted to look upon negativism as prudence, and inferiorities as humility. Strip off these false cloaks and see these attitudes in their nakedness—as enemies of you and of your possibilities.

When a hard thing comes before you, you will take one of four methods in dealing with it, according to Dr. M. S. Congdon, a psychologist: "(1) Flee it! (2) Fight it! (3) Forget it! (4) Face it." The first three ways will end in failure. Only the fourth opens a door.

Your first step is a facing of the facts—the whole of the facts. Don't be like the Scotch minister who began by saying, "This is a difficult text; having looked it in the face we will pass on." Don't pass on until you have really looked your difficulty in the face and have seen it for what it is—not something that must be excused, or defended, or explained away or rationalized, but something that must be ousted.

Are you good at rationalization?

O frank and open-hearted Christ, help me to be frank and open-hearted. Take from my life all negative thinking, all refusal to accept responsibility, all fearful attitudes.

Affirmation: I will face life honestly, confidently, and joyfully.
For further reading: 2 Timothy 1:7; John 6:63, 66-68

AL 102

250 ~ Frustrating Myself

I can do all things through him who strengthens me.
—*Philippians 4:13*

The second step to release is to *let this idea grip you: I am made in the inner structure of my being for creative achievement; when I draw back from that I frustrate myself.*

One of the outstanding ministers of this country was Dr. Shirkey of San Antonio, Texas, a radiant soul and contagious. But he came near living up to his name—or down to it! For he told me that as a lad he had supersensitive fingertips, and at last his mother consented to let him grow long fingernails to protect them. But one day his schoolteacher called him up before the class and made him cut his nails publicly.

This humiliation turned him against school: so he had to invent sicknesses to keep away. One of these make-believe ills was a pain in the hip. The pain became a real pain and grew so serious that a surgeon decided to put him in a cast, for which measurements were taken. Then the lad saw what was happening; he broke down and told his mother the cause. He never went back to the doctor. He became an Apollo in health—but he came near being a cripple all his days. The negative retreatism was arrested in time by an honest facing of the facts.

Is anything frustrating you today?

O God, help this will of mine to will your will. Help me to link my littleness to your greatness, my faintheartedness to your loving aggression, my fear to your faith.

Affirmation: Nothing can stop me when I am linked to God.

For further reading: Galatians 2:21; Colossians 3:9-10; 2 Timothy 3:16-17

AL 103

Shut Your Mind to Negative Thoughts

You are no longer strangers and aliens, but you are citizens with the saints and also members of the household of God.
—Ephesians 2:19

The third step to gaining a positive attitude is *to shut your mind against all negative thoughts the moment they come.* Do not entertain those thoughts and give them a seat; for if they get your attention they will get you. Meet them at the door and slam it in their faces; lock the door and throw the key under a red-hot stove, so you cannot get at it. . . .

A nurse disliked a patient exceedingly. On the threshold of going in to see this repulsive patient, she paused for prayer. The words came, "Inasmuch as ye have done it unto one of the least of these, my brethren, ye have done it unto me" (Matthew 25:40 KJV). Love came. No patient was ever repulsive again. . . .

Don't admit, even to yourself, let alone to anyone else, that you are inferior or afraid. Above all, don't talk about it as a virtue—it isn't; it's a sin. . . . As children of God, we are not inferior. We are capable of infinite possibilities. Our faith in ourselves is not a lifting-ourselves-with-our-bootstraps faith. It is a faith rooted in the fact of our relationship with God.

"The Holy Ghost makes me put back my shoulders."
(Rufus Moseley)

My Father, I am your child, made in your image, enforced by your mind, empowered by your purposes, rekindled by your love, and remade by your redemption.

Affirmation: I cannot be inferior, since God is not, for I am in God.

For further reading: 2 Corinthians 9:8-10; Jeremiah 1:6-10

AL 104

252 —

No Illusions of Grandeur

Scripture

I say to everyone among you not to think of yourself more highly than you ought to think.
—Romans 12:3

If you are to shut your mind against all negative thinking, *you must also shut your mind against all illusions of grandeur.* The temptation will be to swing back from one attitude to its opposite, and, as mental compensation, to indulge in extravagant notions about yourself. You are neither a worm nor a wonder—you are just a bundle of fine possibilities, if developed.

A father said to his daughter who had been slipping in her achievements: "You are not the least bit inferior."

To which the girl replied: "No; the fact is, I'm superior in many things."

That reply showed the secret of her ineffectiveness. She had rebounded from thoughts of inferiority to illusions of grandeur, nursing the idea that she was not like the common herd, and filling her mind with fantasies and daydreaming. From being in the dust, she had gone to living in fairy castles in the air. She had to get back to earth. You don't belong either to groveling in the dust or to soaring in the clouds; but you belong to the earth, with your feet on it, and walking straight into tasks that you can do.

Are you living in reality?

O God, stretch me to my utmost—all I can be in and through you. But don't let me cry for the moon.

Affirmation: With God's help I will use all I have to be God's effective, down-to-earth person.

For further reading: Romans 6:3-8; 1 Corinthians 3:18-23

AL 105

258 — Aspire for Possibilities

*All things are yours ... and you belong to
Christ, and Christ belongs to God.*
—1 Corinthians 3:21-23

The fifth step for getting out of negativism is to *discipline
your aspirations to possibilities.* If you set up too high standards of achievement, beyond the reach of your powers
even when they are used by God, then you may become
discouraged and give up and do nothing.

I know a youth who, because he had such high aspirations of achievement that he couldn't reach those high
goals, would lie on his bed and read. Since he couldn't do
everything, he would do nothing. He should have disciplined his goals to the possible.

A minister felt that he should do the work of evangelist
Dwight L. Moody. He prayed hard and worked hard, but
no spectacular Moody results came. And then he came to
the conclusion that when God got hold of Moody he got
hold of a bigger man, and that God expected him to do his
own work, not Moody's.

Do you know what work you are meant to do?

Dear Father, help me to evaluate what I can be in you and
then go for that goal with all I have.

Affirmation: I will look at all the possibilities before me realistically
and with faith.

For further reading: 1 Corinthians 5:6; 6:19-20

AL 105

263

Your Possibilities in God

"So I tell you, whatever you ask for in prayer, believe that you have received it, and it will be yours."
—Mark 11:24

The next step in leaving negativity behind is to *gauge your possibilities not in yourself but according to what you can be in God.* That leaves you with a disciplined but an ever-expanding possibility; for possibilities in God are infinite. All this is not you, but you plus God.

[After the birth of her son Samuel,] Hannah sang this prayer: "My heart thrills to the Eternal; \ my powers are heightened by my God" (1 Samuel 2:1 Moffatt). Our powers are heightened by our God. True, they are *our* powers, still subject to limitations and not supposed to do the work of someone else, but they are heightened—provided they are surrendered to God and to his purposes. And then anything may happen—yes, anything. . . .

Across the hall from where I am writing once lay a cripple, living in a darkened room. The Little Sister—for so they affectionately called her—set up a home for cripples in China on the site of a pond into which people used to throw crippled children. . . . Her faith inspired others, and money came in and was sent through her loving hands on its healing mission. Everything is "can" to those who believe.

What are your possibilities in God?

O God, I haven't much to offer, but what I have is yours. Heighten these powers, so that I shall be a continuous surprise, even to myself.

Affirmation: In God I cannot be defeated nor fail, for I am now under a living mind and a living will, and the future is open.

For further reading: Mark 9:24-29; 11:20-24

AL 106

255 — Doing What You Can't!

By faith [Abraham] received power of procreation, even though he was too old—and Sarah herself was barren—because he considered him faithful who had promised.
—Hebrews 11:11

Dr. W. V. Kelley spoke at [the Little Sister's] funeral of "the miracle of her healthy mind." It was a healthy mind because a harnessed mind; it was disciplined to the possible, and yet how utterly impossible! Her faith had its feet upon the ground; but sometimes faith walked so fast that those feet seemed to leave the earth. No wonder Dr. Kelley could dedicate his book "To one who through years of suffering bears an illumined face." A crippled body, a healthy mind, an illumined face, a home for cripples—why? In and through it all God worked as she worked. . . .

Jesus answered the question, "What must we do to perform the works of God?" (John 6:28) by saying, "This is the work of God, to believe" (v. 29 Moffatt). When I am believing then I am really working, for I become a channel of the Infinite. . . .

I told [a prayer group] that I had a very difficult assignment that day—I was to see someone I didn't really want to see, yet it had to be done. A layperson quoted this inscription on a tombstone: "She hath done what she couldn't." I went forth with those words ringing in my heart . . . "I'll do what I can't." And I did!

Faith can move mountains.

O God, now I begin to see the way of open possibilities lying before me as I adventure with you. I am following—lead on!

Affirmation: Nothing is too small or beneath my dignity to do; nothing is too large or beyond my powers to do.

For further reading: Hebrews 11:8-12; 35-40; 12:1-3

AL 107

256 — The Person Jesus Sees

Scripture

Jesus gazed at him and said, "You are Simon, the son of John?
Your name is to be Cephas" (meaning "Peter" or "rock").
—John 1:42 Moffatt

There are three people in you: the one your associates see—the outer you; the one you see—the present you; the one whom Jesus sees—the future you.

Everything depends on which "you" you center upon. If you are centering on the "you" your associates see, you will look around before you act to see what effect your action will have on others. You won't act; you will react. You will become an echo and not a voice, a thing and not a person.

If you center upon the "you" you know, then you will be discouraged. For who has not had . . . things in our life that make our cheeks burn with shame and humiliation? If you are centered on this "you," you will be caught in the bondage of inhibitions. . . .

But there is this third "you" that Jesus sees. What a "you" that is! It is a "you" surrendered to God, cooperating with him, taking his resources, working out life together—a "you" loosed from what you've been and done, reinforced with divine energy and insight; a "you" that does things beyond your capacity, amazing both yourself and others—a "you" poised, progressive, and productive. That is the real "you." Center on Christ's "you," and you will become it.

**Jesus always looks not on what we have been or are,
but on what we are going to be.**

God, I'm adventuring in you, pushing back my small horizons as I see yours. I'm exchanging my "you" for your "you."

Affirmation: I will focus on God's greatness and on Jesus Christ as I follow his call.

For further reading: John 1:40-51; Luke 19:1-9

AL 108

Look Beyond Self to God

257

Put on the Lord Jesus Christ, and make no provision for the flesh, to gratify its desires.
—Romans 13:14

The seventh step in leaving negativity: . . . *Don't look too long at this self in God—look at God.* A great many cults center upon self-cultivation and leave behind a multitude of wistful but frustrated people, lifted for a moment and limping for a lifetime. Why? You dare not center on yourself, for if you do, as sure as fate you will lose yourself. "Those who want to save their life"—centering on their life, loving it even for purposes of cultivating it—"will lose it" (Luke 9:24).

As long as Peter looked at himself or the waves around him, he started sinking. Only as he looked at Jesus did he walk firmly on the waters. Look at yourself, or at others, and you will sink; look at Christ, and you can walk on anything.

. . . You must think not of yourself, even to cultivate yourself; but think of Christ, and the self will be cultivated. Glance at yourself in God, but gaze at God.

We are to imitate Christ.

O God, I dare not gaze on myself. When I gaze on you, I find myself. In you I gaze and grow—in myself I cultivate and deteriorate. So now my eye is getting in focus.

Affirmation: When my eye is healthy, my whole body is full of light (Matthew 6:22).

For further reading: Ephesians 3:14-21

AL 109

Don't Gaze
on Problems

...if there is anything worthy of praise,
think about these things.
—Philippians 1:8

Whatever gets your attention gets you.... Our faith is God-centered, not you-centered. So look away from your sins and diseases; look away from yourself—look away to God.

Look away from your sins and diseases. If your gaze is on sin and disease—is sin-centered and disease-centered—you'll never get well.... French airplanes provide a cup in front of each passenger with a sign, "For airsickness." In English planes the notice reads, "In case you feel indisposed, the steward will help you." In English planes scarcely anyone gets sick, but in the French planes almost everyone does! Passengers look at the word *sickness* and the cup—enough! But when they read the sign in English planes they think of a *steward*; the attention is called off from self.

Whatever we focus on determines what we become.

God, my Father, I see where I should be centered. You are my center—and my circumference. In you I am safe and steady and growing.

Affirmation: I am fashioned in my inmost being for God, who is the Homeland of my soul.

For further reading: Philippians 4:8-9; Ephesians 1:17-23

AL 110

The Kingdom Belongs to You!

"Do not be afraid, little flock, for it is your Father's good pleasure to give you the kingdom."
—Luke 12:32

The eighth step in gaining a positive way of life is to *remember that you do not merely belong to the kingdom of God—the kingdom of God belongs to you.* Here is a fact you must lay hold of, for in grasping it you turn the whole tide from defeat to victory. Possess this, and it will possess you.

Three classes possess the kingdom, Jesus said. "Blessed are the poor in spirit, for theirs is the kingdom of heaven" (Matthew 5:3). "Let the little children come to me . . . for it is to such as these that the kingdom of heaven belongs" (Matthew 19:14). "Blessed are those who are persecuted for righteousness' sake, for theirs is the kingdom of heaven" (Matthew 5:10). The poor in spirit, the little children, and those who are sufficiently positive to be persecuted—they all possess the kingdom; its powers are theirs.

The first two classes are alike: "the poor in spirit," literally, "the renounced in spirit," and those who have the spirit of a little child—simple, unaffected, teachable. Here we find the key that unlocks the resources of the storehouse of the universe—the kingdom of God. The wealth of it is all theirs, because they surrender to it. As you surrender to the kingdom of God, you inherit its powers—they are all yours.

How opposite this is to our usual way of thinking!

O God, it seems too good to be true—that all these powers are mine! I surrender now to you, I keep nothing back—absolutely nothing. And giving all, I take all.

Affirmation: As I surrender to God, I take the powers of victory and release and usefulness for my own.

For further reading: Luke 18:15-17; Matthew 5:1-10

AL 111

260

The Kingdom Speaks When You Speak

Scripture

So we are ambassadors for Christ, since God is making his appeal through us.
—2 Corinthians 5:20

We do not merely belong to the kingdom—the kingdom belongs to us. Once you get hold of [this thought] all argument and hesitation and fear are at an end. . . .

An ambassador represents his country—all the powers and privileges of his country center in him. When he speaks, the country speaks; when he decides, the country decides—provided he is not speaking on his own, provided he is surrendered to the will of his country, provided he has merged his interest in the interest of his country. When entirely surrendered, he is entirely masterful—up to the limit of the resources of the country he represents.

If you have merged your interests in the kingdom of God, if you are entirely surrendered to it, if you speak representing not yourself but the kingdom, then all the powers of the kingdom center in you—a universe speaks when you speak; a universe acts when you act; a universe lives when you live. The resources of earthly kingdoms are so limited; the resources of the kingdom of God are so unlimited. That Government which stretches from the lowest cell to the farthest star comes to focus in you—it is all yours!

There is no limit in God.

O God, help me to be unafraid of being great—of being great in surrender, great in responsibility, great in resources, great in myself, because great in you.

Affirmation: I merge my interests in the kingdom; I accept its responsibilities; and—dare I say it?—I inherit its powers!

For further reading: 2 Corinthians 5:17-21; Ephesians 6:19-20

AL 112

Receptivity—The First Law of Life

To all who received him, who believed in his name, he gave power to become children of God.
—John 1:12

We come now to the ninth step on the way out of negativity. Since the kingdom belongs to you, *remember the two conditions for receiving and transmitting the resources of the kingdom: receptivity and response.* These . . . are not only the alternate heartbeats of the kingdom, they are also the alternate beats of the whole of life. John sums up this thought in these words: "to all who received him [the Word, the true light] . . . he gave power to become . . ." How did they get power—power to become? First, by receptivity—they received him. . . .

You and I live physically when we respond to our physical environment: we can take in food and light and air. When response is shut off, we die physically. Our spiritual environment is the kingdom of God. When we respond to it, surrender to it, adjust ourselves to it, receive our very life from it, then we live—and live abundantly. We are in a state of receptivity, which is a state of faith, confidence, appropriation. We absorb kingdom life as the body absorbs food; we breathe in its purifying breath as the lungs breathe in air; we take up its vitality as the skin takes in vitamins from the light of the sun.

To believe is to receive and to receive is to replenish.

O God, you wrap me round as the atmosphere wraps my body. Let me respond to you as my physical body responds to its environment and lives. Help me to live by you, truly live.

Affirmation: I will take deep breaths of God, receiving him into every pore and fiber of my being.

For further reading: John 1:1-14; John 15:1-18

AL 113

Response—The Second Law of Life

Scripture

If by the Spirit you put to death the deeds of the body, you will live.
—Romans 8:13

If receptivity is the first law of life, response is the second law. Perhaps we can say that they are two sides of one law. Jesus revealed the two sides in his summing up of the whole meaning of religion [in Mark 12:28-31]: "You shall love the Lord your God"—receptivity; "You shall love your neighbor as yourself"—response. Love makes you receptive to God and responsive to others. Or better still: love makes you receptive to God and responsive too—two-way traffic. You receive from God, and you give back to God.

In receiving from God you are completed and perfected, and in your responding to God—shall we say it?—God is completed and perfected. For, having created another personality, God is not complete till he gains the love and loyalty of that personality. Our response is as necessary to God as it is to us. For a Love that loves but is not responded to is thwarted. God is all-important to us; we are important to God.

How have you responded to God?

O God, am I—I who thought myself inferior—necessary to you? Then help me never to let you down. Help me humbly to receive from you and humbly to give back to you—a two-way traffic with you.

Affirmation: I shall grow as I get and give.

For further reading: 2 Corinthians 6:1-10; Romans 8:31-39; 12:1-2

AL 114

268

Living in Human Relationships

Owe no one anything, except to love one another, for the one who loves another has fulfilled the law.
—Romans 13:8

If receptivity and response are the two heartbeats of our relationship to God, they are also the two heartbeats of our human relationships. Love lets you receive from the other person; but just as truly it makes you respond in self-giving to the other person. Without this clear two-way traffic, the relationship will break down. One who is always receiving from another and not giving will break down a relationship, and one who is always giving and not receiving will just as truly destroy the relationship. Moreover, the receptivity and the response must be about equal. If one overbalances the other, if you are more of a receiver than a responder, or more of a responder than you are a receiver, you cripple the relationship.

Impractical mysticism is strong on the receiving side, but weak on the responding side, and hence results in a lopsided religion, weak in positive contribution to human welfare. Activism is strong on the responding side, but weak on the receiving side, and hence ends in a religion lacking resources, depth, and permanence. A heart that tries to beat in one direction and not in the other ends in not beating at all.

How is your life balanced between giving and receiving?

O God, my Father, I would follow in your path of giving—giving to others out of the abundance you have given me.

Affirmation: I will love others for what they may become just as Christ loves me for what I may become.

For further reading: Romans 12:9-13; 13:8-10; Ephesians 4:31–5:2; James 2:14-17

AL 114

Never Alone!

"I have said this to you, so that in me you may have peace. In the world you face persecution. But take courage; I have conquered the world!"
—John 16:33

As you turn away from all negativism and inferiority attitudes to positive, abundant living, now take the next step. *Remember that you are not alone—never alone.* At the time of seemingly greatest aloneness, God is closest....

John Wilhelm Rowntree tells how, when he left a great physician's office where he had been told that his advancing blindness could not be stayed, he stood by some railings for a few moments to collect himself. "Suddenly he felt the love of God wrap him about as though an invisible presence enfolded him, and a joy filled him such as he had never known before."

That Presence will manifest himself when most needed. Say to yourself, "I live and move and have my being, in all inner thoughts and outer expression, in the wealth of God every moment." Say this when you least feel the truth of it and keep saying it....

When you lie down to sleep say: "While I sleep I still live and have my being in God. He will guide and purify my dreams and in the morning I shall be further along."

"Those who have the gales of the Spirit are carried forward even in sleep."
(Brother Lawrence)

O God, you and I will work this out together. I am yet weak and can take only a small part of the load—you'll have to take the heavy end.

Affirmation: I live and move and have my being, in all inner thoughts and outer expression, in the wealth of God every moment.

For further reading: Matthew 28:19-20; 14:16-21

AL 115

Handicaps
Become Handles

The Lord ... said to me, "My grace is sufficient for you, for power is made perfect in weakness."
—2 Corinthians 12:8-9

Your next step in climbing out of negativity is to *remember that your very handicaps may be new points of departure.*

Perhaps you may have had a bad start in life—your heredity may be against you. But that need not be other than a spur to you to pass on to others a better heredity.

If you look back into the human heredity of Jesus, you will find some ugly spots: "David was the father of Solomon by the wife of Uriah" (Matthew 1:6). . . . What a tragedy to have such a label stuck on one's life. But what a glory it is that both David and Solomon survived that tragedy and contributed in spite of it! And think of the honest courage it took to put that statement into the genealogy of Jesus Christ. He who was going to begin a new humanity had the blood of the old humanity in his veins. But the divine inheritance so overcame the human inheritance that he passed on a new inheritance to humanity. Through his divine inheritance you can begin a new heredity. . . .

**Make up your mind to use your handicaps
as handles for achievement.**

Father, what I lack by nature I shall make up by grace, drawing heavily on you. Make my very weakness into your strength.

Affirmation: I will take hold of my handicaps and convert them into handiwork.

For further reading: 2 Corinthians 10:10; 11:5-6; 12:7-12

AL 116

Flee Forward!

*"When they persecute you in one town, flee to the next;
for truly I tell you, you will not have gone through all the
towns of Israel before the Son of Man comes."*
—Matthew 10:23

Handicaps [can also be] spurs that drive us forward. Jesus told his disciples that when the people turned them out of one village, they were to "flee to the next." In other words, if you have to flee, flee forward—to the next opportunity on your list. Some flee backward; but the Christian who has to flee always flees forward.

So the next step out of negativity is: *If you have the impulse to flee, then flee forward....*

A young woman...had not accomplished as much as she was capable of doing in her teaching of voice, and so lost her own voice to give her an excuse for her failure. The trouble was not in her vocal cords, but in her defeatist mentality. She...fled backward....

Not having a college education made Rabindranath Tagore India's great poet....He fled from the lack of a college education—forward! He could have drawn back and bemoaned his inferior education; instead he turned that lack into a spur, became superior in himself and founded a new type of educational institution.

**Life will be made or broken
at the place where we meet and deal with obstacles.**

Father God, help me not to run away from the obstacles in my life, but to run toward them, tackle and overcome them.

Affirmation: When I feel the impulse to flee, I will compel it to make me flee forward to the next opportunity.

For further reading: Acts 5:40-42; Philippians 1:12-19; 1 Peter 4:12-14

AL 117

Nobodies Become Somebodies

God chose what is low and despised in the world, things that are not, to reduce to nothing things that are.
—1 Corinthians 1:28

Your next step: *Remember it is never too late to be a creative personality.* No matter what happens to you, or when it happens to you, it is never too late to become creative. I know a woman, wife of a professor, who did not touch a paintbrush until she was fifty. Then she awakened, began to paint, and her paintings are being exhibited here and in other countries....

Some artists gathered on a farm to paint the landscape. The farmer, becoming interested, painted the landscape on his own. The teacher, seeing the painting, asked who had done it. The farmer was "discovered" and became a famous landscape artist. His awakening had come at sixty-eight.

Jesus is the great Awakener.... In his company we begin to see farther, feel for people on a wider scale, and act more decisively. Jesus takes the nobodies and turns them into the somebodies.... No one can be in his company long without feeling an irresistible impulse to roll up their sleeves and say, "Where do I begin?" For the creative impulse comes from contact with the creative God.

Where will you begin?

O Christ, creator of living thoughts in dead brains, giver of life, I ask you to enter into me and quicken every fiber and nerve cell that I too may become creative.

Affirmation: I will open my mind and heart and will to the infinite possibilities available to me in God.

For further reading: 1 Corinthians 1:26-31; 6:9-11; Philemon 10-16

AL 118

Plan for Creative Achievement

Work out your own salvation with fear and trembling;
for it is God who is at work in you, enabling you both to
will and to work for his good pleasure.
—Philippians 2:12-13

We come now to the last step in our climb out of negativity: *Plan for creative achievement and put your plan into operation by however small a beginning.*

Say with Jesus, " 'Do not weep for me' [Luke 23:28]—I'm through with asking for pity, for compassion. I don't want sympathy, I want a task, an open door. I'm through with living on a no. I'm going to live on a yes. I'm not inferior since I have hold of a superior God and he has hold of me. I no longer belong to those who look back, for those who look back cannot fit into the kingdom of God, and I belong to the kingdom of God, the kingdom of the forward looking."

Say to yourself: "What God suffers for he means to have, and what he takes hold of he never lets go. He has taken hold of me, and he will never let me go, even though I stumble. He will save me again and again even though I fail."

When we trust God,
we can look forward and live positively.

O Christ, at last the doors of my life are turning outward instead of inward. At last I have lifted my feet out of the quicksand of self-pity. At last I have love in my heart, courage in my will, and faith in my inmost being. Thank you.

Affirmation: God has taken hold of me and will never let me go. He is giving me strength to act.

For further reading: 1 Peter 4:2-11

AL 119

How to Deal with Negative Thoughts

269

The Spirit entered into me, and set me upon my feet.
—Ezekiel 3:24 RSV

As part of your plan for creative achievement, you will need to write down your negative thoughts and then tear them up as a symbol that they no longer exist. Then write down your positive thoughts about what you can do, and begin at once to express these thoughts, to act on them in however small a beginning. If you cannot do one thing, flee forward and do the next thing. Then decide to do what you have decided to do, and do it now.

The prophet Ezekiel testified that God's Spirit entered him and made him stand up, stand on his feet. The Spirit of God has entered into you; now you are to stand upon your feet and do an adult's work in the world.

Say as you go out each day, "I can do all things through Christ which strengtheneth me" (Philippians 4:13 KJV). Repeat it the last thing before you fall asleep at night and the first thing in opening your eyes in the morning. The subconscious mind is very susceptible at those two periods. It will get into the subconscious and work with you, making you positive and creative.

**Will you write out and then
discard your negative thoughts?**

O Jesus, come into my soul, my mind, my body, into every brain cell to keep me moving forward.

Affirmation: I will to do God's work in the world.

For further reading: Philippians 2:13-15; Ephesians 5:6-10

AL 119

279

Our Resources

Where sin increased, grace abounded all the more.
—Romans 5:20

Someone has said, "The early Christians did not say in dismay: 'Look what the world has come to,' but in delight, 'Look what has come to the world.' " They saw not merely the ruin but the Resources for the reconstruction of that ruin. They saw not merely that sin did abound but that grace did much more abound. On that assurance the pivot of history swung from blank despair, loss of moral nerve and fatalism, to faith and confidence that at last sin had met its match, that something new had come into the world, that not only here and there, but on a wide scale, human beings could attain to that hitherto impossible thing—goodness. And not only goodness, but health of mind and body—rhythm and harmony in their total being.

That same sense of confidence must possess you if you are to pass from an anemic, noncreative, nay-saying type of person to one who is master of self, circumstances, and destiny.

But this confidence and faith must not be based on a self-hypnosis, a mental and spiritual fool's paradise. It must be based on the solid confidence that your life is related to the sum total of Reality, and that that Reality is working with you and not against you.

**Goodness, health, harmony, confidence:
what an inviting description of a full life!**

O gracious God and Father, my heart beats a little faster at the prospect of being the person that, now and again, in my highest moments, I have felt I might be. I follow you to be that very person.

Affirmation: The secret of abundant and positive living: It is not my responsibility, but my response to God's ability.

For further reading: Romans 5:20-21; Colossians 2:6-10

AL 183

Grace in the Dungeon

Thus says the Lord:
"The people who survived the sword
found grace in the wilderness. . . .
I have loved you with an everlasting love."
—Jeremiah 31:2-3

There are many who say: "I am caught in a web of circumstances that bind me hand and foot. How can I have abundant living under these circumstances?" In answer I refer you to a passage which tells of those who "find grace in the dungeon" (Jeremiah 31:2 Moffatt). If you find grace at all, you must find it in the dungeon. You are caught—you are not able to get out of the dungeon; then the only thing to do is to get the dungeon out of you—to find grace in that very dungeon.

The people to whom this passage was addressed did find grace in the dungeon—they were purified in the Exile and became the instrument of God. The dungeon became a door! You needn't accept your circumstances as from God, but you can accept them as an opportunity for God to use them to make you creative. . . .

Among the most beautiful of Paul's writings are these lines: "This salutation is in my own hand, from Paul. 'Remember I am in prison. Grace be with you'" (Colossians 4:18 Moffatt). You would have expected him to say, "I am in prison—God give me grace." But no; . . . . I have found grace in the dungeon—enough and to spare—I pass it on to you.

Do you feel caught?
Will you ask for grace?

Gracious God and Father, help me not to whine or complain when my circumstances become a dungeon, but to find the resources of your grace enough to pass on.

Affirmation: God's grace is sufficient for me not merely when life is free and open but also when life turns into a dungeon.

For further reading: Jeremiah 31:1-9; Acts 16:19-34; Philippians 1:12-14
AL 337

Freedom Through Limitations

We know that all things work together for good for those who love God, who are called according to his purpose.
—Romans 8:28

I have always been grateful that I went to a small, obscure college, for it left me with the sense of being uneducated. I suppose that those who go to great institutions feel secure; to mention the name of the great university they attended brands them as educated. I have felt no such security; so I have endeavored all my life to become an educated person. I gather from every moment, every occasion, and every conversation something that will help educate me. On the tombstone of a man were these words: "He died climbing." I would like to have this inscription on mine: "He died learning." The limitation has been a liberty. I have found grace in the dungeon.

The person who has discovered and revealed to the people of Arkansas their wildflowers is shut-in, a woman crippled with arthritis. Although her hands are gnarled and twisted, she has painted exquisitely five hundred specimens.... Her cheer and her skill are beyond words. She has found grace in the dungeon. A shut-in knows more about the wildflowers and where they grow than anyone in the state!

In every situation there is always something we can do.

Christ, you have shown me how to take hold of the nettle of life when it stings and make those very stings into sensitiveness to the hurts of others. I am plunged into a dungeon. Perhaps I am in this dungeon so that I can see the stars.

Affirmation: Nothing can defeat me if I remain undefeated within.

For further reading: Romans 8:26-39

AL 339

The Dungeon
Makes or Breaks Us

. . . this is evidence of their destruction, but of
your salvation. And this is God's doing.
—Philippians 1:28

The dungeon experience can make us or break us. Some it crushes; others it solidifies. . . .

It was said of Jesus that he went into the wilderness "full of the Holy Spirit," and came out "filled with the power of the Spirit" (Luke 4:1, 14)—mere fullness turned to power under the stress of temptation. The dungeon of temptation resulted only in his being strengthened. . . .

A gracious Christian lady said to another: "I know you dislike being ill. But I find the only thing to do is to get something out of every experience that comes to me. So make your illness give you something."

I find it hard to wait for people, but I've learned to make waiting contribute by forming the habit of immediately turning to prayer whenever I have to wait. I find that praying keeps my temper from getting ruffled and that I am also not wasting my time. It always leaves me an open door out of every dungeon.

The possibility of prayer is always open,
anywhere,
at any time.

Gracious Father, if I don't know what else to do, help me to turn naturally to prayer. So life will be held together by poise and calm and victory, and I can always find grace in every dungeon.

Affirmation: I will let no moment be empty and fruitless but will fill it with prayer.

For further reading: 2 Corinthians 1:1-11; Philippians 1:12-20

AL 338

Living with Maturity

What Is Maturity?

*Solid food is for the mature, for those whose faculties have
been trained by practice to distinguish good from evil.*
—*Hebrews 5:14*

A mature person [is] one who is able to function happily,
usefully, and at maximum capacity in a given situation.
The definition needs correction at the place of "maximum
capacity," for it is possible to lay hold of capacities not
your own, and to make them your own, through grace. But
we will let the definition stand for the time being.

If this definition of maturity is somewhere near being
accurate, then it is obvious that many of us are not
mature; for we do not function happily, usefully, and at
our maximum powers in our situation. Why? The temptation will be strong, and very ancient—the most ancient of
temptations—to lay the blame on someone else: "The
woman whom you gave to be with me, she gave me fruit
from the tree, and I ate" (Genesis 3:12). Adam blamed God
for giving him the woman and he blamed the woman for
giving him the fruit; God and the woman, not Adam were
to blame. Such an attitude showed immaturity. To blame
others and our surroundings shows our immaturity.

Are you living at maximum capacity?

O God, forgive me when I put the blame elsewhere than on
me for the way I am. I want to grow into maturity. Help me.

Affirmation: From now on I will not blame anyone or anything else
for what I am.

For further reading: Genesis 3:1-19; Luke 15:11-24

CM 1

Accepting Responsibility

Scripture

*" 'I will get up and go to my father, and I will say to him,
"Father, I have sinned against heaven and before you." ' "*
—Luke 15:18

The first step in gaining maturity is to accept the responsibility for being what we are. I do not deny that our surroundings of people and place can and do influence us. But only that part of our environment to which we respond influences us. We do the responding. The choice is always ours. If you are a half-person with a half-life output, then it is because by a series of choices you have consented to be that half-person. But no one need be a half person.

For both God and life will maturity. Life wills maturity. Within everything, from the lowest cell to the highest human, is an urge after completion, after fuller, more abundant life—everything reaches up after maturity. If, therefore, we are not mature, it is obvious that we are blocking the life urge within us. Somehow, some way, we are choking those urges.

**All God's resources are behind those
who will to be mature persons.**

O God, my Father, I cannot bear being what I am—half-made, half-baked, a half person. Today I put my feet upon the way that leads me out of immaturities into your wholeness.

Affirmation: My first step in maturity—I accept responsibility for what I am.

For further reading: Ephesians 4:12-24

CM 1

276 — God Wills Maturity

We must no longer be children...
—*Ephesians 4:14*

What kind of Father would God be if he did not disturb us toward maturity? No earthly parent could be content to have a child who refused to grow up. The parents' joy is in development, in growth, in going on toward maturity. God cannot be otherwise and still be God, our Father. So the disturbances we feel in our immaturities are not signs of his anger, but a manifestation of his love. He loves us too much to let us settle down in halfwayness.

But if God should stop at the point of making us discontented, then he would stop this side of being God, our Father. To be our Father, he must provide literally everything for our maturity. And he has! He has put at our disposal all the resources for our being what we ought to be—everything except coercion. There he draws the line, for if he coerced us into maturity—took us by the back of the neck and shook us into maturity—then of course we couldn't be mature. The will to be mature must be at the center of our maturity.

Are you willing to grow toward maturity?

Father, show me the restrictions in me and the resources in you. I put my feet on the Way. Amen.

Affirmation: Since I am destined to be mature, I accept that destiny as my own.

For further reading: Ephesians 4:1-16; James 3:13-18

CM 2

Life Wills Maturity

*Speaking the truth in love, we must grow up in every
way into him who is the head, into Christ.*
—Ephesians 4:15

God and life...conspire in every possible way, short of
breaking down our wills, to make us mature. Life makes us
discontented and unhappy in our immaturities. Suppose
we could settle down happy and contented in being a
half-person, that would be a tragic situation. But we cannot. That divine discontent is a part of our salvation. It is
a goad that impels us into higher, fuller life. . . .

If God and life and we ourselves will maturity, then
there is nothing in heaven or earth that can stop us from
being the mature persons we ought to be. We are destined
to be mature, and that destiny is written in every cell of
our bodies. We can slow down or block that destiny. The
choice is always ours.

Thank God for divine discontent!

Father, hope begins to spring up in me, for if I am destined
to be mature, then I can and do accept that destiny and
make it my own. Show me the restrictions in me and the
resources in you.

Affirmation: I will to grow into maturity, to live in God's Way and in
the Way of life.

For further reading: Ephesians 4:1-16

CM 1, 2

The Way

Lord, . . .
You it was who fashioned my inward parts;
you knitted me together in my mother's womb.
—Psalm 139:1, 13 REB

The Christian way, often called in early days, "the Way," is the way to live. . . . [It] is written in our nerves, our blood, our tissues, in the total organization of life. If we live according to that Way, we live; if we don't we get hurt. . . . The Christian Way is written not merely in texts of Scripture but in the texture of life. It is the way we are made to live.

How different would your life be
if you truly believed this?

O God, I am grateful that you have written this demand in my physical being. Please fulfill it in me.

Affirmation: I want to live in God's Way, the way of maturity.

For further reading: Psalm 139

WPP 1

A Mature Faith

*The gifts he gave were . . . to equip the saints . . .
until all of us come to the unity of the faith and
of the knowledge of the Son of God, to maturity.*
—*Ephesians 4:11-13*

If we are to be mature we must get hold of a mature faith—or better, it must get hold of us. For the immaturities of our faith will soon show themselves in immaturities in our actions and our attitudes. . . . Nothing can be more immature than the oft-repeated statement: "It doesn't matter what you believe just so you live right." For *belief* is literally *by-lief, by-life*—the thing you live by. And if your belief is wrong your life will be wrong.

. . . I don't mean to say that if you have a correct belief you'll necessarily have a correct life. That doesn't follow. The creed, to be a creed, must be a vital rather than a verbal one. For the only thing we really believe in is the thing we believe in enough to act upon. Your deed is your creed. But it does matter what you hold as the basic assumptions of your life. If you have no starting point, you'll have no ending point.

What do your actions say about your beliefs?

O God, my Father, I am all eager to begin, for I feel that I am about to be introduced to Reality itself. Help me to be real as I do so. Amen.

Affirmation: Since a mature faith is the first necessity, I am an open candidate for a mature faith.

For further reading: Colossians 2:6-10

CM 3

The Starting Point

We declare to you what we have seen and heard
so that you also may have fellowship with us...
with the Father and with his Son Jesus Christ.
—1 John 1:3

Where do we start?...[In] the first epistle...John sums up the Christian revelation. The Gospel of John gives the facts, the Epistle of John gives the fruits of those facts. Here in this epistle John has graphically depicted the most mature living ever seen upon our planet....

John didn't begin with the word *maturity* or with the word *love*. He began with a Person....John has no hesitancy in pointing straight to the heart of the matter: The center of [mature faith] is a Person and that Person—Jesus. "We declare to you what was from the beginning, what we have heard, what we have seen with our eyes, what we have looked at and touched with our hands, concerning the word of life—this life was revealed" (1:1-2). Here, over against human speculations about God, John pointed to God's authentic self-revelation: Jesus.

Jesus Christ is our pattern.

Jesus, you are our alpha and our omega, the beginning and the end of all our maturities. I want to be mature according to your pattern.

Affirmation: As Jesus is the center of my faith, he shall be the center of my loyalty and love.

For further reading: 1 John 1:1-4; 1 Timothy 3:16

CM 3, 4, 5

God-Salvation or Self-Salvation?

We have seen and do testify that the Father has sent his Son as the Savior of the world.
—1 John 4:14

The most important question we can face is does salvation, and hence maturity, come up from human beings through their striving, illuminated by the Divine; or does salvation, and hence maturity, come from above—from God—through the act of God and our receptivity of that act?...

Over against speculations, John sets the vitalities of gospel sureties.... All religions are humanity's attempt to climb to God; Jesus is God's descent to humanity. All religions are our search for God; Jesus is God's search for us. Therefore there are many religions, but there is but one gospel. Jesus did not bring a religion to set alongside of other religions, one a little better, more moral, more spiritual. He came to set the gospel over against human need. ... The gospel lies in his person—he himself is the Good News.

Are you looking for a sure thing?

O Jesus, my Lord, I am grateful that you yourself are my salvation.

Affirmation: My attachment shall be a personal attachment to the personal Jesus with all my person.

For further reading: Acts 17:22-28

CM 5, 6

Jesus Is God Incarnate

By this you know the Spirit of God: every spirit that confesses that Jesus Christ has come in the flesh is from God, and every spirit that does not confess Jesus is not from God.
—1 John 4:2-3

In order to be sure that we see that the Word really became flesh, John piles statement upon statement in 1:1-3....

"What we have heard"—but hearing may be at such a distance that it can be almost hearsay.

"What we have seen with our eyes"—that brings the speaker in range of the eye—nearer.

"What we have looked at"—not a fleeting glance, but a steady gaze.

"And touched with our hands"—referring to Jesus' statement after his resurrection when he invites the disciples to touch him, to handle him, to thrust their hands in his side!

In these four statements involving three of the senses, John nails down the fact that the Word actually did become flesh. So important is this fact that John makes it the test of whether the Spirit of God is present (4:2-3). Everything hinges on Jesus as Incarnate, not Jesus as inspiration, not Jesus as moral teacher, not Jesus as philosopher. But Jesus as Incarnate God—that is the issue!

God became one of us!

Father, your unveiling in Jesus makes me see what lies back in eternity, and makes me grateful that you have entered our human world.

Affirmation: If Jesus is the life of God made manifest, I shall be the life of Jesus made manifest.

For further reading: Philippians 2:5-11

CM 7

The Eternal God Becomes Like Us

God's love was revealed among us in this way: God sent his only Son into the world so that we might live through him.
—1 John 4:9

The center of the Christian faith is the Incarnation—God becoming human flesh, becoming truly human. Beside this central fact of the divine invasion of us, all else is comparatively irrelevant.

Miracles? This is the central miracle—the Eternal God become like us that we may become like him.

Teaching? What greater teaching could there be than this teaching of God in action? For in it we see as in a flash the meaning of humility, of service, of self-giving goodness, of love of everything.

Morality? This is morality, not thundering the law, but washing our feet.

Spirituality? This is spirituality, not aloof and lifted up on some Olympus, but walking in sandals.

God walking in sandals—amazing!

O Jesus, you come into our lowly doors out of the eternities touching both. You are so high and so lowly, so terrible and so tender, so like God yet so like us. I worship you. Amen.

Affirmation: As Jesus is the opening of the meaning of God to me, I shall be the opening of the meaning of Jesus to others.

For further reading: Colossians 1:13-20

CM 7, 8

The Highest
Definition of Love

*In this is love, not that we loved God but that he loved us
and sent his Son to be the atoning sacrifice for our sins.*
—1 John 4:10

"This life was revealed" (1:2). John comes right to the heart
of the whole matter here. God has spoken, not in words but
in the Word. And in that speaking he reveals his heart.
Jesus is the heart of God wrapped in flesh—revealed....

Doctrine? This is a doctrine that is a Deed.

Ritual? Here ritual is not in form but in fact, the free
flowing of love in adoration.

Sermons? Here we do not merely hear one—we see one—
every act, every word, every attitude a living sermon....

Religion? He never mentioned the word, but if you were
to ask my definition of religion I would point to him: he is
religion.

Law? Here law becomes love.

Love? The highest definition of love. The love of the
cross. Sacrifice? Not the sacrifice of giving animals, or
fruits, or deeds to God to appease him, but the very God
himself giving himself in sacrifice for us on a cross.

In Jesus we see God's heart—love in action.

O Father, your unveiling in Jesus makes me see that you are
good and only good, purity and only purity, love and only love.

Affirmation: God gave himself for me in love. I will give myself to
him in love and gratitude.

For further reading: 1 John 4:7-21

CM 7, 8

God on a Cross

And the Word became flesh and lived among us.
—John 1:14

The whole of John's epistle revolves around the Person and work of Jesus, anticipating the controversy that would arise [later]. . . . The Ebionites said Jesus was a mere man; the Docetists said that Jesus was a phantom—he was a God who just seemed to be a man; the Cerinthianists . . . endeavored to combine these two opinions and supposed that the divine element, Christ, was united with the man Jesus at his baptism but left him before the cross. All three . . . were attempts to obviate the difficulty of God dying on a cross. "God on a cross" scandalized the ancient world of philosophy wherein matter was evil and God the ineffably aloof. . . .

The controversy . . . is still going on. A letter received a few days ago protested against my "attempt to unite all the Christians around the alleged deity of Jesus Christ." . . . Why try to unite all around one Person? . . . But suppose that person turns out to be the Person, the Absolute Person, the meeting place of the human and the Divine, then it is inevitable that we get together around him, or perish. This is the Eternal God confronting us. . . .

The ancient [explanations] perished. . . . The Christian affirmation of "God on a cross" lives on.

"Amazing love! how can it be
That Thou, my God, shouldst die for me?"
("And Can It Be," Charles Wesley)

O God, the unfolding of your meaning and purpose through Jesus leaves me awed. All my heart is aglow with gratitude.

Affirmation: Since Jesus is the Word become flesh, I shall be that same word become flesh again.

For further reading: John 1:1-5, 14-18; 1 John 5:6-11

CM 10

Jesus in a Cosmic Setting

We declare to you what was from the beginning.
—1 John 1:1

John placed Jesus in a cosmic setting.... "Jesus, knowing that the Father had given all things into his hands, and that he had come from God and was going to God... began to wash the disciples' feet" (John 13:3-5). The consciousness of greatness was the secret of humility. All things had been given into his hands, so he used those hands to wash the disciples' feet. Knowing he was God, he could become man....

Since he had a cosmic setting, he could choose the setting of a stable. Since he held all power in heaven and on earth, he could become powerless in the hands of men and let them crucify him. Since he had a name which was above every name, he could take the name of a criminal. He who had everything could choose to have nothing. He who was deathless could choose a tomb.

All of this, *provided* he is love. No other motive would or could make him do what he did except one—love....

The Incarnation is the incredible—except on one basis— love. If love is at the heart of God, then you can expect him to do anything, anything that love would do. And love did this: he who was the Cosmic became the Carpenter.

Jesus Christ gave up all for love.

O Jesus, you stooped to conquer. And you have conquered me, conquered me to my depths. If you hold the world in your hands, you hold me too—your glad, willing, and eternal slave.

Affirmation: Love will do anything for the loved one. I am identified with love, so I am ready to do anything.

For further reading: Hebrews 1:1-3; Philippians 2:5-7

CM 12

The Emphasis on "This"

Scripture

We know love by this, that he laid down his life for us.
—*1 John 3:16*

In John's epistle, the word *this* is used twenty-nine times. The emphasis is not on "that" or "the other"—things far away—but on "this"—the near, the available, the now, the here. The "thisness" of God in Jesus is a surprise to everyone who really tries it. It hits you like a bolt out of the blue, or it wells up from within like the breaking forth of a sealed fountain, or the settling upon you of an infinite Quiet that tells you he is here.

Peter, standing up after receiving the gift of the Holy Spirit, said to the multitudes: "This is that" (Acts 2:16 KJV)—that which had been prophecy was now fact, glorious, bubbling, self-authenticating fact.

This is just the difference between the way of Christ and the other ways: other ways are all "that"—something just beyond the fingertips, something hoped for but not possessed, something in the realm of idea. But Jesus is the word become flesh, not only in his flesh, but in your flesh and mine...provided we take it by receptivity. God is no further away than yes—your "yes" to his "yes." So that no one is further than one word from God—"yes."

What a powerful word—*yes!*

O Jesus, you are God at the lintel of the doorstep of my being, with nothing between you and me except my opening the door from within.

Affirmation: Jesus Christ is my maturity. I know maturity as I know him. I shall know him more deeply today.

For further reading: 1 John 4:10, 13; 5:2-5, 11

CM 18

Maturity—A Gift and a Growth

*Little children, let us love, not in word
or speech, but in truth and action.*
—1 John 3:18

Salvation and maturity are near at hand—at our doors in Jesus. "Yes," someone suggests, "I can see that salvation may be at hand, but I thought that maturity was a long, slow growth." It is in one sense, but in another it is not. For the moment that you get into vital contact with Jesus, the most mature Fact of the universe, then you have maturity in its essence. . . .

Mary[1] . . . was accustomed to run to the telephone and listen in on a party line. . . . Everybody did it. The morning after she was converted, she automatically went to the telephone to listen in. But pausing a moment before lifting the receiver, she found herself saying "Why, I don't need to any more." And she didn't pick up the receiver. That was maturity—straight off. . . .

Maturity is primarily a gift, then it is a growth. The gift makes maturity possible now.

Jesus Christ makes change possible.

O Jesus, I thank you that the depth of my receptivity is the depth of my maturity. The Way is an open Way and I can put both feet on it now.

Affirmation: I reverse all my immature attitudes and receive all Jesus Christ's mature attitudes.

For further reading: Luke 19:1-10

CM 19

---

[1]Not her real name.

289 — All Self-Centeredness Is Immaturity

Abide in me as I abide in you. Just as the branch cannot bear fruit by itself unless it abides in the vine, neither can you unless you abide in me.
—John 15:4

A tree is mature only when it is bearing fruit. Until then it is immature. A person is immature until he or she is outgoing and sharing. And how does a tree bear fruit? By struggling, trying, working itself up into a lather? By tense anxiety, by trying harder? No. It bears fruit by receptivity.

"The branch cannot bear fruit by itself," Jesus said. That verse is the death knell to all attempts at maturity by self-tinkering, striving for self-salvation. All these attempts leave you centered on yourself, and when you are centered on yourself, you are immature, however religious you may be and however psychological you may be. Something has to break the tyranny of self-preoccupation, and only a mighty flux of love from Christ can do that. . . .

The inmost self must be offered on the altar and then, and then only, can we be redeemed.

What is the motivating factor of your life?

Jesus, you are redemption. You do not give redemption—you are redemption. For to have you is to be redeemed from sin and immaturity—from everything that makes me little. So I open my being wide to you. Come—it's all yours.

Affirmation: Jesus, you are the center of my preoccupation. I am in love with you, wholly and forever.

For further reading: 1 Timothy 3:1-5; John 15:1-17

CM 23

Immaturity Keeps Us Out of Fellowship

We declare to you what we have seen and heard so that you also may have fellowship with us; and truly our fellowship is with the Father and with his Son Jesus Christ.
—1 John 1:3

The basis of our immaturity is a self-centeredness that keeps us from fellowship with God, ourselves, others, nature, and life itself.... So the first thing in the Christian purpose is to produce fellowship.

First of all with God. John seems to say that the fellowship is "with us," but he hastens to add that "our fellowship is with the Father." Those who have no fellowship with God are immature. They feel, consciously or unconsciously, that they are cut off from the very root of their being. The prodigal son in Jesus' parable (Luke 15:11-24) saw that he had sinned in three directions (v. 18): "I have sinned against heaven"—the impersonal moral law: "and before you"—against the personal love of his father: and "I am no longer worthy to be called your son"—against himself, against his own sonship. The center of the three broken relationships was against his father's love. So that was the first relationship to be restored. The father ran and kissed him. Restored to the father he was restored to the moral law and he was restored to himself.

What a problem self is!

O God, we are homesick and heartsick for you and we don't know it. Make our sickness so acute that we will arise, like the prodigal, and go to you, our Father.

Affirmation: I cannot produce this fellowship by trying harder; I can only take it by trusting more.

For further reading: Colossians 4:7-15; 2 Timothy 4:9-11

CM 25

God Comes to Us

"[Mary] will bear a son, and you are to name him Jesus,
for he will save his people from their sins."
—Matthew 1:21

There are just two types of religion: one tries to meet God in reconciliation and realization at the top rung of a long ladder; the other meets God at the lowest rung. In the one we go to God, climbing up by our good deeds, by our prayers, by our mortifying of ourselves, by our gaining of merit, by our obedience to rites and ceremonies, and by our faithfulness to law and duty—we can earn our maturity and our realization of God. Every way, except the Christian way, belongs to that category. It is our search up for God.

The Christian way is quite different. We do not climb to God and meet him at the top rung. He comes down the ladder to us and meets us on the lowest rung—he receives us as sinners. . . . That is new and revolutionary. It reverses all the values of all the religions. . . .

Only One dared reverse all this, and they crucified him for it—Jesus. He rendered vain all these attempts at self-salvation. He shows us that God isn't at the top of the ladder—he is at the bottom. Breathtaking.

We don't have to become perfect in order to find God.

O Jesus, what can I say? I am speechless before the wonder of this. I am in the dust. But there I find you—in the dust before me, ready to receive me and lift me to the highest heaven. I belong to you—forever.

Affirmation: Only empty hands can take this Gift—my uplifted hands are empty.

For further reading: Matthew 1:20-23; 1 John 4:7-12; Luke 5:29-32

CM 26

He Welcomes Sinners

If we say that we have no sin, we deceive ourselves.... My little children, I am writing these things to you so that you may not sin.
—1 John 1:8, 2:1

"This fellow welcomes sinners and eats with them" (Luke 15:2). That was scandalized religion's most bitter complaint about Jesus. The complaint is now a compliment. For if Jesus received sinners, they didn't remain sinners—they became saints, straight off. And if he ate with them they were soon eating with him—the bread of Communion.

The elder brother in Jesus' parable (Luke 15:25-32) represents the attempts at fellowship with the father at the highest rung of the ladder of goodness...through keeping the Law. "I have never disobeyed your command" (v. 29). ...It failed. The younger son met the father at the lowest rung of the ladder, the rung of grace. He succeeded....When the parable ends, the one who tried to *earn* the fellowship with the father was on the outside sulking, and the one who took the fellowship through grace was on the inside rejoicing.

God cannot be found at the top of the ladder, for he is not there. He is at the lowest rung receiving sinners. If you feel you are not a sinner, then there is no place for you. But if you do, everything is open to you—especially the Father's heart.

You cannot earn God's love.

Jesus, I know you are the way to the Father, for you are the way of the Father to all of us. I cannot be grateful enough that you have met us at the lowest rung of the ladder, for I could not have met you anywhere else.

Affirmation: The Way is not in me, nor in others, nor in things—the Way is in Christ. Jesus Christ is the Way.

For further reading: Luke 15:11-32; 19:1-10; Romans 5:8

CM 29

Fellowship—The Central Thing in Maturity

We declare to you what we have seen and heard so that you also may have fellowship with us.
—1 John 1:3

The measure of our maturity can be and is measured by the breadth and depth of our capacity for fellowship. We are as mature as our fellowships. So if we cannot fellowship with other races, we reveal our immaturity. . . .

This statement holds good in regard to our capacity to fellowship with other Christians. If we can fellowship only with those who belong to our group, our denomination, our particular set of doctrinal beliefs, then in such measure we are immature.

What, then, is the basis of our fellowship? One thing and one thing only: everyone who belongs to Christ belongs to everyone who belongs to Christ. The basis of our fellowship is not around this doctrine, that doctrine, the other doctrine; or around this group, that group, or the other group. It is around Christ and only around Christ. . . . If we shut out our brother or our sister, we shut out Christ.

What is the basis of your fellowship with other Christians?

O Christ of the stretched-out arms, help me to open my arms and my heart to everyone who names your name. For if I do not fellowship with them, I refuse fellowship to those for whom you died.

Affirmation: When prejudice shuts out my fellow Christian, then penury sits in my soul.

For further reading: Luke 9:49-50

CM 33

"Why Does She Act This Way?"

Beloved, since God loved us so much,
we also ought to love one another.
—1 John 3:14

Sometimes particular people...make us draw in on ourselves. With them we find it difficult to be outgoing and friendly and generous. How do we overcome this inner withdrawal?

Perhaps in two ways. First, by saying to ourselves, "This person is someone for whom Christ died. Christ loves him, Christ lives with her; so must I." Say that over and over to yourself. Second, ask the question, "Why does she act this way? I will have to try to understand her." Then project yourself into that person's situation and see life from that standpoint....

If you find someone who sets up a barrier to fellowship, find out the reason; and if the reason is unreasonable, then dissolve it by your love. If that amount of love doesn't dissolve it, give more love, and still more love.

**Are you willing to try to see life
from someone else's standpoint?**

O Father, you fellowship with me, not because I am worthy of that fellowship but because of who you are. Help me to fellowship with everybody, everywhere, because of what I am—a lover of you.

Affirmation: If God fellowships with me in spite of what I am, I'll fellowship with everybody.

For further reading: 1 John 3:7-21; Matthew 7:11-12

CM 35

Joy, a Mark of Maturity

We are writing these things so that
our joy may be complete.
—1 John 1:4

Joy is a mark of maturity. The sad, morose type of person is immature. For that unhappiness is being caused, almost entirely, through inner conflicts and wrong attitudes toward life. When we get rid of inner conflicts and wrong attitudes toward life, we will almost automatically burst into joy. For we are made for joy—made for it in the inner structure of our beings. And when we are truly ourselves by being truly his, then we are joyous, constitutionally.

Rendell Harris says: "Joy is the strength of the people of God; it is their chief characteristic." Where there is no joy there is no Christianity, and where there is Christianity there is joy. "So there was much joy in that city" of Samaria where "Philip . . . proclaimed to them the Christ" (Acts 8:8, 5 RSV). Christ and joy go together. Where he is, there is joy; and where he is not, there is sadness. The rich young ruler "went away sorrowful" (Matthew 19:22 KJV). Everybody goes away from Christ sorrowfully. For when you go away from Christ you go away from joy. He is joy—a fountain of joy. The Christian way is piety set to music. It is fun!

A fountain of joy—do you have it?

To know you, Jesus, is to know joy, a continuous joy. For as long as you are within, joy is within, and any little thing sets it off.

Affirmation: All my deepest joys will be joys of creative sharing with others. I will begin today.

For further reading: Mark 9:17-22; Galatians 5:22-23

CM 36

296

"Joy Surging"

*"I have said these things to you so that my joy
may be in you, and that your joy may be complete."*
—John 15:11

The wife of a missionary who had suffered much in China
wrote me these lines:

> Holding Your hand I walk the Way,
> You understand all I would say;
> Holding Your hand I need not pray.
>
> Lord, I belong here at Your side,
> Singing Your song, swinging Your stride,
> Joy surging with the strength of a tide.
>
> Beside us each tree shines against the blue,
> No need to see some distant view,
> The future must be here, now, with You.

When you sing Christ's song and swing his stride, then
automatically joy surges with the strength of a tide. You
don't seek happiness—it seeks you. But when you sing
your own song and take your own stride, gloom automatically surges within you.

Joy will keep you going.

O Master, may I be mastered by you, wholly and completely—no pockets of rebellion left. Then I shall know the
joy of being yours and the joy of inward oneness.

Affirmation: I am joyous in his joy, because unified in his unity I am
at one with him, and hence with myself.

For further reading: John 15:1-17; 1 John 3:1

CM 37

306

The Joy of Creative Sharing

*Welcome one another, therefore, just as Christ
has welcomed you. . . . May the God of hope fill
you with all joy and peace in believing.*
— Romans 15:7, 13

Joy comes as a result of inner harmony. When there is no civil war within, when everything is under a single control, Christ; when everything is directed toward a single end, his will—then joy is a natural concomitant. You do not seek it; it is there inherently. And it is there permanently. It does not come and go, for the conditions that produce it are there as a permanent part of us. Those conditions are us. So we don't have joy—we are joy.

In John's epistle the joy is of a particular kind (1 John 1:4). It is the joy of creative sharing. "We are writing these things so that our joy may be complete." It was a joy, not of what happened *to* him, but of what happened *through* him. If our joy is the result of what happens to us—success coming to us, people giving us gifts, being held high in the esteem of others, the market going our way—then our joy is immature and precarious. It is egocentric. And anything, including joy, if it is egocentric is off-center and will not and cannot abide.

Only that joy abides which is a creative joy. It creates joy in others and therefore brings joy to the creator.

**If our joy is creatively outgoing to others
it will always be incoming.**

O God, I want to taste and know your joy—the joy of continuous creation. Make me this day the instrument of your creation.

Affirmation: Perhaps I cannot create in the big, but I can always create in the little acts of creative love.

For further reading: Luke 10:21-22; Romans 12:9-21

CM 38

Joy Seeks Us

*I thank my God every time I remember you,
constantly praying with joy...because of your sharing
in the gospel from the first day until now.*
—Philippians 1:3-5

You can be in the midst of very unfavorable circumstances and be full of joy. Dorothy[2] was. Her husband had married three times. The first wife turned to drink to escape his torments. The second wife turned to sex. And Dorothy, his third wife, turned to God. When she found God, then her husband lost all power to torment her. She slipped out from under his control when she went under God's control....

Her husband didn't know what to do with her. He said to a friend in a baffled way: "Dorothy and her friends are praying for me and I have to act like a hellion or they will get me."...She rose in one of our meetings and said, "I'm the woman who is living in heaven and in hell at the same time." But really there was no hell; it was all heaven—in spite of!

So Joy is not to be sought; it seeks us when we are creative and outgoing. We become incorrigibly happy, for our happiness is not based on happenings.

Do you let circumstances get you down?

O Father God, you are trying to share your joy with my small, joyless heart. Help me to open wide to your creative love. Then I will know the joy of being outgoing and helpful and loving.

Affirmation: My eyes and my heart will be wide open today to seek situations in which I can love.

For further reading: Luke 15:3-7; Philippians 1:12-25

CM 39

---

[2]Not her real name.

Joy Makes Us Immune

As servants of God we have commended ourselves in every way... as sorrowful, yet always rejoicing; as poor, yet making many rich.
—2 Corinthians 6:4, 10

Overflowing joy makes us immune to unconscious slights, to pinpricks, to the daily rubbing of events, to the intentional hurts, to the drabness of things, to disease. And when I use the word *immune*, I mean "immune."...

We have in our Ashram in India a Greek woman who is an expert masseuse, filled with the love of God and people. She massages the patients who have contagious diseases, lepers included, and she is more than immune—she is life-giving. I tell her she gives a massage and a message at the same time. She rubs hope and life and love into withered souls and bodies...without regard to what contagious disease they may have had. She herself is...not only healthy, she is health-giving. She can look at a physical body and tell whether it belongs to God or to egoism....She rubs God and self-surrender into the souls and bodies of people, and does it joyously and without tiring.

Self-surrender is a joyous word!

O Jesus of the joyous heart, I bury my sadness in your joy. I leave my gloom at the foot of the cross. I drink deep of your resurrection victory and I am whole again.

Affirmation: Today I will give my life in joy to the resurrected Christ.

For further reading: 2 Corinthians 4:7-18; 6:4-10; 1 Thessalonians 2:19-20

CM 40

Self-Acceptance

300

We are writing these things that our joy may be complete.
—1 John 1:4

John frankly says he is writing for a dual purpose. First
... to share ... with others (1:3)—this is social. Second,
"that our joy may be complete"... to share this joy with
ourselves—this is personal.

... John, shows a very mature attitude—toward himself.
He didn't try to be overly spiritual and say that he had no
interest in himself, that he was thinking only of others....
Self-acceptance is as necessary as other-acceptance. Those
who ... are always insisting that they don't think about
themselves are unconsciously revealing their self-interest in
talking about their self-denial. You have to accept yourself
and provide for yourself in the scheme of redemption.

The only question is, In what order? Are you first, Jesus
second, and others third? Then that is egotistic immaturity.
But here the order is right: Jesus first, others second, and
you third.... The self is there, but last. Such an attitude
made John a Christ-centric, other-centric, self-centric person, in that order. It made him mature. Reverse the order
and you have immaturity. And you have no joy. J-O-Y—
Jesus first, others second, you third.

**You can safely talk about yourself
after you have talked about Jesus and others.**

O Father, you accept me, so I accept myself. I cannot reject
what you have accepted. I can accept my self and love it,
because I love you more.

Affirmation: I accept and love myself for God accepts me and loves me.

For further reading: 2 Corinthians 2:14-17; Philippians 1:12-19

CM 41

Self-Surrender

301

If we confess our sins, he who is faithful and just will forgive us our sins and cleanse us from all unrighteousness.
—1 John 1:9

Christianity teaches self-surrender, not self-abasement. Self-abasement means self-debasement. The self is the gift of God and was never intended to be debased. It is an insult to the Creator to treat his gifts with contempt. . . .

In teaching self-surrender, Christianity leads us to self-realization. For in losing one's self in surrender, it is found—found a different and enhanced self. It is given back to us—heightened. It is cleansed from a thousand conflicts and contradictions by surrender, and then it is given back again unified. Your self is never so much your own as when it is most God's. Bound to him it is free. Since it is his, it is yours. You can live with God; therefore you can live with yourself. . . .

If you love God supremely, you can love yourself subordinately. Love yourself—and like yourself and enjoy yourself. For it is a self accepted by him and therefore accepted by you. The renounced self becomes, strangely enough, the realized self.

"My power is faint and low
Till I have learned to serve."
("Make Me a Captive, Lord," George Matheson)

Father God, I thank you that you have not given me a self only to cancel it out. But out of gratitude I lovingly yield it back to you. And now it is mine because it is wholly yours.

Affirmation: Myself, not canceled but consecrated, is now free—free to live and serve.

For further reading: 1 John 1:5-9; 3:1-3; 1 Corinthians 4:1-4

CM 53

302 — No Self-Seeking

Even if I am being poured out as a libation over the sacrifice and the offering of your faith, I am glad and rejoice with all of you.
—Philippians 2:17

The Christian demand seems to be a central no to the self. "I am crucified," says Paul (Galatians 2:20 KJV). The essential self is crucified. . . . But note he added two words: "I am crucified with Christ." Those two words make all the difference. If you make yourself the center of yourself, if you seek your own, if you look after Number One, as society bids you to do, if you are, in short, a self-centered person, then do you escape crucifixion? Not at all. You run straight into it. You will be crucified upon the cross of your own frustrations, conflicts, and unhappiness. All self-centered persons are unhappy and frustrated, even though outwardly successful. Why? Because they have made themselves God. And the commandment is: "You shall have no other gods before me" (Exodus 20:3). A person breaks that commandment and is broken by it—inwardly.

The Christian answer is in the two words "with Christ." How was Christ crucified? Deliberately and by his own choice. "I lay down my life" (John 10:15). The Divine Love loved us enough to die for us. Lost his life—and found it!

Living—and dying—with Christ will save my life.

O Christ, thank you for showing us the way of self-giving love—love that gives its all and then finds its all. I give my life to you.

Affirmation: Jesus Christ owns my life.

For further reading: 1 John 3:16-22; 4:7-21

CM 267

Maturity in Love

The commandment we have from him is this: those who love God must love their brothers and sisters also.
—1 John 4:21

To see whether our love is mature love...put "I" in the place of "love" ("charity" KJV) in a portion of Paul's description of love (1 Corinthians 13:4-7): "I am patient; I am kind; I am not envious or boastful or arrogant or rude. I do not insist on my own way; I am not irritable or resentful; I do not rejoice in wrongdoing, but rejoice in the truth. I bear all things, believe all things, hope all things, endure all things."

How do I come out? Am "I" and "love" identical? Our growth in maturity is a growth in that very identification.

And the love must be "love in shoes." Love must be first, last, and always my method. . . . Love that is not expressed is not love.

Only to the extent that we love do we live.

Dear Lord and Father, you have made me for yourself and since you are love, you have made me for love. When I give myself to loving everybody, then I find myself in that love.

Affirmation: Today I will give out love and only love, with God's help.

For further reading: 1 John 4:7-21; 5:1-5; 1 Corinthians 13

CM 338, 339

The Pattern of Maturity

> *Beloved, we are God's children now; what we will be has not yet been revealed. What we do know is this: when he is revealed we will be like him, for we will see him as he is.*
> —1 John 3:2

How do we change and become mature?

First, we must get straight, and get it straight once and for all, the pattern of our maturity: "into [Christ's] likeness." . . . Until we get the pattern fixed we are at the mercy of every suggestion.

The two greatest interpreters of the Christian Way, and the two best illustrations of it, were Paul and John, and they both agree on the goal. John says that "we will be like him"—nothing less than and nothing other than *that*. Paul's goal coincides. We "are being changed into his likeness" (2 Corinthians 3:18 RSV). We are certain now as to where we are to head—into his likeness. Is there anything higher, or better, in heaven or on earth, than to be changed into Christ's likeness? I have scanned the horizons of the earth and the horizons of thought . . . for over half a century to see if there is any other comparable pattern. It's a life conclusion: there is none.

**There are no alternatives in maturity—
it is maturity according to Christ.**

O Jesus, Master, you are our standard. Every time I think your thoughts, feel your feelings, do your will, I am in tune with you, with God, with myself.

Affirmation: "Into his likeness"—that is my destiny and that shall be my direction.

For further reading: Hebrews 8:5-7; 12:1-3; 2 Corinthians 3:17-18; 4:1-11

CM 345, 344

Adjusted to the Highest

For those whom he foreknew he also predestined to be
conformed to the image of his Son, in order that he
might be the firstborn within a large family.
—Romans 8:29

The first step in maturity is to get the pattern clear. To take the pattern of society in which one lives as the standard and adjust to that . . . is to adjust to maladjustment . . . to immaturity. . . .

We are to be adjusted to nothing this side of the highest—the Highest in heaven and earth—Jesus Christ. In Christianity sin is *hamartia* (literally, "missing the mark"). Applied, it means that sin is missing the mark—Jesus Christ. All departure from his mind and spirit is sin. That is not a legal definition of sin but a life definition. It is an unfolding Standard and therefore never outgrown. Our code is a Character. That is fixed and yet unfolding—fixed in history and yet unfolding as the Spirit unfolds him more and more.

Do you think this kind of maturity is possible
for the ordinary person?

O blessed Jesus, what an amazing possibility that the latchstring is low enough for all of us—even for me—to reach, so that I can accept your offer to be made into your likeness and image.

Affirmation: That word *all* takes me in just as blessedly as the *whoever* of John 3:16.

For further reading: Colossians 1:15-29

CM 346

Maturity Open
to All of Us

*All of us, with unveiled faces, seeing the glory of the
Lord as though reflected in a mirror, are being transformed into the same image from one degree of glory to
another; for this comes from the Lord, the Spirit.*
—2 Corinthians 3:18

The second step: *This pattern of maturity as in Christ's likeness is open to all—open to a person as a person, and the ordinary person especially.* The passage says, "All of us...are
being transformed."...In his "all" Paul included the
Corinthians to whom he was writing:

> Fornicators, idolaters, adulterers, male prostitutes,
> sodomites, thieves, the greedy, drunkards, revilers,
> robbers—none of these will inherit the kingdom of
> God. And this is what some of you used to be. But
> you were washed, you were sanctified, you were jus-
> tified in the name of the Lord Jesus Christ and in the
> Spirit of our God. (1 Corinthians 6:9-11)

To these people he says, "All of us...are being transformed." This open-to-all possibility regarding maturity is
the most breath-taking and nerve-tingling fact about
Christianity. It doesn't ask anything about origins, only
about destinations: "Where do you want to go?"

**Maturity is open to all.
Will you aim for it?**

O my Lord, thank you that wherever human nature opens
its depths to your healing grace, there the miracle of
change takes place. Help me to open everything in my life
to your healing as I aim for maturity.

Affirmation: Wherever Jesus Christ is, anything can happen—and he
is with me.

For further reading: Psalm 40:1-3; Colossians 3:5-14

CM 346, 347

Beholding the Glory of the Lord

And we all... beholding the glory of the Lord,
are being changed into his likeness.
—2 Corinthians 3:18 RSV

The third step: *You are made into the image of that on which you habitually concentrate your attention—"beholding the glory of the Lord."* If you concentrate your attention on the faults of people around you, you become a faulty person. If you look with the eyes of creation upon people, you become a creative person. If you look at yourself, you will become a self-conscious person....

The process of Christian maturity is the process of the redemption of the imagination—redeeming it from self-concentration, sex concentration, herd concentration, money concentration, past-failure concentration, sin concentration—and concentrating it on "the Lord." You become Christ-conscious instead of self-conscious; you become future-conscious instead of past-conscious; you become creative-conscious, since your attention is concentrated on the Creator and the Re-Creator. The imagination is redeemed, and with it the whole person....

The person who gazes and keeps on gazing at Jesus becomes like him in appearance.

"Turn your eyes upon Jesus,
Look full in his wonderful face."
("Turn Your Eyes Upon Jesus," Helen Howarth Lemmel)[3]

O Jesus, my Lord, when I look at myself I feel collapsed and inadequate, but when I look at you and your glory, I feel that anything is possible. Help me to look long and longingly.

Affirmation: If I look at Jesus I shall see his glory.

For further reading: John 1:14-16; Colossians 1:15-19: 3:1-4

CM 351, 352

308 — With Unveiled Face

Scripture

*We all, with unveiled face, beholding the glory of the
Lord, are being changed into his likeness.*
—2 Corinthians 3:18 RSV

Jesus is now the glorified Lord, and when we plug in to
him we plug into glory. But if we are to see that glory in
the face of Jesus Christ, we have to take the next step: *We
must look at him "with unveiled face."* . . .

[That] means that we must be completely honest with
God, with ourselves, with others, with life. We must come
clear—absolutely clear. We must have unveiled faces—no
masks, no putting on of fronts, no make-believe. . . .

What are some of the veils? . . .

(1) Acceptance of responsibility for what we are. . . .

(2) . . . Let down the veils of fear, of resentments, of pride,
of envy and jealousy, of self-centeredness, of bad temper, of
inferiority, of guilts—and anything else not included in this
list of which you may be conscious—or unconscious. . . .

(3) Let down the last veil—doubt of acceptance. It is not
enough to give up; you must take. Faith is the leap in the
dark . . . that will land you in his arms. . . . You will see with
cleared vision the most beautiful sight this world holds—
the sight of his reconciled face.

Never doubt the love of Christ.

O Christ, my Lord, your face is the object of my life quest.
I see it, not through my goodness, but through your grace.
I've only taken down the veils—you are always there. It is
I who have been away.

Affirmation: As I look at Christ and his glory, I am being changed into
his likeness.

For further reading: Psalm 32:5-61; John 3:2-3

CM 353, 354, 355

The Way of Grace and Discipline

The Gospel Starts with Grace

Therefore, since we are justified by faith, we have peace with God through our Lord Jesus Christ, through whom we have obtained access to this grace in which we stand.
—Romans 5:1-2

The gospel starts with God's redeeming love, with grace. It is God's initiative that redeems us. . . . In other religions we have man's search for God, in the gospel we have God's search for man. "We love him because he first loved us" (1 John 4:19 KJV).

Francis Thompson's poem "The Hound of Heaven" depicts the love of God pursuing us down the years. . . . We do not find God, we put ourselves in the way of being found by God.

But the first thing is grace. "The gospel is not good advice but good news." It is not primarily a teaching us how to live but an offer of Life. Jesus did not come to show us the Way, but to show himself as the Way.

God is always the initiator.

O Christ, I bow my head and heart in deepest gratitude for your initiative in seeking me, for your grace that gently presses upon me, awaiting the dropping of barriers. I will respond.

Affirmation: "The grace of God has appeared" (Titus 2:11 Moffatt). My eyes are open to see it.

For further reading: Romans 5:1-11; Ephesians 2:4-10   TW 208

Grace or Law?

You are not under law but under grace.
—Galatians 6:14

We can live by grace or we can live by law. Peter speaks of "the grace of Life" (1 Peter 3:7 Moffatt). If you will not take the grace of Life, then you must take the law of life. You can live by the grace of Life—you surrender to and are ruled by the processes of Love. You are receptive to this invading Grace. You do not struggle and try, but surrender and trust and obey. Your little life is caught up into the purposes of Life, you are redeemed by Life, replenished by Life. Faith is a yieldingness to Love.

But if you do not live by the grace of Life, then you live by the law of life. . . . You reap what you sow. You get back from life what you give to life . . . a very strict bargain. You have to watch each deed, for you know you will get back an exact equivalent. Life therefore works on a strictly "cash and carry" basis—you lay down the cash of your deed and carry away the result of the consequences of that deed. There are no surprises in life, no going beyond on either side. It is all very just and all very dependable, and all very dead.

There are no surprises in living by the law.

O Christ, I want to live by the grace of Life, instead of the law of life. I want the gaiety of a life fully surrendered to Love.

Affirmation: "Never think, 'I will treat him as he treated me. I will pay back the man for what he did' " (Proverbs 24:29 Moffatt). God thinks grace—so shall I.

For further reading: Romans 5:12-21

TW 209

Bargaining or Loving?

The free gift is not like the trespass. For if the many died through the one man's trespass, much more surely have the grace of God and the free gift in the grace of the one man, Jesus Christ, abounded for the many.
—Romans 5:15

[This] is the gospel of the marketplace religion. You bargain with life and life bargains with you and holds you to the bond. There is no Good News in it, for life is grim-faced and so are you. Religion based on give and take has no spontaneity in it, no bubbling joy, no freedom. It plods—it cannot soar. It sighs—it cannot sing. It is the religion of the elder brother [who complained to his father]: "You have never given me even a young goat so that I might celebrate with my friends" (Luke 15:29). How could he? The elder brother was living by legalism, so when the scene closes he was on the outside, living by the law, and the younger brother was on the inside, living by Love.

In a home, if life were lived by the law of each insisting on getting what he or she gives, what a deadly, dull house—I cannot call it a home—it would be. In a real home, love reigns, You go beyond law, and spontaneously express love in a thousand beautiful little ways, never thinking of anything in return.

Love does not demand.

O God of grace, you shower me with your love in a thousand ways. Help me not only to recognize your gifts of love but also to be your loving child, expressing love without demanding anything in return.

Affirmation: Because God loves me, I love.

For further reading: Romans 5:18-21; 8:1-4; Matthew 5:43-48

TW 209

The Discipline of Grace

For the grace of God has appeared, bringing salvation to all, training us to renounce impiety and worldly passions, and . . . to live lives that are self-controlled, upright, and godly.
—*Titus 2:11-12*

This grace of Life is the most exacting discipline. It disciplines you far more deeply than any law could discipline you. When you keep a law, it's kept—kept in the outer conformities. But when you keep a love, it's not kept by outer conformities—it's kept only in the inner conformities. Love is ten times as exacting as law. When you fulfill a law you are off duty, but you are never off duty from love. It's got you every moment, impelling you to go beyond.

"The grace of God . . . schools us to renounce . . . and to live a life of self-mastery" (Titus 2:12 Moffatt). . . . Here free grace puts us to school! And the severest of schools. It disciplines the inmost thought and the outmost act and everything between. You accept the grace of God and by that very act you accept self-control, rather self-control through God control. You are free to act within his control. His control is perfect freedom.

In the grace of Life
the law becomes your runway
from which you take off
to soar in the heaven of freedom.

O Christ, I want to grow in the grace of surrendering to Grace, in the love of surrendering to Love. For your will is my deepest will, and when I do your will, I do my own.

Affirmation: Today I shall walk in "the perfect law of liberty" (James 1:25).

For further reading: Romans 6:1-11; James 1:22-25; Titus 2:11-14

TW 210

Grace and Reality

*This grace was given to us in Christ Jesus before
the ages began, but it has now been revealed
through the appearing of our Savior Christ Jesus.*
—2 Timothy 1:9-10

Is grace something imposed by religion on life, or is it inherent in life itself? . . .

The gospel says that grace is rooted in reality: "We have seen his glory . . . seen it to be full of grace and reality. . . . Grace and reality are ours through Jesus Christ (John 1:14, 17 Moffatt). Here grace and reality are connected.

Is grace part and parcel of the make-up of reality? It is. . . . Jesus "brought life and immortality to light through the gospel" (2 Timothy 1:10). Life and immortality were inherent in the nature of reality, but they were "brought to light," lifted out of the nature of things, made overt where they were covert. He brought them to light in his own person. He brought grace to light again in his own person. . . . This grace was "given ages ago" (v. 10 Moffatt). It was written into the structure of reality but has now been revealed in the appearance of our Lord Jesus Christ.

**The most beautiful revelation of reality
is grace.**

O Christ, your power over me is the power of grace, the power of love. I'm glad to be conquered by love.

Affirmation: Today God's grace toward me will make me gracious toward others.

For further reading: Ephesians 2:1-8; Romans 6:12-19

TW 211

The Cross Inherent

3/4

God...chose us in [Christ] before the foundation of the world,...having predestined us to adoption as sons by Jesus Christ....In Him we have redemption through His blood.
—Ephesians 1:3-7 NKJV

If grace and reality are connected inherently, what does "the Lamb slain from the foundation of the world" mean (Revelation 13:8 KJV)? Is the cross built into the structure of things...?

If the cross were suddenly imposed on history at a given point, something extraneous, then it would lack a cosmic validity. But if the cross is the scarlet thread that runs through the whole garment of existence, then it would have inescapable meanings. "The Lamb slain from the foundation of the world" points to the cross as inherent.

"The cross is the ground plan of the universe." If so, we would expect to see intimations of that ground plan everywhere. We do....The seed dies that the plant may live. The mountains are barren that the valleys may be rich. The white corpuscles circulate through the blood stream watching for infection. When they find it, they absorb it if possible; but when they cannot, they fling themselves upon the intruder and die that the rest may live.

The cross is in our blood.

O Lamb slain from the foundation of the world, we see you everywhere. You suffer with our sufferings. Eternally you take upon your heart our sins and sufferings. You died that I might live.

Affirmation: I will live for Christ today.

For further reading: Hebrews 9:23-28; 10:15-25; Romans 5:6-11

TW 212

3/5 Grace Did Much More Abound

Where sin abounded, grace did much more abound.
—*Romans 5:20 KJV*

The cross is inherent, lifted up in history that we might see in a point of time something that is timeless. If a spotlight from Mars were to be pointed at the most important place on our planet it would fall upon a hill called Calvary. But there are lesser calvaries everywhere. Everywhere Christ is hungry in the hunger of the hungry, sinful in the sin of the sinner, he takes it all on himself.

That means that grace is everywhere, healing, redeeming, saving. "Where sin abounded, grace did much more abound." Where disease abounds the grace of health much more abounds. "The grace of . . . Jesus Christ overflowed far more richly" (Romans 5:15 Moffatt). The grace was unrestrained, it overflowed. Or as Paul puts it again, "The grace of our Lord flooded my life" (1 Timothy 1:14 Moffatt).

A little girl, a refugee from bombed England, wistfully asked her American hostess, when a full glass of milk was placed before her, "How deep may I drink?" She wasn't sure it was *all* for her. How deep may we drink of grace? Is it *all* for us? It is! "Take what you want," says God, "and pay for it." And the paying? it is not our goodness but our gratitude. Not our worthiness but our willingness.

Grace abounding, flooding, overflowing!

O Christ, I open my heart to your grace that seeks, searches, saves. Fill every fiber of my being so that I too may abound and overflow.

Affirmation: Grace sought me, grace bought me, grace taught me, grace caught me—now grace has me.

For further reading: Romans 5

TW 213

Grace Everywhere,
to Everybody

Therefore just as one man's trespass led to condemnation for all, so one man's act of righteousness leads to justification and life for all.
—Romans 5:18

The Christian Way is not the way of karma, but the way of grace. And yet there is a truth in karma. The fact is that grace is in karma too. Karma says that you reap what you sow. This is true, but only partly true, for other people reap what we sow. Bound up in a bundle of human relationships, we pass on to others the good and evil results of our sowing. The good results? yes!

So Jesus, standing at the center of existence, passes on to all of us his good karma—his deed of the cross lets grace overflow to everybody. The fact that others reap what we sow opens the way to the vicarious. So "the Lamb [was] slain from the foundation of the world." He is everywhere. . . . I see his cross in every telegraph pole with its cross beam. And the message of grace is coming over every wire to us. . . .

Grace is written in the Scriptures, but also in the texture of reality. It is written everywhere, in everything.

> **"Grace is flowing from Calvary, . . .**
> **Grace enough for me."**
> **(E. O. Excell[1])**

O Christ, I accept your grace in place of my striving. Your grace is sufficient for me in every part of my life. I am grateful—so grateful.

Affirmation: I am not under law but under grace (Romans 6:14).

For further reading: Romans 6:15-23; 8:1-4; 2 Corinthians 12:7-9

TW 213

---

[1]"Grace, Enough for Me," E. O. Excell, copyright 1933, renewal, Hope Publishing Co.

Grace Makes Us
Reign in Life

Where sin increased, grace abounded all the more, so that just as sin exercised dominion in death, so grace might also exercise dominion through justification leading to eternal life through Jesus Christ our Lord.
—*Romans 5:20-21*

There is a fear...that this emphasis on grace weakens one....But this notion is deeply mistaken. Paul puts it this way: "Much more shall those who receive the overflowing grace and free gift of righteousness reign in life...through Jesus Christ" (Romans 5:17 Moffatt). Those who receive this grace "reign in life"—"exercise dominion" (NRSV). They reign not only in this little marginal victory or that sideline accomplishment, but they reign *in life*. Life centrally and fundamentally is under their control. They know how to live, life is theirs. Just as airplane pilots reign over the sky because they obey the laws of flying, so Christians reign over life because they obey the laws of life.

Grace binds you with far stronger cords than the cords of duty or obligation can bind you. Grace is free, but when once you take it you are bound forever to the Giver, and bound to catch the spirit of the Giver. Like produces like. Grace makes you gracious, the Giver makes you give.

In Christ, we are more than conquerors.
(Romans 8:37)

O Christ, thank you that you come to me not as teacher first of all, but with grace, grace for my sins, for my weakness, for my ignorance—for everything. I accept your grace.

Affirmation: Where sin has abounded in me, grace now much more abounds. I live by that "much more."

For further reading: Romans 8:28-39; 2 Timothy 2:1

TW 214

327

Grace Is the Key

*Grow in the grace and knowledge of
our Lord and Savior Jesus Christ.*
—2 Peter 3:18

Grace strengths you. "Be strong in the grace of Christ
Jesus" (2 Timothy 2:1 Moffatt). The grace of Christ Jesus
produces strength, strength of character and strength of
love....Karma weakens you, makes you legalistic, bar-
gaining. It produces the Pharisee and the proud Brahman.
Both are discredited—life can't use them....Those who
are swayed by grace do ten times as much as those who
are swayed by karma. They have no limitations and no
inhibitions. Their grace overflows to everybody.

Grace is not only the key to strength, it is the key to knowledge. We are to "grow in the grace and knowledge
of...Christ." Grace is first, and knowledge is second. You
don't know unless you know grace. Knowledge without grace
is ignorance—you haven't the key to unlock the mysteries of
the kingdom. But when you start with grace, then everything
is open to you. Life is one glad, glorious, opening surprise.

**Growing in grace means
that there is always more grace available.**

O God of all grace, you have called me to your eternal glory
in Christ, and you promise to restore, support and strengthen
me. Continue to teach me and to help me grow.

Affirmation: Grace and peace is mine in abundance from the God of
all grace (2 Peter 1:2).

For further reading: 2 Peter 1:1-11; 1 Peter 5:10

TW 214

A Disciplined Life

*You were bought with a price;
therefore glorify God in your body.*
—1 Corinthians 6:20

The acceptance of grace is a privilege, a blessed privilege, provided it is permeated with discipline.... Very often "free grace" has been preached in such a way that it has weakened character. Paul warns against this in these words, "Do not make your freedom an opening for the flesh" (Galatians 5:13 Moffatt). Here liberty had become license....

We must learn to be disciplined persons. While the Way is the way of [grace and] dependence, drawing strength from Another, nevertheless to do that we must be disciplined.... Dependence plus discipline equals dependable disciples. This combination was shown in this incident in which God apparently showed a sense of humor. A woman writes that she had been healed . . . of paralysis in the legs and arthritis when she surrendered it all to God. Then she said: "Now Lord, you've healed me, what are you going to do about my overweight?" The answer: "This kind goeth not out save by fasting" (see Matthew 17:21 KJV). Where only dependence could heal, that was the answer. Where only discipline could heal, that was the answer.

The Christian life is the balanced life.

O disciplined Christ, so disciplined and yet so free, teach me your secret. For only as I am disciplined can I dance the dance of freedom.

Affirmation: "Happy are they who follow his injunctions, giving him undivided hearts" (Psalm 119:2 Moffatt).

For further reading: 1 Corinthians 6:12-20; Galatians 5:13-25

TW 236

320 — The Way of Discipline

Athletes exercise self-control in all things; they do it to receive a perishable wreath, but we an imperishable one.
—1 Corinthians 9:25

The Christian Way is the way of discipline. Yesterday I saw a beautiful elm tree which had been blown over in a storm because some of the roots had strangled the tree. They had twined themselves around the base of the tree underground, so that the very things which were intended to sustain the tree had strangled it.

Our natural urges are given to sustain us, but if they get out of place they can strangle us. Sex dedicated is sustaining. But sex out of place, an end in itself, coils about the rest of life and strangles it. Self dedicated is sustaining, but if the self becomes the center of life it can strangle the personality. The trouble with the roots of that fallen tree was that, instead of reaching out beyond themselves, they turned back on themselves and the trunk. They were not disciplined to their original purpose. The natural became the unnatural. . . .

I glanced up from my writing on a train and saw on a lever these words: "Lift up to release." We have to lift up to release. If we think we can turn our powers to lower purposes and be free, we are mistaken.

You have to lift up to release.

O Christ, help me to lift up my powers to your purposes and plans; then I shall be released and free.

Affirmation: "I am the Eternal . . . training you for your good" (Isaiah 48:17 Moffatt).

For further reading: 1 Corinthians 6:12-20; 9:24-27

TW 237

Disciplined to the Highest

321

I urge you ... to ... instruct certain people not to teach any different doctrine, and not to occupy themselves with myths ... rather than the divine training that is known by faith.
—1 Timothy 1:3-4

The Christian way is a discipline and not merely a doctrine. The doctrine gives direction and content to the discipline. Doctrine that does not discipline is dead. Christianity is therefore not merely something that you believe, but something that you believe in enough to act upon. Your deed is your creed—the thing you believe in enough to put into practice. You do not believe in what you do not practice. Theory and practice are one. Your theory is your practice.

The future of the world is in the hands of disciplined people ... who are disciplined to the highest. ... The Christian is disciplined to what? ... "The divine order which belongs to faith" (1 Timothy 1:4 Moffatt). The divine order is ... the kingdom of God ... embodied in the divine Person—Jesus Christ. We are, therefore, disciplined by a Person who embodies an order, an embodiment which makes our discipline at once personal and at once social.

**We can give ourselves without question
to the Christian discipline!**

O God, help me to be disciplined to this Way with no reservations and with no hesitations.

Affirmation: I take the yoke of Christ's kingdom, for his yoke is easy and his burden is light (Matthew 11:30).

For further reading: 2 Timothy 1:6-10; 2:1-5; 4:2, 5

AL 344

Discipline
and Freedom

The Christian discipline is the highest discipline because it is disciplined to the highest—the divine order embodied in the divine Person. This discipline is complete and totalitarian, reaching in to control and redeem the inmost thought and aspiration, and stretching out to the utmost rim of relationships. Then does it produce the robot, the marionette dancing to the invisible strings of the divine Master...? No! The exact opposite is true. For when you fulfill this will, you fulfill yourself.... "The aim of the Christian discipline is the love that springs" (1 Timothy 1:5 Moffatt)—it produces spontaneity—it "springs."

Here is what the totalitarians are aiming to achieve and cannot. They cannot produce a love that springs. Their methods produce a hate that springs. They have to sit on a lid. God takes off the lid. "Love God, and do what you like." You are perfectly free, for you are free to do what you ought.

**The disciplined person is attuned to life—
to the highest in Christ.**

God and Father, I surrender my lesser, uncontrolled loves of self in order to find a disciplined love in you. Gather up my discords into your harmony, so that I may be truly free.

Affirmation: Loving God and disciplined by Christ's kingdom, I am harmonizing with my true nature.

For further reading: John 4:13-14; 7:37-39; 2 Corinthians 2:1-4

AL 345

Discipline Produces
Spontaneity

*The aim of the Christian discipline is
the love that springs from a pure heart,
from a good conscience, and from a sincere faith.*
—1 Timothy 1:5 Moffatt

"The aim of the Christian discipline is the love that springs from a pure heart." Strange that the end of discipline is defined as spontaneity—"love that springs." And that is the end of discipline, to make you free.

There is a false idea of freedom prevalent in modern civilization: "You are free to do as you *like*." The Christian answer is, "You are free to do as you *ought*."... Liberty comes through obedience to law....

Love can "spring," be spontaneous and free, only if it comes a pure heart, a good conscience, a sincere faith. On other words, from a disciplined life. Any supposed freedom that leaves you with an impure heart, a bad conscience, and an insincere faith ends not in springing and singing, but in sighing and dying.

**The Christian discipline produces
the most truly spontaneous and natural person in the world.**

O Christ, teach me your way, the way of discipline, for I would sing. When I take my way, I end in a mess. When I take your way, I end with joy and spontaneity.

Affirmation: "Spurn not the Eternal's schooling" (Proverbs 3:11 Moffatt).

For further reading: 1 Corinthians 9:24-27; 2 Timothy 1:7

TW 238, AL 345

Discipline
Produces Courage

Rekindle the divine gift...for God has not given us a timid spirit but a spirit of power and love and discipline.
—2 Timothy 1:6-7 Moffatt

The aim of discipline is to produce discipline...to hide it away into habit, into the subconscious, so that the disciplined person appears to be and is spontaneous....The first result of that discipline is courage, not a timid spirit. Disciplined people have a sense of courage. They are afraid of nothing, for they know that the sum total of reality is behind them. They have a sense of power for they know they are working with God....

If I had one gift to give myself and others, I would unhesitatingly give courage. For more people grow dim and need rekindling of the divine gift through lack of courage than through any other thing. First of all, the courage to take from God what he offers...to pay the price and take the gift. That takes courage, for it shifts the whole basis of life from self-sufficiency to God-sufficiency. Then the next step: the courage to face up to the world with this appropriate gift of God and to believe that this and this alone will meet every need—and to say so, when others are apathetically trying unworkable ways.

Many of us lose our souls for lack of courage.

O God, my Father, give me the even courage of Jesus, who went quietly on, unruffled and unafraid, even though the end of that road meant his death. Success and failure are in your hands.

Affirmation: I do not have to succeed—only to be true to the highest I know.

For further reading: Joshua 1:5-9; Acts 4:13, 29

TW 238, 243, AL 350

Discipline
Produces Liberty

Thy statutes are my songs, as I wander through the world.
—Psalm 119:54 Moffatt

Discipline . . . is discovering the laws of our being and finding that they are the laws of God. . . . Statutes become songs! Laws become a liberty—to sing! The idea of the disciplined person as a disagreeable person is false. The disciplined person is full of rhythm and song—attuned to life.

It is true that Jesus said, "Everyone has to be consecrated by the fire of the discipline" (Mark 9:49 Moffatt), but this "fire of the discipline" only burns away the fetters. When the three Hebrew children fell bound into the fiery furnace, the fire did nothing to them except to burn their bonds. They walked around free in the fire. And form of the Fourth was with them. The fire of discipline does nothing to you except to burn every clinging fetter and make you walk free with the Fourth. You are consecrated by the fire of discipline.

Someone has said, "Beauty is the purgation of superfluities." Discipline takes away superfluities, confines us to the essentials, and makes life beautiful, for nothing clutters up the picture.

Discipline is development in harmony.

O Christ, I know I will surrender myself to the discipline of something—the discipline of the pressures around me or the discipline of your will and purposes. If I do the first I will pass away; if I do the second I will remain forever. Help me.

Affirmation: "Happy is he who has thy discipline and thine instruction, training him calmly to wait on, in adversity" (Psalm 94:12-13 Moffatt).

For further reading: Psalm 119:73-80, 97-104; Romans 8:1-2, 5-6

TW 239

Discipline Begins at the Center

The one who doubts is like a wave of the sea,
driven and tossed by the wind ... being
double-minded and unstable in every way.
—James 1:6-8

We must take these steps in becoming a disciplined person.

1. Let discipline begin at the center, not at the margin. The center is you. You must be undivided in affection. It was said [of King Asa that his] "mind was undivided all his life" (2 Chronicles 15:17 Moffatt). That is at the basis of all successful, effective character.... "Purify your hearts, you double-minded" (James 4:8). "Keep, then, an undivided mind for the Eternal our God, to live by his rules and to obey his orders" (1 Kings 8:61 Moffatt).

One of the greatest tragedies of history is this: "When [Solomon] grew old, he had no undivided mind for the Eternal his God.... His wives seduced him to follow foreign gods" (1 Kings 11:4 Moffatt). Solomon was a wise man turned foolish because of a lack of inner discipline— discipline at the place of his affections.... "Keep your heart with all vigilance, \ for from it flow the springs of life" (Proverbs 4:23). Solomon must have said that with a wistful sigh, for it was the very thing he did not do.

"Guard above all things,
guard your inner self."
(Proverbs 4:23 Moffatt)

O Christ, you are relentless in seeking me for you cannot be satisfied with my marginal allegiances. I give you now my inner self.

Affirmation: "The Eternal's law is in his heart, his footsteps never falter" (Psalm 37:31 Moffatt).

For further reading: 2 Timothy 1:6-7; 2:1-4; Psalm 119:33-40

TW 240

Discipline
and Surrender

Give me understanding, that I may keep your law
and observe it with my whole heart.
—*Psalm 119:34*

Many people accept grace and rise to a new life, and then it leaks out because of a lack of discipline. A brother prayed very often, "Fill me, Lord." A man nearby was overheard to say, "You can't Lord. He leaks." Many of us are not "filled," because if we were we would leak out. God isn't going to pour the water of his grace down the ratholes of undisciplined living. . . .

[We must] discipline the inner self by a complete self-surrender to God. Don't give up this thing, that thing. Give up the self and that carries everything else with it. God has *you*—and that means all you've *got*. I know of a man who is a marginally surrendered person. He is centrally unsurrendered, the self sticks out through all he does for God. A very discerning friend commented, "He came near being a great man." He surrendered the marginal, kept back the central.

Where might you be leaking?

O God, I fling away every doubt and fear and hesitation and surrender my whole self—mind and heart, body and soul—to you. I surrender my lesser, uncontrolled loves of self in order to find a disciplined love to you. Make me your disciplined person.

Affirmation: In God's love I shall walk the earth a conqueror, wanting nothing but God.

For further reading: 2 Corinthians 2:14-16; 5:14-21; Psalm 119:97-120

TW 240, AL 345

328 — Discipline Your Habits

Shun youthful passions and pursue righteousness, faith, love, and peace.
—2 Timothy 2:22

2. Discipline your habits. Having surrendered the center, you may now deal with the margin. Go over your life and see if there is anything that is incompatible with that fundamental surrender of the self. Someone has defined a preacher as "one who preaches a whole gospel and wholly lives it. ". . .

Perhaps the habit may be . . . a sex habit that saps the lifeblood from the central purposes of life; or a habit of taking the line of least resistance instead of standing up for your principles; or a habit of evading responsibility, excusing yourself when opportunities are presented; or a habit of negativism, of always raising objections to positive plans; or a habit of criticism and faultfinding; . . . or a habit of comparing yourself with others instead of with the will of God. Discipline all these.

"Vanished the ripe fruit of thy soul's desire!"
(Revelation 18:14 Moffatt)

O Christ, you are making me a disciplined person and I am glad. I feel that these barnacles which have accumulated through the years and have slowed down the progress of my ship are being sloughed off. I'm getting ready for action. Thank you.

Affirmation: "Happy are they who hold to what is right, who do their duty at all times!" (Psalm 106:3 Moffatt).

For further reading: 2 Timothy 2:20-26; Psalm 119:1-16

TW 241, AL 346

Replace the Old by the New

The good person brings good things out of a good treasure, and the evil person brings evil things out of an evil treasure.
—Matthew 12:35

Someone said to the exuberant nineteenth-century evangelist Billy Bray, who was always praising the Lord, "Isn't it possible to get into the habit of praising the Lord?"

"Yes," replied Billy, "and it's a very good habit, and so few have it."

You can build up a set of good habits so that you habitually take the Christian way without thought. Every act repeated drops into the subconscious mind and becomes an attitude that easily repeats itself. Jesus says, "The good man brings good out of his good store" (Matthew 12:35 Moffatt). The good... store is the sum total of accumulated good habits which have passed into attitude and character. No good action, therefore is lost. Even though it seems to have no effect on the other person, it does something to you, becomes a part of your good store.

Every good action becomes a part of inevitable goodness.

O Christ, teach me to watch day by day the little things that make me the person I am. I want to be a truly disciplined person, to be good inevitably.

Affirmation: "I know that his orders mean eternal life" (John 12:50 Moffatt).

For further reading: Matthew 12:33-37; Psalm 119:25-48; 2 Timothy 2:15

TW 242

Discipline
Your Courage

Knowing that trouble produces endurance,
endurance produces character, and character
produces hope—a hope which never disappoints us.
—Romans 5:3-5 Moffatt

Salvation is by grace through faith—salvation is by Christ. It is a gift. But if it is a gift, it is also a growth, a growth in character. And character is developed through discipline.

That leads us to this step:

3. *Discipline your courage.* Every time you refuse to face up to life and its problems you weaken your character. Character needs courage to make it real character. If we have no courage, we are what Nietzsche called "moral cows in our plump comfortableness." Present-day civilization is suffering from a lack of moral courage. . . . We are in the process of being standardized morally—and at a very low level. "Everybody does it," is the new moral code. . . .

Many of us lose our souls for lack of courage. . . . Paul speaks of four steps in development [in Romans 5:3-5]. (1) Trouble leads to (2) endurance; endurance to (3) character; and character to (4) hope. Character is formed out of endurance which is formed out of trouble, and character brings forth hope—the only hope that will never let us down.

If you are on the Way
you must get used to the sight of your own blood.

O Christ, I see that the trouble that comes from courage is strengthening my fiber, giving me hope. Give me your gentle courage that will be disciplined to face life bravely and cheerfully.

Affirmation: "The Eternal is my light and aid; whom shall I fear?" (Psalm 27:1 Moffatt).

For further reading: Philippians 2:12-13; Romans 5:1-5; 1 Peter 3:13-17

TW 243

Discipline
Your Beginnings

"It is better for you to enter the kingdom of God with one eye than to have two eyes and to be thrown into hell."
—Mark 9:47-48

4. *Discipline your beginnings.* When Jesus spoke of the fire of discipline, he did so after mentioning three possible hindrances—hand, foot, eye. If any of these offends, that is, cuts across the purposes of your life, cut it off or pluck it out....

The hand is the thing that takes hold, the thing that grasps what we want. Don't take hold of a thing unless you want that thing to take hold of you. For your possessions often end in possessing you. Be careful of what you grasp....

The foot approaches the thing desired. Don't walk toward a thing unless you are willing to take hold of the thing and have the thing take hold of you. Discipline your approaches to life.... You destine yourself to the deed when you decide to approach it.

The eye looks at the thing which you may approach and then may grasp and possess. Watch what you see. You first see, then seek. For seeing creates desire and desire creates emotion, and in the battle between the emotion and the will the emotion nearly always wins.... In temptation flight is better than fight.

**Discipline the beginnings
and the ends will take care of themselves.**

O Christ, help me to discipline my beginnings, to look at life through your eyes, to see and to seek what you see and seek, to follow you wholeheartedly.

Affirmation: "When I think my foot is slipping, thy goodness, O Eternal, holds me up" (Psalm 94:18 Moffatt).

For further reading: Mark 9:43-48; James 1:12-16; 1 John 2:15-17

TW 244

Discipline
Your Persistence

*Do not, therefore, abandon that confidence of yours;
it brings a great reward. For you need endurance,
so that when you have done the will of God,
you may receive what was promised.*
—Hebrews 10:36-37

5. Discipline yourself at the place of carrying through. A great many good but ineffective people discipline their beginnings. They take up good things, but they don't carry through. Their lives are strewn with the wreckage of good beginnings and poor endings.

Don't take up everything that comes along. Save yourself for the best.... " Get guidance from God, know your call, and then stay by it till you hear the recall....

"I am staying on.... I have wide opportunities here... and there are many to thwart me" (1 Corinthians 16:9 Moffatt). Many of us would have said, "I am quitting. ...I have wide opportunities here, but there are too many things against me."

... " 'Where is the trusty, thoughtful steward whom the lord and master will set over his establishment?' " (Luke 12:42 Moffatt).... "Trusty" means not only honest, but that he can be trusted to go through to completion.

In a long distance race, it is finishing that counts.

O Christ, I know you want to use me. Give me the strength to be both trusty and thoughtful—to go through clear to the end with unwavering persistence.

Affirmation: "Never will he let you slip; he who guards you never sleeps" (Psalm 121:3 Moffatt).

For further reading: Hebrews 10:32-39; 12:1-6; Philippians 3:13-16

Discipline Your Time

Be careful then how you live... making the most of the time.
—Ephesians 5:15-16

6. *Discipline your time.* If, in discussing the last point of disciplining yourself to carry through to completion tasks taken up, your rationalization is, "Well I haven't the time," then the answer must be: Discipline your time. If you actually haven't time for it, then you ought not to do it; it isn't your task. You must exercise the duty of refusing to do good. . . .

But perhaps the real difficulty is that you don't use to best advantage the time you have. Your time is undisciplined. You carry on conversations long after they have run out of intelligence, for most conversations run out of intelligence in half an hour! You do not tackle your tasks decisively and get them done and out of the way. You daydream instead of think; you dawdle instead of do. You waste hours of time at games which are supposed to be recreation but which wreck time and you.

Time is distilled opportunity. Don't waste it, for in doing so you lay waste yourself. . . . Budget your time. Plan your work, and work your plan.

What reason do you give for lack of time?

O Christ, when I look at you I see that you were never in a hurry—you always had time for the pressing necessities of the day. Give me that disciplined, poised life with time always for the things that matter.

Affirmation: " 'He who believes [in him] will not be in haste' " (Isaiah 28:16 RSV)—"One who trusts will not panic" (NRSV).

For further reading: 1 Thessalonians 5:14; Ephesians 5:15-20

TW 246

Discipline Yourself to "What Is"

Let each of you lead the life that the Lord
has assigned, to which God called you.
—1 Corinthians 7:17

7. *Discipline yourself to "what is."* There are many who are uselessly beating themselves upon the bars of life... because they cannot fly. "If I were only there, or anywhere but here, I'd be all right." They dream of what they would do if they were not here.

But we've always got to live on what is....I was off-loaded in Trinidad on my journey back from South America ...by two local passengers. I was a "through" passenger. It meant my missing important mass meetings in Miami, long planned. The priority officer agreed that I had had "a raw deal." But these words came to me as clear as crystal: "Lord, I do not ask for special treatment; I ask for power to take any treatment that may come, and use it." Peace settled within me. That sentence itself has lingered like a benediction within me ever since. I lived by it during that waiting period...have lived by it in many a situation since....

You can rescue out of every unjust, impossible situation something that makes that situation not confining, but contributing. You can live on "what is."

Are you living in the present or in the future?

O Christ, thank you that you lived through the silent years of obscurity in Nazareth—and lived gloriously. Help me to live on what comes, good, bad, indifferent.

Affirmation: If I don't get what I like, then I shall like what I get.

For further reading: 2 Corinthians 1:4-6; 4:15-18

TW 247

Discipline
Your Tongue

Scripture

How great a forest is set ablaze by a small fire!
And the tongue is a fire.
—James 3:5-6

8. *Discipline your tongue.* Jesus said, "By your words you will be justified, and by your words you will be condemned" (Matthew 12:37). This always sounded superficial until I saw that you become what you say. If you tell a lie, you become a lie. The deepest punishment of a lie is—the liar. He has to live with someone he cannot trust. That is an uneasy hell. There are therefore no "white lies," for they leave a black mark—on the soul. "Isn't a lie ever justifiable?" No, absolutely no. Evil means produce evil ends always. . . .

Discipline your tongue not only to the truth but to the relevant truth . . . to concise, straightforward speech . . . that says what it means and means what it says.

Discipline your tongue to the loving. When in doubt, say the most loving thing and you will not be wrong. . . . "This is how I write. 'The grace of our Lord Jesus Christ be with you all' " (2 Thessalonians 3:18 Moffatt). Is that how we write and speak: "grace . . . all"?

"The adjective is the enemy of the noun."

O Christ, nothing but gracious words came from your mouth. Discipline my tongue to the truth, the relevant, the loving. For my words will condemn me to be what they are. Help me.

Affirmation: "Set a watch upon my mouth, O Thou Eternal, guard thou the door of my lips; may I have no mind to evil" (Psalm 141:3 Moffatt).

For further reading: James 3:1-12; Proverbs 18:4-8, 20-21; Matthew 12:34

TW 248

Discipline
Your Disciplines

"He let you hear his voice out of heaven, for discipline."
—*Deuteronomy 4:36 Moffatt*

Discipline is not something imposed on a reluctant human nature by an arbitrary God.... The "voice out of heaven" is exactly the same as the voice out of our needs. For the voice out of heaven only voices what we need but often cannot voice. God's voice and our needs are one. Our choosing of disciplines is the choosing of the laws and demands of our beings. If this is true, then we must:

9. *Discipline our disciplines.* We must not allow them to become too obvious, too ... stilted. A person who is obviously trying to be disciplined is not rhythmical and winsome. The disciplines must be buried in the subconscious where they work naturally as a part of you. In the beginning you may have to impose them until they take root within you. But the end is to make them artesian instead of artificial.... [They] will then function as spontaneous habit. For the disciplines have become *you.*...

"If he [the disciple] is perfectly trained, he will be like his teacher" (Luke 6:40 Moffatt). The end of the discipline is to make you "perfectly trained" so that you may be like your Master.

You are being disciplined into Christlikeness.

O Jesus Christ, thank you that your disciplined heart sang its song of freedom. Give me the song of freedom through discipline. Bring every desire into captivity to the obedience of your will.

Affirmation: "As a parent disciplines a child so the Lord your God disciplines you" (Deuteronomy 8:5).

For further reading: Acts 20:28-35; Hebrews 12:5-11

TW 249

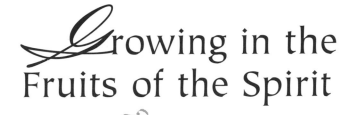

Growing in the Fruits of the Spirit

The Fruit of the Spirit

The fruit of the Spirit is love, joy, peace, patience, kindness, generosity, faithfulness, gentleness, and self-control. There is no law against such things.
—Galatians 5:22-23

To be filled with the Spirit is often looked on as a magical power...making one a seven-day wonder—healing the sick, stopping tornadoes, changing the weather—signs and wonders. The Spirit-filled person becomes a dispenser of miracles. Now miracles do happen in the Christian impact...but nowhere as a central emphasis. They are by-products of something deeper. When you emphasize the by-product and underemphasize the product, you will lose both the by-product and the product. The product is life characterized by nine qualities, all of them moral, not one of them magical...the natural outcome of the Spirit within.

The Christian impact is redemptive, creating moral and spiritual changes in character.

O God, thank you for the possibility of being fruitful in moral qualities that enrich me and my relationships.

Affirmation: The central miracle is happening in me, as I change and grow.

For further reading: 2 Corinthians 6:4-20; 1 Corinthians 1:20-23; Ephesians 4:18-20

GS 120

888 — The First Fruit Is Love

*Thus "faith and hope and love last on, these three,"
but the greatest of all is love. Make love your aim,
and then set your heart on spiritual gifts.*
—1 Corinthians 13:13–14:1 Moffatt

Having the Spirit within results in a quality of being with nine characteristics. And the first one is "love" (Galatians 5:22). This emphasis on the firstness of love fits in with Paul's emphasis in 1 Corinthians 13:13.... The primacy of love in the spiritual life is not an arbitrary, imposed condition; it is inherent. If you have the Spirit, you have love, and if you do not have the love, you do not have the Spirit. And this love is not an occasional attitude of life. Love is the first outcome of the Spirit within, and if it is lacking, everything is lacking.

To grow spiritually is to grow in love. Without love all other growth is a cancer growth, consuming instead of constructing.

Lack love and you lack maturity.

O Father, help me to grow in love as my primary growth. Reinforce me there and then I shall truly grow.

Affirmation: I make love my life aim. I cannot be less than love and still live.

For further reading: Ephesians 4:30–5:2, 25; 1 John 4:7-12

GS 120, CM 99

339 — Smashing and Melting

Love...bears all things, believes all things,
hopes all things, endures all things.
—1 Corinthians 13:4, 7

According to the Christian faith all motives of life, if they are to be sound, are reduced to one motive—love...the love of Christ. The greatest of Christians said, "I am controlled by the love of Christ" (2 Corinthians 5:14 Moffatt). This cuts deep. It is possible to be controlled by the love of achievement, of success, of a cause. . . . To be controlled by the love of Christ is different not only in degree but in kind, in quality. . . .

There are two courses to take to get rid of a block of ice. One is to try to smash it with a hammer, in which case you only succeed in scattering it, not destroying it; the other is to melt it, in which case you really do get rid of it. . . .

Jesus on the cross is God not smashing his enemies but melting them. There is only one way of getting rid of your enemies, and that is to turn them into your friends.

Christians don't smash situations and people;
they melt them.

O Jesus, teach me your way, the way of love. Help me to melt every situation by love—your love.

Affirmation: What I cannot get around I shall melt with love. And what I cannot melt with love will get more love.

For further reading: 2 Corinthians 5:13-21; 1 Corinthians 13

GS 124

340 — "Make Love Your Aim"

"This is my commandment, that you love one another as I have loved you."
—John 15:12

How do we grow in love?

Let us remember that the capacity and necessity of love is inherent within us. . . . If a child is only self-interested, turning to selfishness, it is automatically an unhappy child. The happy child is the other-interested child. We are destined to love and this destiny is written within us. . . . [Paul says that] God "destined us in love to be his sons through Jesus Christ" (Ephesians 1:5 RSV). We are destined to be Christians . . . and that destiny came through his love . . . then it must hold within it a destiny to love. . . .

Since to be a man or woman of love is your destiny, then . . . "Make love your aim," your life purpose (1 Corinthians 14:1 RSV). This will . . . make it the central controlling purpose of your life. . . . If love be hindered here, it will break out there; if it is thwarted here, it will find a way there. "Love never fails" (1 Corinthians 13:8 KJV), for it always finds a way of expressing itself. . . .

Your life purpose is fulfilled even if you see no results of your loving, for you have become a loving person. There is nothing higher.

**In expressing itself,
love makes you more loving.**

O God, my Father, thank you that the real thing, love, has taken hold of me. Let it possess me. I consent.

Affirmation: I cannot fail if I love, even if my love fails to accomplish its ends.

For further reading: John 15:12-17; 1 Corinthians 13

GS 127

350

Let Christ Love You into Loving

God is love, and those who abide in love abide in God, and God abides in them.
—1 John 4:16

Do everything for the love of Christ. [This] transforms the menial into the meaningful, the sordid into the sacred. One of the richest meanings of the Incarnation is here. The carpenter's bench, the struggle in the wilderness, the healing of the sick, the feeding of the hungry, the torture of the cross—all these were not obstacles but opportunities for showing the love of God.... The love of God is the biggest thing in the universe, and when that love is incarnate in a deed, then the deed is big.

Doing everything for the love of Christ will dull the edge of disappointment and make us invulnerable to lack of appreciation....

Don't strain to love, but let the love of God love within you. John puts it this way: "Yet if we love each other God does actually live within us, and His love grows in us towards perfection" (1 John 4:12 Phillips).... We don't try to love; we just let Love love. And as we do, we grow in love toward perfection. His perfect Love perfects our love and perfects us in the process.

"In each small task...see an opportunity of saying, 'I love you, Jesus.' "
(Mary)[1]

O Father, thank you that all I have to do is to surrender to Love in order to become a perfected being.

Affirmation: God's love grows in me toward perfection; then no blocking of that love today.

For further reading: 1 John 4:7-21

GS 129, 208

---

[1]Jones's name for a woman whose life was transformed as a result of his ministry. His books contain a number of references to her testimony.

Joy Is Inevitable

342

Rejoice in the Lord always; again I will say, Rejoice.
—*Philippians 4:4*

In the list of the fruit of the Spirit in Galatians 5:22, it is no mere chance that the order is "Love, joy." Joy comes after love. . . . Joy is a by-product of love. If you seek joy first, it will elude you. But if you go out to love everybody in the name of Jesus, joy will seek you out. . . .

Joy is . . . the very essence of our faith. If there is no joy, there is no Christianity, for Christianity is joy. The empty tomb takes away our empty gloom. When we can sing in the face of death, we can sing in the face of everything.

These passages (from Moffatt's translation) show our privilege of being joyful. "Let us enjoy the peace we have with God" (Romans 5:1). Some have peace with God but don't enjoy it! . . . "We enjoy our redemption" (Ephesians 1:7). To be redeemed and not enjoy that redemption is a contradiction in terms. Again: "We both enjoy our access to the Father in one Spirit" (Ephesians 2:18). And finally: "We enjoy our confidence of free access" (Ephesians 3:12). Here joy seems to be overflowing because of peace, redemption, access to the Father, and confidence of free access. Joy is inevitable.

Are you rejoicing in the Lord?

Gracious Father, with all this as the basis of life, how can I help but offer the tribute of my joy? I do.

Affirmation: My greatest joy is in something beyond joy, but including joy—free access to the Father.

For further reading: Deuteronomy 12:18; 1 Chronicles 16:27; Colossians 1:11-14

CM 254, GS 134, 135

The Solid Glory

The more grace abounds, the more thanksgiving may rise and redound to the glory of God.... The slight trouble of the passing hour results in a solid glory past all comparison.
—2 Corinthians 4:15, 17 Moffatt

Christians' joy is not in what we possess, nor in what we do, nor in what others do for us. It is in relationships that abide amid the flux of possession and nonpossession, of success and failure, of good treatment and ill treatment. Christians can do without anything on earth—even life on earth, for we have a permanent eternal life now which is rooted in eternity.

Rendel Harris says: "Joy is the strength of the people of God; it is their glory; it is their characteristic mark." And when the mark is absent, then the characteristic of a Christian is absent. Joy is the natural fruit of Christian living. And because it is natural, it finds joy in simple things.

... Jesus said of himself: "Foxes have holes, and birds of the air have nests; but the Son of Man has nowhere to lay his head" (Luke 9:58), and yet "he thrilled with joy at that hour in the holy Spirit" (Luke 10:21 Moffatt). His joy was not in his circumstances, but in his inner-stances. They remained the same no matter what happened on the outside. Therefore his joy was invulnerable.

Are you glad you are a Christian?

O Father, thank you that I have found an ultimate joy, unshakable, immeasurable, eternal—a solid glory that far outweighs today's trouble.

Affirmation: My joy will outlast all earthly joys and will still be singing when they are silent and gone.

For further reading: Ephesians 5:18-20; 2 Corinthians 4:15-18; Acts 16:25-34

GS 140

— # Joy Is Your Birthright

*May his glorious might nerve you with full power
to endure and to be patient cheerfully, whatever
comes, thanking the Father who has qualified us
to share the lot of the saints in the Light.*
—*Colossians 1:11-12 Moffatt*

Make up your mind that joy, not gloom, is your birthright as a child of God and is the natural way to live. You are made for joy, and if there is gloom, there is something wrong. Joy is blocked. Clear away the blocks, and joy comes automatically. If you are gloomy, then don't look around for the cause; look within. If you have an unhappy home, explore the possibility of the cause being in the person your mate married. Stop blaming your circumstances. . . .

We can make life woeful or wonderful according to the way we take it. You're natural if you're joyous and happy; you're unnatural if you're unhappy and gloomy.

**Give up gloom.
Accept happiness.**

O Father, help me to take my birthright of joy and live the life for which I'm made—in right relationship with you and with myself. I will cease being unnatural.

Affirmation: I will be joyful and rejoice in the Lord in every circumstance today.

For further reading: 1 Peter 4:13; Romans 5:1-5

GS 141

Joy in God

Through him [Jesus], then, let us continually
offer a sacrifice of praise to God, that is,
the fruit of lips that confess his name.
—Hebrews 13:15

Make up your mind where your joy is going to center—in God.... Only in one place in this universe can you put your whole weight down—on God. Everything else is a staff upon which, if you lean too hard, it will break and pierce your hand—and your heart. But you can lean on God, absolutely, and he will hold you, absolutely.... Make up your mind that there is an absolutely trustable spot in the universe—and only one—and that spot is God.

...Now surrender yourself and all you have into his hands. If God is going to make the total you joyful, he must have the total you. Let him make you over from the ground up. I saw a sign over a garage which specialized in repairing broken car springs, saying: "Limp in and leap out." That's what surrender of yourself and your sorrow and gloom to God will mean; you will limp in, and you will leap out.

When you pass through the valley of weeping,
make it a place of springs.
(See Psalm 84:6.)

O Father, help me not to withhold myself and thus impoverish myself. Take me. I give all freely and gladly.

Affirmation: I am not withholding myself; God is not withholding himself. Where these two meet, joy is inevitable.

For further reading: Psalm 84:5-7; Philippians 4:8-13

GS 142

Turn Your Sorrow into Joy

Rejoice insofar as you are sharing Christ's sufferings, so that you may also be glad and shout for joy when his glory is revealed.
—1 Peter 4:13

Don't try to protect yourself against sorrow, for it is bound to come. Face it in Jesus' name and turn it into joy. The attempt to stop up all the holes against sorrow is bound to fail. It will get behind our armor in spite of all that we do. . . .

[The followers of Gautama Buddha] spread the message that life is fundamentally suffering, that the only thing to do is to escape it into Nirvana, the state of the snuffed-out candle—extinction of personality.

Here was a . . . tragic example of trying to protect oneself from suffering. The result was a system of philosophy based on a vast pessimism. The Christian faith is the opposite of that. It exposes one straight off to the very heart of suffering, to a cross. And then it proceeds to take that suffering and turn it into salvation; the cross becomes an Easter morning. The worst is met and changed into the best. Pains are turned into paeans. A singing optimism is won out of a dark pessimism.

The Christian sings in spite of.

Father, thank you that everything helps those who follow you, that we can learn from pain—and learn to sing with your joy.

Affirmation: When disasters come, I shall make them doors—doors into richer, fuller, more effective living.

For further reading: 1 Peter 1:6-9; 4:12-19

GS 144

Growing in Peace

...let your requests be made known to God. And the peace of God, which surpasses all understanding, will guard your hearts and your minds in Christ Jesus.
—Philippians 4:6-7

The third fruit of the Spirit is peace.... First, love—love is preeminent; then joy—joy comes as a result of love; and then peace—peace is joy grown quiet and assured. Joy simmers down into peace. Joy is peace with its hat in the air, and peace is joy with its arms folded in serene assurance....

Let us get one thing straight.... [The] using of God to give us peace of mind and to make us healthy is a species of self-idolatry which is very prevalent and very popular—and very shallow. It makes God serve us instead of our serving God....

The phrase "peace of mind" in itself reveals the shallowness of the quest. You cannot have peace of mind unless you have something deeper than peace of mind. When you have peace at the depths of your spirit, then peace of mind is an outcome of that deeper peace. You cannot have peace in the mind if there is conflict in the spirit.... You yourself in your essential make-up must be a harmonized person. Then and then only will there be peace of mind.

Christian peace, a tough-fibered kind of peace,
can stand anything that can happen.

O Father God, give me the peace that surpasses all understanding—a peace that I do not possess but that possesses me.

Affirmation: "Thou wilt keep him in perfect peace, whose mind is stayed on thee" (Isaiah 26:3 KJV).

For further reading: Proverbs 16:7; Colossians 1:19-20; 3:12-17

GS 148, 149

"Serene Assurance"

"Peace I leave to you, my peace I give to you;
I give it not as the world gives its 'Peace!'
Let not your hearts be disquieted or timid."
—John 14:27 Moffatt

[The Christian's] peace is based on a solid security—the security of knowing that every hurtful thing can be turned into a helpful thing, every injustice into an opportunity for witnessing. This brings what Peter calls "serene assurance": "Be eager to be found by him unspotted and unblemished in serene assurance" (2 Peter 3:14 Moffatt).

Any peace based on mental tricks will let you down. This will hold you up because it has the universe behind it. This is solid peace.

It is the kind of peace Jesus had . . . [and gives to us. We] can walk straight up to life confident that it can find some good in the worst that comes. . . . "I have said all this to you that in me you may have peace; in the world you have trouble, but courage!—I have conquered the world" (John 16:3 Moffatt). And within that world which he has conquered is included every single thing you have to meet in your life.

In Christ, you are secure,
absolutely secure.

O Jesus, I know that in you I have peace. Help me to abide in you, knowing that together we can meet anything that may happen.

Affirmation: All that I am and hope to be I place lovingly in the hands of my Father, knowing full well that what is for my best good will come to me, and no power on earth can prevent it.

For further reading: 1 Peter 3:9-17; Romans 5:1-5

Make Peace
Possible for You

For he is our peace. . . . So he came and proclaimed peace
to you who were far off and peace to those who were near.
—Ephesians 2:14, 17

[Since peace is a gift, and therefore possible for all], make peace possible for you. Stand in the way of allowing peace to invade you. Peace is knocking at the door. Lift the latch and let peace come in. . . . John Calvin put it this way: "God in a sudden conversion reduced my mind to a teachable frame." "A teachable frame"—a frame where you are receptive. There anything can happen; everything can happen.

"In His will is our peace,"[2] and when we bring everything into submission to that will, our peace begins and is assured. The Phillips translation puts it this way: "Let the harmony of God reign in your hearts" (Colossians 3:15). God is harmony, and when we are in harmony with God, we are in harmony with harmony. "Chaos is God saying, 'No,' to what we are doing in pride and ignorance." Harmony is God saying "Yes."

With our lives aligned to God's will,
we live in a state of "Yes."

Father, thank you that you will my peace. Help me to accept the will that wills my peace.

Affirmation: Harmony within will tend to produce harmony without.

For further reading: John 16:33; Colossians 3:12-17; 2 Corinthians 13:11

GS 156

---

[2]Dante Alighieri, *The Divine Comedy, Purgatorio*, canto III, 1, 85, translated by John Aitken Carlyle, The Temple Classics, 1900. Cf. Ephesians 2:14.

350 — Constructive Tensions

"What a tension I suffer, till it is all over."
—Luke 12:50 Moffatt

The next fruit of the Spirit [is] "good temper" (Moffatt), "patience" (NRSV), "longsuffering" (KJV). Someone has suggested that longsuffering is love stretched out. It is so elastic and tough that it doesn't break down into bad temper. It maintains good temper amid the flux and flow of human events....

Christians [are] not free from suffering...[or] from tensions. The violin string free from the violin is free from tensions and hence incapable of music. Jesus had tensions....But his tension was...harnessed not to fear and anxiety and self-interest, but to redemption. He was on his way to a cross, and that tension was not loosed until he said, "It is finished" (John 19:30). That tension did not leave him frustrated and bad-tempered; it left him calm and composed with a prayer for forgiveness upon his lips for his enemies. It drove him, not to pieces, but to peace—the peace of achievement and victory. This was so because the tension was harnessed not to self-will but to God's will.

**Do your tensions drive you to goals,
or do they drive you nuts?**

O Father, harness my tensions to your purposes, and then they shall pass into rhythm and song.

Affirmation: With God's help, I will reexamine my life, so that all my tensions, redeemed from selfish conflicts, will be harnessed to kingdom purposes.

For further reading: Luke 9:21-25; 12:49-52; 1 Corinthians 13:4-7

GS 159

Did the Poise
of Jesus Snap?

*[Jesus] said to them, "Is it lawful to do good
or to do harm on the sabbath, to save life or to
kill?" . . . He looked around at them with anger;
he was grieved at their hardness of heart.*
—Mark 3:4-5

Didn't the peaceful tension of Jesus snap when in the synagogue he looked around on them in anger . . . when he blistered the souls of the Pharisees with his burning words of "Woe unto you" (Matthew 23)? Were these manifestations of bad temper? Hardly. . . . [In the synagogue] the anger was grief—grief at their insensibility to human need. It was grief at what was happening to someone else and not personal pique at what was happening to himself. That changed the anger from destruction to construction.

In the case of the Pharisees his burning words were an uncovering of the sordid depths of a self-seeking, soured religion. . . . So his words were redemptive. His words were like a surgeon's knife—the cutting was not to hurt but to heal. That this was so can be seen in the climax. He turns from "woes" to weeping: "How often have I desired to gather your children together as a hen gathers her brood under her wings" (Matthew 23:37). This redeemed the woes from personal spite into collective salvation.

**The redemptive temper burns with a steady fire
of redemptive intention.**

O Father, give me the redemptive intention in all my attitudes and acts. That will save me and them.

Affirmation: Renouncing bad temper, all my temper will be tempered to kingdom purposes alone.

For further reading: 2 Timothy 2:24-26; Mark 3:1-6; Matthew 23

GS 160

352 — Changing Bad Temper

*For man's temper is never the means
of achieving God's true goodness.*
—James 1:20 Phillips

The greatest single influence in changing bad temper to good temper is the grace of God. A Christian businessman tells how he started life on a small farm in Mississippi. He had a high temper and would get mad and rave and rip when things went wrong.

He went to an altar one night and was converted. The next day he went back to plowing new ground with a mule. When the roots hit him on the shins and the plow hit rocks, causing the handle to gouge him in the side, instead of cursing and yelling and beating the mule he just said, "Lord, help me."

This went on for some time, and finally the mule of his own accord stopped, twisted around in the traces, and just looked at him in surprise! Later a neighbor who was working in another field came over and said: "Charley, I saw you plowing, but I couldn't hear you. Are you sick?"

"No," he replied, "I'm not sick. God saved me last night."

**Breathe a prayer for yourself
when you are about to lose your temper.**

O God, give me the temper that is unperturbed amid provocation. Help me to meet all impatience with patience, all frustration with joy.

Affirmation: I shall be the peaceful exception amid disturbed surroundings—at rest amid restlessness.

For further reading: 1 Timothy 2:1-8; James 1:19-26

GS 162, 161, 165

Growth in Kindliness

The harvest of the Spirit is love, joy, peace, good temper, kindliness, generosity, fidelity, gentleness, self-control.
—Galatians 5:22-23 Moffatt

The next fruit of the Spirit [is] kindliness. This is a very homely virtue, homely in the British sense of belonging to the home—a very commonplace, ordinary virtue. And yet it is ordinary as salt, and as essential. Without kindliness there is no virtue in the other virtues. It puts a flavor into all the other virtues; without it they are insipid and tasteless; or worse, they degenerate into vices. Love, joy, peace, good temper, without kindliness are very doubtful virtues. So it is no chance that this is the middle virtue of the nine, putting flavor into all the others.

So to grow in kindliness is to grow in virtues that are flavored with a certain spirit.... "Treat one another with the same spirit as you experience in Christ Jesus" (Philippians 2:5 Moffatt). Not merely the same actions, but the same spirit.... This saves kindness from mere maudlin sentimentality. It can be very severe—severe because he loves so deeply that he often has to save us by hard refusals. And his kindness can cut... when, like a surgeon, he insists on cutting out of us moral tumors and cancers.

Christ's severity is security.

O Christ, show your kindness to me this day, even if it be a cutting kindness, for I don't want leniency; I want life.

Affirmation: I want God to be kind to me in the form that my deepest necessities demand.

For further reading: Colossians 3:12-14; Ephesians 4:30-32; Philippians 32:1-11

GS 169

Kindness a Must

*She opens her mouth with wisdom,
and on her tongue is the law of kindness.*
—Proverbs 31:26 NKJV

Kindness is not a luxury virtue, but a moral and spiritual and physical must. By its very nature kindness is an outgoing attitude. It breaks the tyranny of self-preoccupation and gives you the attitude of other-interest.

A doctor wrote out a prescription for a sick man—emotionally sick, hence physically: "Go down to the New York Central Station and find there someone who needs you and do something for him." The businessman thought the doctor crazy but didn't know what else to do, so he went. He found a woman in a corner seated on her suitcase weeping.... Her daughter was to have met her but hadn't, and she didn't know her address and was frightened by this great city. The man got the daughter's address from the telephone directory, got the mother into a taxi, bought some flowers for her on the way, delivered her to the daughter amid the tearful gratitude of both, and then came back and called up the doctor and said, "Say, Doc, that was great medicine! I feel better already."

Put kindness into your life, not as an occasional deed, but as a life attitude... set in [the] will.... The kind thing is always the wise thing.

Unkindness is spiritual sickness.

O Father, in the legislature of my heart I pass the law of kindness. I come under its sway, forever.

Affirmation: I can never heal a hurt with another hurt. Kindliness is the one and only balm.

For further reading: Proverbs 31:10-31; 1 Peter 4:8; 2 Peter 1:5-8; James 2:14-17

GS 173

364

The Generous Eye

The eye is the lamp of the body:
so, if your Eye is generous,
the whole of your body will be illumined.
—Matthew 6:22 Moffatt

Six out of the nine [fruits of the Spirit] are related to our attitudes toward others—love, good temper, kindliness, generosity, fidelity, gentleness. Only three can be said to refer to oneself alone—joy, peace, self-control.... Jesus said that we are to love our neighbor "as" ourselves (Luke 10:27)—the self-interest and other-interest are to exactly balance....

But in this surrendering to the Spirit and letting the Spirit have sway over us, does it turn out that we find ourselves twice as interested in others as ourselves? Is this the second-mile attitude in human virtues? [See Matthew 6:39-41.] And if we do go the second mile, do we become lopsided personalities?... Strangely enough, no. The more we love others, the more beautiful we become in ourselves....

If your Eye—your outlook on life, your whole way of looking at things and people—is generous, then your whole personality is illumined, is lighted up.

Jesus was generous toward all—the poor, the meek, the sinful, the unlovely. And his whole personality was full of light.

Let Jesus generate that generosity within you.

O Jesus, clarify my sight so that I may look at others with the illumination of generosity, in the same way that your generous Eye sees me.

Affirmation: With Christ's help, I will view life through a generous Eye, and live life with a loving spirit.

For further reading: Matthew 6:22-23; 7:1-5; Romans 13:8-10

GS 176

356 — Growing in Generosity

Give liberally and be ungrudging when you do so,
for on this account the Lord your God will bless
you in all your work and in all that you undertake.
—Deuteronomy 15:7-8

To grow in generosity, first, decide that you own nothing. God is the owner, and you are ower. This puts God in his place and you in yours. You are not free to manage your material possessions as you like, but as he likes. This gives you a sense of accountability to Another. You get your life orders not from whim, notion, self-impulse, but from God.

Second, since God is owner, go over your life under his guidance and see what belongs to your needs and what merely belongs to your wants. Your needs are important. He has promised to supply them—not your wants. [See Philippians 4:19.] And what are your needs? You need as much as will make you more physically, mentally, and spiritually fit for the purposes of the kingdom of God. Beyond that belongs to other people's needs.

. . . In his presence go over your life, and item by item decide which belongs to which. . . . Go over the matter with some member, or members, of society, who have a similar sense of accountability to God and man, and check up with them. But the final decision must be with you.

What is your attitude toward your possessions?

O Father, I confess that too often I confuse my wants with my needs. Help me to be clear and honest with you and with myself—so that I may grow in generosity.

Affirmation: I shall take out of my earnings what I need. The rest is at God's disposal.

For further reading: Deuteronomy 15:7-11; Philippians 4:10-19

GS 180

Tithe Your Earnings

Each of you must give as you have made up your mind, not reluctantly or under compulsion, for God loves a cheerful giver.
—2 Corinthians 9:7

Third, since the central issues are fixed as to ownership and as to need, now decide to have the generous Eye toward people and things. You now have a framework for generosity. ...Within that fixed framework let your love operate as generosity. This will not now be so difficult, for generosity is the native air of this framework. In it you will live and move and have your being. It is the homeland of your soul.

Decide that your very outlook on everything and everybody will be to find the good, further the good, and to do good in every situation with every thought and act. You're naturalized in generosity.

Fourth, fill in this framework with specific attitudes and habits—give a tithe of your earnings. The giving of the tithe, or one-tenth, is a symbol of acknowledgment that the nine-tenths belongs to God. Just as you give rent as an acknowledgment that the rent house belongs to another, so you give one-tenth as acknowledgment that the nine-tenths belongs to God.... When one sincerely gives within this framework of generosity, something happens [in society and to you].

What happens to your money happens to you.

O Father, so that my money and property may not be dead money and dead property, I dedicate them to you, so that you may work in me and in the world.

Affirmation: My property is the extension of my person. My person belongs to God; so does my property automatically.

For further study: Genesis 14:20; 28:18-22; Leviticus 27:30-33; Deuteronomy 14:22-28; Matthew 23:23-24; 1 Corinthians 16:1-4; 2 Corinthians 8–9   GS 180, 181

Fidelity

*He who is faithful with a trifle is
also faithful with a large trust.*
—*Luke 16:10 Moffatt*

Paul, instead of putting honesty first . . . puts love first and
fidelity toward the last. Is he right? Yes, for the primary
basis of the Christian faith is love. The first and second
great commandments begin "Thou shalt love." The primary question is: What do you love supremely?

If the primary thing is honesty, then the root of religion
is in the will. But if the primary thing is love, then the root
of religion is in the emotions. If the center of religion is an
act of the will, then religion means a whipping up of the
will—a demand of duty. But if the center of religion is not
in the will, then we surrender the will to the object of the
emotion—God. Then religion is not a straining to be
good; it's a surrender to Goodness. Fidelity [is] a fruit of
surrender to the Spirit. Jesus said: "He who is faithful with
a trifle is also faithful with a large trust, and he who is dishonest with a trifle is also dishonest with
a large trust. So if you are not faithful with dishonest
mammon, how can you ever be trusted with true Riches?
And if you are not faithful with what belongs to another,
how can you ever be given what is your own? (Luke 16:10-
12 Moffatt).

How are you handling trifles?

O Father, you are letting me be tested day by day with the
little. Help me to be faithful there.

Affirmation: Fidelity in thought and deed shall be the hallmark of my
character.

For further reading: Proverbs 28:20; 1 Corinthians 4:1-2; Ephesians
4:15-16, 25

GS 183, 184

Growing in Fidelity

359

So then, putting away falsehood, let all of us speak the truth to our neighbors.
—Ephesians 4:25

First, determine to be basically honest and faithful in thought and speech and act. Lay this down as a basic cornerstone of your life. Begin building from there. And admit of no exceptions. . . . God cannot lie, and he cannot delegate you the privilege of lying for him. The New Testament is flat-footed on this matter: "Do not lie to one another" (Colossians 3:9). And [it] ends by declaring that "for . . . all liars, their place will be in the lake that burns with fire" (Revelation 21:8). When you take lies and dishonesties into your bosom, you take fire into your bosom, here and hereafter.

Second, fix it as an axiom in your thinking: Nobody gets away with anything, anywhere, at any time, if that "anything" is dishonest or untrue. The whole history of humanity is a commentary on this. . . .

Third, where you have been unfaithful and dishonest, face it frankly with yourself and God. . . . There is absolutely no other way to get rid of it.

Dishonesty brings death.
Honesty brings freedom and life.

Dear Father, give me the strength to take the hard way of honesty, for the hard way turns out to be the easy way of life and freedom.

Affirmation: No dishonesty is worth the price I will have to pay for it.

For further reading: Romans 13:7-10; Acts 5:1-6

GS 187, 186

360 — Look for Loose Ends

Scripture

"As for the seed in the good soil, that means those who hear and hold fast the word in a good, sound heart, and so bear fruit steadfastly."
—*Luke 8:15 Moffatt*

Fidelity will mean that I will carry through in God's entrustments to me; I will keep faith until the end.

When I asked the leading members of a large church what was the outstanding need of their church, they replied: "Fidelity." Fifty percent of church members are hangers-on, getting a free ride, contributing nothing from purse or person; 25 percent promise to do something and then after a few stabs at it drop out. They lack fidelity. The life of the church is carried on by the remaining 25 percent....

Go over your life and see where there are loose ends, broken promises, half-fulfilled tasks; and begin to complete the incomplete, fulfill the half-fulfilled, and gather up the loose ends. When you do so, there will be a sense of well-being, a sense of being whole.... Don't live under that haunting sense of the incomplete. Don't take up too much, but what you do take up, complete.

Only the steadfast are the finally fruitful.

O Father, I am good-intentioned and weak-willed. Take my intentions and turn them into driving convictions.

Affirmation: As far as possible, my half-finished jobs shall all be finished today, for I don't want to be a half-finished person.

For further reading: 2 Timothy 4:5-8; Hebrews 10:23-25; 12:1-2

GS 189

370

Adaptability

*The Spirit, however, produces in human life fruits
such as these: love, joy, peace, patience, kindness,
generosity, fidelity, adaptability and self-control.
—Galatians 5:22-23 Phillips[3]*

"Adaptability" ("gentleness" KJV) seems a strange fruit of
the Spirit. Is it thrown in as a second thought or is it integral to the spiritual life? I am persuaded it is integral and
fundamentally necessary to the best human living....

We always have to adapt ourselves to a new situation,
[either] destructively or constructively. We adapt. But how?

Some adapt to their surroundings by succumbing to
them; they fit in and echo. They don't stand for anything,
and hence they become nothing. They have all morality
and spirituality flattened out of them. This is the wrong
kind of adaptability; it is adaptability downward. Those
who adapt in this manner perish morally and spiritually.

...Nevertheless we must have adaptability. While we
refuse to compromise the center...of our moral convictions,
we must, however, learn to be adaptable persons—adaptable
in the things which are not vital convictions.... Those who
can [do so] survive.

**To put conviction and adaptability together
in a proper blend makes a strong person.**

Dear Jesus, you had these two things in your character.
Give them to me, for I too would be strong.

Affirmation: I shall have to have a trained insight to know when to
be adaptable and when to be adamant.

For further reading: Luke 9:12-17; Acts 15:1-21; Philippians 4:10-13

GS 190, 191

---

[3]J. B. Phillips, *Letters to Young Churches* (New York: The Macmillan Company, 1953), p. 101.
In later editions, Phillips used the translation "tolerance." The Greek word *chrēstos*, the root of
the word Paul used—*chrēstotēs*—in addition to meaning, good, pleasant, kindly, also has the
meaning of useful, suitable, worthy.

Able for Anything

I have learned how to be content wherever I am. I know how to live humbly; I also know how to live in prosperity. I have been initiated into the secret for all sorts and conditions of life . . . for prosperity and for privations; in Him who strengthens me, I am able for anything.
—Philippians 4:11-13 Moffatt

Did [Paul] know adaptability by experience? He did, and that made him an evangelist to the Gentiles. . . . Paul became "all things to all people" (1 Corinthians 9:22), and as a result was powerful in his appeal to all.

Paul's greatest passage describing his adaptability is Philippians 4:11-13. [It] shows the essential greatness of the man—a man who could take both privation and prosperity in his stride, making them both contribute toward the ends for which he lived. . . . Paul called his secret being "initiated into the secret for all sorts and conditions of life"—an initiation into a secret society!

And what was the initiation fee? The old word again: *self-surrender!* He had sustained a central loss, the loss of himself! What could lesser losses do to him now?

The initiation fee is yourself.
But the "secret" is worth it.

O Father, thank you for this glorious secret—the secret of being able to meet anything that comes. Glory be!

Affirmation: Penury or plenty leaves me undismayed; I am rich in God, very rich indeed.

For further reading: 1 Corinthians 9:19-22; 10:23-33, Philippians 3:7-11

GS 193

Self-Control

One who is slow to anger is better than the mighty, and one whose temper is controlled than one who captures a city.
—Proverbs 16:32

It is interesting that Paul puts self-control last. Most systems ancient and modern would put it first. . . . Modern cults through mind-control strive to produce "the happy person." The Christian Way produces through Christ-control the self-controlled person. But note that self-control is not so much a means as an end. You do not gain Christ through self-control; you gain self-control through Christ.

"The love of Christ constraineth us" (1 Corinthians 5:14 KJV)—or, literally, "narrows us to his way," controls us. If you begin with self-control, then you are the center, you are controlling yourself, and will be anxious lest yourself slip out from beneath your control.

But if you begin, as Paul does with love, then the spring of action is love for a Person, someone outside yourself. You are released from yourself and from self-preoccupation. "The "expulsive power of a new affection" breaks the tyranny of self-love and releases your powers. This means that you are a relaxed and therefore a released person. When you begin with love, you end in self-control.

**"Love Christ and do as you like,"
for you'll like what he likes.**

O Christ, I will move over and let you take the wheel, and then I'll get through this business of living without mishap.

Affirmation: My self-control will be rooted in Christ-control, and therefore no longer precarious.

For further reading: Proverbs 14:29; 19:11; James 3:1-12; 4:19-20; Galatians 5:13-18

GS 197

364 Growing in Self-Control

Whoever avoids slips of speech is a perfect man; he can bridle the whole of the body as well as the tongue.
—James 3:2 Moffatt

Fix it in your mind that you as a Christian cannot control the margin if something other than Christ controls the center. Be sure that fears, resentments, self-centeredness, inhibitions, guilts do not control the center. At the center let there be Christ-control. . . .

Don't allow conflicting loyalties in your life. . . . If you tolerate conflicting loves, then sooner or later one or the other of the loves will rise up and assume control. Have one supreme control—the love of Christ—and fit into that central love all the lesser loves. . . .

Have self-control at the place of the tongue . . . [which is] an index of whether you have real self-control. There are three stages: impulse, consideration, speech. Many leave out the second and jump from impulse to speech. Disciplined persons pause between impulse and speech and give themselves to consideration. . . . If in the heat of an impulse you write a stinging letter, don't send it. Sleep over it, and see how it looks the next morning when your passion has subsided and you enter the state of consideration. You'll probably tear it up.

No consideration, no character.

Dear Father, help me to tolerate no competing loves within me, so that I may be a disciplined person in thought, word, and deed, under your control.

Affirmation: Because the love of Christ controls me, I will think before I speak.

For further reading: Matthew 10:37-39; Proverbs 12:13-26; 15:4, 7; James 3

GS 200, 202, 201

A Daily Exercise

*Furnish your faith with resolution ... intelligence ... self-control
... stedfastness ... godliness ... brotherliness ... Christian love.*
—2 Peter 1:5-7 Moffatt

Begin the day with God:
    Kneel down to Him in prayer;
Lift up thy heart to His abode
    And seek his love to share.

Open the Book of God,
    And read a portion there;
That it may hallow all thy thoughts
    And sweeten all thy care.

Go through the day with God,
    Whate'er thy work may be;
Where'er thou art—at home, abroad,
    He still is near to thee.

Converse in mind with God,
    Thy spirit heavenward raise;
Acknowledge every good bestowed,
    And offer grateful praise.

Lie down at night with God,
    Who gives His servants sleep,
When thou tread'st the vale of death
    He will thee guard and keep.

O Christ, help me to draw on the power of habit to reinforce these resolves. Help me to become natural in good, at home in the kingdom.

Affirmation: My habits, being dedicated, work with me to make me active and fruitful. Soon they shall make me automatic in my Christian responses.

For further reading: 2 Peter 1:1-11

TW 381